THE PROBLEM OF BLAME

T0372599

This book makes a case for the permissibility of reactive blame – the angry, harmful variety. Blame is a thorny philosophical problem, as it is notoriously difficult to specify the conditions under which an agent *is* deserving of blame, is deserving of blame in the basic sense, and furthermore why this is so. Kelly McCormick argues that sharpening the focus to reactive, angry blame can both show us how best to characterize the problem itself, and suggest a possible solution to it, because even reactive blame is both valuable and deserved in the basic sense. Finally, she shows how, despite the many facets of the dark side of blame, adopting an explicitly victim-centered approach high-lights a powerful argument from empathy for retaining reactive blame and its attendant attitudes and practices.

KELLY MCCORMICK is Associate Professor of Philosophy at Texas Christian University. She has published a number of articles on blame, desert, and moral responsibility in journals including *Philosophical Studies*, *The Journal of Value Inquiry*, and *The Journal of Ethics & Social Philosophy*.

THE PROBLEM OF BLAME

Making Sense of Moral Anger

KELLY MCCORMICK

Texas Christian University

Shaftesbury Road, Cambridge CB2 8EA, United Kingdom

One Liberty Plaza, 20th Floor, New York, NY 10006, USA

477 Williamstown Road, Port Melbourne, VIC 3207, Australia

314–321, 3rd Floor, Plot 3, Splendor Forum, Jasola District Centre, New Delhi – 110025, India

103 Penang Road, #05–06/07, Visioncrest Commercial, Singapore 238467

Cambridge University Press is part of Cambridge University Press & Assessment, a department of the University of Cambridge.

We share the University's mission to contribute to society through the pursuit of education, learning and research at the highest international levels of excellence.

www.cambridge.org
Information on this title: www.cambridge.org/9781108827416

DOI: 10.1017/9781108907071

First published 2022
First paperback edition 2024

A catalogue record for this publication is available from the British Library

Library of Congress Cataloging-in-Publication data
NAMES: McCormick, Kelly (Kelly Anne), author.
TITLE: The problem of blame : making sense of moral anger / Kelly McCormick, Texas Christian University.
DESCRIPTION: Cambridge, United Kingdom ; New York, NY, USA : Cambridge University Press, 2022. | Includes bibliographical references and index.
IDENTIFIERS: LCCN 2021060109 (print) | LCCN 2021060110 (ebook) | ISBN 9781108842259 (hardback) | ISBN 9781108827416 (paperback) | ISBN 9781108907071 (epub)
SUBJECTS: LCSH: Faultfinding. | Blame. | Justice. | BISAC: PHILOSOPHY / Ethics & Moral Philosophy
CLASSIFICATION: LCC BJ1535.F3 M33 2022 (print) | LCC BJ1535.F3 (ebook) | DDC 158.2–dc23/eng/ 20220301
LC record available at https://lccn.loc.gov/2021060109
LC ebook record available at https://lccn.loc.gov/2021060110

ISBN   978-1-108-84225-9   Hardback
ISBN   978-1-108-82741-6   Paperback

For Susan & Anne

Contents

Acknowledgments

Many people have provided helpful discussion, comments, and other invaluable support on this project. To begin at the beginning, I want to thank Mark Heller for first introducing (subjecting?) me to the free will debate as a student. Mark will be amused to know that I finally understand his advice, "Never ask someone writing a book how their book is going!" I get it now. It was good advice. So, thanks Mark.

I am grateful to many philosophers and colleagues who have provided extensive conversations and feedback on many of the ideas developed in this book. Foremost among them are Manuel Vargas, Derk Pereboom, and Michael McKenna. I am deeply indebted to all of them for their support and encouragement at various stages of this project, and for their incredibly helpful feedback on earlier drafts of many portions of this book. Their own work has been a great inspiration to me, and I am grateful to have had the chance to discuss it with them on so many occasions. I am especially grateful to Manuel for responding to that very first email years ago from a confused graduate student wanting to write about revisionism. Many would not have taken the time, I am sure. Your incredibly helpful feedback, respect, and kindness have always been invaluable at every stage of my philosophical development.

Earlier versions of many of the arguments in this book were presented at various conferences and workshops and benefited immensely from comments from the audience and other participants. Earlier versions of the arguments concerning the methodological burdens for eliminativism in Chapter 5 were first presented at the Moral Responsibility: The Next Generation conference organized by Michael McKenna and hosted by the Arizona Center for Freedom in December 2017. I am extremely grateful for many helpful comments, criticisms, and suggestions that I received at this workshop, and for wonderful and insightful discussions with all of the participants: Santiago Amaya, Macalester Bell, Justin Capes, Christopher Evan Franklin, Meghan Griffiths, Robert Kane, Elinor

Mason, Kristin Mickelson, Dana Nelkin, Mirja Pérez Calleja, Michael Robinson, David Shoemaker, and Chandra Sripada. I also received helpful comments on these arguments from participants at the Early Career Metaphysics Workshop at the College of William & Mary in April 2018. Thanks here are owed to Ricki Bliss, Sam Cowling, Robin Dembroff, Aaron Griffith, Kevin Richardson, Noël Saenz, and Alex Skiles. Thanks also to the participants at the San Francisco Free Will Conference on Reference, Conceptual Change, and Free Will organized by Manuel Vargas in 2013, especially Gunnar Björnsson, Joe Campbell, and Chris Weigel. Finally, thanks to Justin Coates and Neal Tognazzini for feedback on an earlier version of this manuscript, and especially to Neal for his incredibly helpful and detailed comments on the completed manuscript. This book is much better thanks to them, and Neal I owe you a beer for those twenty-seven misuses of a certain word.

Work in several chapters was inspired by or improved upon at various sessions of the Pacific Division Meeting of the American Philosophical Association (APA). Commenting on Tammler Sommers' "Philosophical Busybodies" at the meeting of the Society for Philosophy of Agency Group Session in April 2016 helped to inspire a shift to a more victim-centered approach to my thinking about free will, responsibility, and blame. My views about Shaun Nichols' discretionary approach were significantly influenced by participating in the Author Meets Critics session on *Bound* at the Pacific APA in 2015, along with Manuel Vargas and Bob Kane. I am also grateful for feedback from the audience at the 2014 meeting of the Pacific APA, where I presented earlier versions of the parity of reasons arguments offered in Chapter 4.

I have made use of my own previously published work in various parts of this book. Chapter 2 is based on my chapter "Basic Desert and the Appropriateness of Blame," which first appeared in Joseph Keim Campbell, ed., *A Companion to Free Will* (Hoboken, NJ: Wiley-Blackwell, 2022). Chapter 3 includes most of my article "Companions in Innocence: Defending a New Methodological Assumption for Theorizing about Moral Responsibility," published in *Philosophical Studies*, 172 (2015), pp. 515–533. Chapter 5 is a revised version of my article "Meeting the Eliminativist Burden," in *Social Philosophy and Policy*, 36 (2019), pp. 132–153. And Chapter 6 includes most of my article "Why We Should(n't) Be Discretionists about Free Will," in *Philosophical Studies*, 174 (2017), pp. 2489–2498.

I am lucky to be a member of a supportive philosophy department with consistently wonderful students at Texas Christian University (TCU).

Many of the ideas in this book have benefited from thinking them through with those students in several iterations of my seminar on Free Will & Moral Responsibility, and my seminar on Blame. While considerations of space do not allow me to thank them all here, I am especially indebted to Jaclyn Barber, Jordan Hittesdorf, and Hannah Vu. The many hours of working with each of you on your own projects on free will, blame, and responsibility helped me to improve many of my own arguments here. I count those meetings among the most enjoyable and rewarding parts of my teaching career thus far.

I am also grateful to my colleagues at TCU, Ley Cray, Richard Galvin, Blake Hestir, John Harris, and Bill Roche, for countless hours of discussion about many of the ideas found here. Special thanks are due to Ley for always offering to let me bounce ideas off of them in conversation, including some that became the earliest seeds of this book. And to John, to whom I am forever indebted for taking the time to provide detailed feedback on a full draft of this manuscript. And a special thanks also to John and Tracie both, for all of your encouragement and for being such fantastic friends.

Finally, while the ideas in this book have been jostling around in my head for many years, the process of actually writing it happened to coincide with a particularly difficult set of circumstances. The universe, as always, has a sense of humor. Even the best-laid plans could not have anticipated a worldwide pandemic and the roadblocks it created for completing this project. I cannot thank my family and friends enough for their patience, support, and encouragement, without which completing this project would not have been possible.

To Kirsten Egerstrom, Rachel McKinney, and Meghan Page, I am beyond lucky to have found such a badass group of women, colleagues, and friends to navigate all the stages of this profession with. To Katelyn McKenna, Shannon Ostwald, Stephanie Dowling, Tim Livedalen, and Rachel Livedalen, thank you for always cheering me on. To my family, Kevin McCormick, Carly McCormick, Shawn McCormick, and Hannah McCormick, thank you for keeping me grounded, and for your willingness to always pack up and hide out in the middle of the woods when I needed a break. To my parents, Sue and Shawn, and my grandparents, Anne and Art, thank you for everything. You have always made me feel like I can accomplish whatever I set out to do, and supported me every step of the way. And to Byron, thank you for your love and support, and for getting me across the finish line. You are the best.

Finally, many thanks to Hilary Gaskin at Cambridge University Press for believing in this project. Thanks also to Renée Cleghorn for her indexing magic. And to those who have offered feedback and support on this project who I have not been able to name here, thank you. I hope that you will not blame me, but I fully understand and I am quite sure that I deserve it if you do.

Introduction

Blame is a puzzling phenomenon. When we find ourselves on the attributing end of things, blame and its attendant practices can strike us as both practically invaluable and as a pervasive feature of our emotional lives. It seems to play an important role in holding one another responsible (both interpersonally and legally), properly valuing and defending the victims of wrongdoing, and perhaps even in sustaining the distinctly moral norms that compose our shared moral communities. It is the kind of thing that we would be hard-pressed to imagine giving up entirely.

On the other hand, when we find ourselves on the receiving end of blame, matters are quite different. With this perspectival shift, blame often takes on a darker character. As targets of blame, we are all familiar with the unpleasantness of even the most innocuous instances of blame. A coworker becomes a bit standoffish when you forget to refresh the office coffee pot, or a significant other issues a barely noticeable sigh when you tell them you will have to cancel tonight's dinner plans. No one wants to be blame's target, and the unpleasantness that goes along with such common, relatively minor infractions is just the tip of the iceberg. In many contexts, blame is not only unpleasant but also *hurts*.

These dual faces of blame give rise to a tension. Blame is both something we value – a surprisingly effective tool in our moral lives – and something we may also wish we could be rid of. Does the value of blame outweigh its corresponding harms? Or does the potential pain caused by blame give us reason to abandon at least some of its forms? In light of this tension, what ought we to *do* when it comes to blame and its attendant practices – is blame, even in its harmful guises, ever really *permissible*? And, even if we have reason to doubt that it is, does this entail that we should endeavor to *eliminate* blame from our lives, if not entirely, then at least insofar as we can?

These are the central questions of this book. In what follows, I take an emerging group of *blame curmudgeons* as my central opponents.[1] Many of these curmudgeons have offered powerful arguments against the permissibility of blame, and in favor of eliminating blame from our lives insofar as we are able.[2] These concerns highlight two important aspects of the curmudgeonly view that are often run together – *skeptical* arguments about permissibility, and *eliminativist* arguments about what we ought to do, practically speaking, in light of the plausibility of skeptical conclusions. I take a full blown defense of reactive blame to require a response to *both* aspects of the curmudgeonly position. A successful argument for the permissibility of reactive blame as we find it in our moral lives would be a shallow victory if it did not also address full blown eliminativist worries.

In what follows, I will offer a defense of reactive blame in two parts, roughly corresponding to these skeptical and eliminativist aspects of curmudgeonly concerns about blame. Part I focuses on the skeptical aspect, and the question of whether reactive blame is ever permissible as we find it in our moral lives. I call this question about the permissibility of reactive blame *the problem of blame*, and argue that this problem can ultimately be resolved.

In Chapter 1, I attempt to explicate the problem itself, making use of an analogy with another more familiar problem relevant to permissibility and harm – the problem of punishment. I argue that this comparison serves to highlight two clear desiderata for a normatively adequate account of blame, one concerning the value of blame and another concerning desert. In this chapter, I also argue that the problem of blame concerns the *reactive* varieties of blame in particular, offer some principled strategies for distinguishing between reactive and nonreactive varieties of blame, and discusses the role that the negative reactive attitudes play in characterizing the former.

In Chapter 2, I turn my focus to the desert-based desideratum for a normatively adequate account of reactive blame. I begin with an issue that

---

[1] I credit Christopher Franklin (2013) for coining this colorful way of describing the position of various skeptics about blame.

[2] Here, I offer a stipulative characterization of curmudgeonly views about blame. While there is now a wide array of descriptively skeptical views about free will, moral responsibility, and blame (see, e.g., Ishtiyaque Haji (2016), Neil Levy (2011), and Galen Strawson (1993)), curmudgeons are those who argue further for some prescriptive variety of eliminativism whereby we ought to eliminate blame from our lives insofar as we can. The paradigm curmudgeonly views that I have in mind as targets here are Pereboom (2001, 2013), Caruso (2012, 2015, 2020), and Waller (1990, 2011, 2015, 2020).

often plays a central role in obscuring whether the problem of blame can be resolved, namely how we ought to understand the concept of *basic desert*. Adjacent to the problem of blame, debates about free will and moral responsibility often bottom out in appeal to whether or not the account on offer can deliver basic desert of blame. However, little progress has been made in explicating precisely what basic desert of blame amounts to. I argue that once we have restricted our focus to reactive blame in particular, a clearer picture of basic desert emerges. I go on to offer an analysis of basic desert of reactive blame which I call *the fittingness account*, and argue that it can provide the first step in resolving the problem of blame.

In Chapter 3, I focus on the nature of reactive blame itself. In order to see how the fittingness account of basic desert might help to resolve the problem of the blame, we need a clearer picture of the reactive attitudes whose conditions of appropriateness this solution will ultimately depend on. In this chapter, I canvass three of the prominent views of reactive blame (P. F. Strawson's, R. Jay Wallace's, and David Shoemaker's) that I take to be most helpful in further explicating what meeting the desert-based desideratum for normative adequacy might look like. Here I argue for a cognitivist view of the reactive attitudes, and that we ought to restrict the scope of the relevant class of reactive attitudes at issue quite narrowly. With a sharper view of the reactive attitudes in hand, I then return to the fittingness account of basic desert and offer a first pass at an account of the right kind of reasons to reactively blame.

In Chapter 4, I return to the problem of blame, and argue that both the desert-based and value-based desiderata for a normatively adequate account of reactive blame can be met. First, adopting a *victim-centered* approach highlights the importance of blame for appropriately valuing other persons, and for protecting and defending them against actions and attitudes that disvalue them.[3] I then argue that reactive blame is the variety of blame that is uniquely suited to serve this function. Thus, the value-based desideratum for a normatively adequate account of reactive blame can be met. I then offer two arguments for thinking that the desert-based desideratum can be met. The first is a parity of reasons argument. Given epistemically relevant similarities between the negative reactive attitudes and a privileged subset of our moral judgments, we ought to extend the same privileged status to beliefs about the object of the propositional content of the negative reactive attitudes. The second argument appeals

---

[3] See Franklin (2013).

to another similarity; this time between our emotional experiences (of which the negative reactive attitudes are a subset) and perceptual experiences. While there are also important *dissimilarities* between these two kinds of experience, explicating their nature in fact suggests that we have good reason to think some of our emotional experiences – those constitutive of the negative reactive attitudes in particular – provide indirect evidence for the existence of moral reasons that would render their content correct. Thus, we have reason to think that the desert-based desideratum for normatively adequate reactive blame can be met.

If the arguments in Part I are successful, then the problem of blame can be resolved. We have good reason to think that – contra blame skeptics – even reactive blame is both valuable and sometimes deserved in the basic sense. Reactive blame, therefore, is permissible. If in fact reactive blame is both valuable and deserved in the basic sense, it is not at all clear what further defense of permissibility skeptics might reasonably demand.

In Part II, however, I turn my sights on those still intent on holding onto the problem of blame. For those who reject my arguments for permissibility, would the fact that reactive blame is impermissible be sufficient to motivate not only skepticism, but full blown eliminativism? Addressing this prescriptive question requires a deeper dive into thorny issues regarding free will and moral responsibility. In particular, what are the methodological burdens for eliminativism in this domain, and how do theories of reference ultimately inform and influence disagreement about existence claims about free will and moral responsibility and in turn whether we ought to retain or abandon reactive blame?

In Chapter 5, I take up the first question. Here I explicate two methodological burdens for the kind of eliminativist views about free will and moral responsibility that might threaten a prescriptive preservationist view of reactive blame. The first burden is that eliminativists must *fix the skeptical spotlight*, and offer at least some comparative support for their claim that the error they identify for free will and moral responsibility that threatens blame cannot be resolved by abandoning some other assumption, belief, or feature of our concept that it is in tension with. But fixing this spotlight is not enough. The fact that we are stuck with an error still does not entail by itself that we ought to abandon free will, responsibility, and reactive blame. As countless historical and philosophical examples show, we often realize that our thinking about some target feature of the world has been deeply mistaken, yet rather than eliminate that thing from our ontological, conceptual, and practical frameworks we instead opt for preservation by way of *revision*. Eliminativists, therefore, must meet a second methodological burden and explicitly motivate elimination over some variety of revisionist preservation. I call this second burden *the motivational challenge*, and examine two possible eliminativist strategies for meeting it. The first involves appeals to gains and losses intended to directly motivate elimination, and the second involves explicit appeal to some claim about the essence of free will and moral responsibility. What both of these strategies reveal is that their success ultimately depends on thorny issues about reference and essence.

In Chapter 6, I attempt to tackle these issues head-on by making explicit the way that theories of reference influence the plausibility of existence claims about free will and moral responsibility.[4] I begin by canvassing some early work on the way various reference-fixing conventions might inform existence claims about free will offered by Mark Heller (1996) and Susan Hurley (2000). I then turn to one of the most systematic attempts to analyze the way that "free will" refers currently on offer, Shaun Nichols' discretionary view. While Nichols' account of how "free will" refers is already quite hospitable to eliminativism in allowing that eliminativists' claims that free will does not exist are sometimes true, I also take up a further argument from Gregg Caruso that Nichols' view actually suggests that eliminativists' claims are *always* true.

If Caruso is right, then Nichols' discretionary view would offer a clear path to motivating eliminativism. However, I argue that Caruso's proposal for the target of our initial baptism of "free will" on a causal-historical account of reference is implausible. I then go on to argue that Nichols' discretionary view in fact lays the groundwork for motivating full blown preservationism, due in large part to the role that our all things considered practical interests must play in fixing the appropriate reference-fixing convention for "free will." So, while Heller and Hurley's arguments show that traditional approaches to reference are not hospitable to at least some varieties of eliminativism, even Nichols' elimination-friendly account fails to offer the resources to motivate eliminativism over preservationism. I conclude that eliminativists' prospects for meeting the motivational challenge look grim.

I conclude in Chapter 7 first with a return to the kinds of concerns that often motivate attempts to defend descriptive skepticism and prescriptive eliminativism – those that highlight the high costs of reactive blame. While

---

[4] Here, I restrict my focus to the way that "free will" refers in particular, as this is the only term in the constellation of free will, responsibility, and blame that has thus far received much attention in regard to its operative reference-fixing convention.

I take my arguments in earlier chapters to have defused the force of these arguments, I anticipate that these initial concerns about "the dark side" of free will, moral responsibility, and especially reactive blame will continue to linger among those inclined toward a curmudgeonly position. I also think that these concerns are well taken, and so in this final chapter, I attempt to address them head-on and examine what I take to be two of the *worst* potential costs of free will, responsibility, and blame: their apparent connection with a constellation of deeply troubling political beliefs, and concerns about harming the innocent undeservedly. I argue that neither of these concerns can successfully motivate any kind of brute pragmatic argument for eliminativism over preservationism. However, in the final section, I sketch the contours of just this kind of argument in favor of *preservationism*. Here I conclude on a more personal note, by emphasizing my own *victim-centered* interests in theorizing about free will, responsibility, and blame, and suggest that when we adopt a perspective that places the testimony of actual victims at the forefront, eliminativism appears to have a dark side of its own. There is in fact an *argument from empathy* that ought to be considered more explicitly in our attempts to adjudicate between eliminativists and preservationists, and it counts heavily in favor of preservation.

Before getting started, it is worth noting that while Part I remains focused exclusively on reactive blame, the discussion in Part II will often slide between talk of free will, moral responsibility, and blame. This is not ideal, as it allows for potential points of confusion and misunderstanding regarding whether or not claims made about one of these things apply equally to the other two. Here I admit that I am not entirely sure how best to address this concern. On the one hand, it is now commonplace in the literature to use "free will" to discuss the kind of control necessary for moral responsibility, and to assume that moral responsibility is the kind of thing that makes us deserving of moral praise and blame in the basic sense. I think, therefore, there is nothing especially dubious about sometimes sliding between these terms, at least for ease of exposition.

On the other hand, it always feels a bit philosophically reckless to be imprecise with one's terms. Perhaps, then, a brief *mea culpa* will go some way toward defusing any potential initial ire. Here I can report that I take these concerns seriously, but have chosen to prioritize the value of taking a broad approach to these issues over the value of maximizing precision. When it comes to free will, my own thoughts are that dialectical shifts that narrow the conversation and prioritize precision can sometimes lose sight of the forest for the trees.[5] Many of the most significant shifts in the literature have come when we take a step back, and think more carefully about whatever it is we are trying to get at with the term "free will."[6] It seems to me, for example, that the progress that has already been made since the titanic shift initiated by P. F. Strawson in understanding the ways that moral responsibility and blame seem to be what *grounds* our interest in free will in the first place suggests that a broader approach is worth pursuing. But the cost of trying to reconceptualize any particularly intractable philosophical issue is often some degree of imprecision. Perhaps others will be able to address these questions without sacrificing quite so much, but here the best I can do is acknowledge this cost and offer the reader a promissory note that I have done my best to minimize it.

---

[5] I say this having myself weighed in on questions about Frankfurt-style-cases involving time travelers.
[6] Here of course P. F. Strawson's (1962) work comes to the forefront.

PART I

The Permissibility of Blame

CHAPTER I

The Problem of Blame

Part of what makes the problem of blame so difficult is the fact that there is little consensus on the nature of blame itself. For example, some take blame to be a mere judgment with no necessary emotional sting accompanying it. Others take blame to be essentially accompanied by some angry emotional charge. The varieties of blame come packaged with very different accounts of the *sting* of blame, and thus the corresponding degree of discomfort or harm that blame causes differs drastically depending on the details.

In what follows, I will be restricting my focus almost exclusively to one particular variety of blame: *reactive blame*. The motivation for this restriction is that it is the kind of blame that motivates blame curmudgeons' skeptical worries about permissibility. As noted in the Introduction, I am assuming a stipulative characterization of curmudgeonly views about blame. While there are now a wide array of descriptively skeptical views about free will, moral responsibility, and blame (see, for example, Ishtiyaque Haji (2016), Neil Levy (2011), and Galen Strawson (1993)), curmudgeons are those who argue further for some prescriptive variety of eliminativism whereby we ought to eliminate reactive blame from our lives insofar as we can. The paradigm curmudgeonly views that I have in mind as targets here are Pereboom (2001, 2013), Caruso (2012, 2015, 2020), Strawson (1994), and Waller (1990, 2011, 2015, 2020).

Curmudgeonly worries do not arise for *every* kind of blame. It is not at all clear, for example, why one might be concerned about the permissibility of merely holding the belief that a wrongdoer is blameworthy. But, matters are different when we consider varieties of blame that are clearly harmful. The idea that we ought to avoid harming others without justification is among the bedrock of our moral intuitions, and so as we consider more harmful varieties of blame, the justificatory stakes creep higher, and concerns about permissibility naturally begin to emerge. And reactive blame appears to be the *most* harmful variety of blame.[1] It is the kind of blame that is intimately tied to one of our most unpleasant moral emotions – moral anger.

Some attempts to defend blame from curmudgeonly skepticism have adopted the strategy of *avoiding* this kind of blame, arguing that there are less harmful, *sanitized* varieties that can sustain the valuable features of our blaming practices without the emotional costs of moral anger.[2] While there are merits to this kind of approach to defending blame against skepticism – for example, it carves out conceptual space for salvaging at least *some* variety of blame if such skeptical worries ultimately prove decisive – one might worry that this kind of sanitizing approach gives far too much away to skeptics from the start. For my part, I think that this strategy avoids the problem of blame by merely sidestepping it, leaving the real *hard problem* of blame largely untouched. No one – including the staunchest of blame curmudgeons – is losing much sleep over the permissibility of sanitized, painless blame. It is the nasty, reactive, angry kind that is controversial, and so the real challenge of defending blame against skeptical worries is to defend the reactive variety in particular.

My goal throughout this book is to meet this challenge head-on, and offer a defense of reactive blame in particular. If this defense succeeds, then it is not at all clear what further worries about the permissibility of blame could remain. If a case can be made for thinking that even the *worst* kind of blame is sometimes permissible, and that our all things considered reasons count in favor of retaining this kind of blame, then the most serious skeptical threats to blame will have been defused.

But what counts as reactive blame, and how ought we to distinguish this kind of blame from other more innocuous varieties? In Section 1.1, I trace a fault line between reactive and nonreactive varieties of blame and identify some of the features that unify reactive accounts. In doing so, I attempt to clarify a feature of reactive blame that has thus far led to a great deal of confusion – how we ought to understand the kind of *central role* played by the reactive attitudes for such accounts. I identify and set aside one particularly implausible (yet seemingly widespread) way of understanding this role, and identify two far more plausible alternatives.

---

[1] At least among plausible contemporary accounts. Here, I set aside accounts tied directly to retributive theological views or theories of punishment.

[2] Scanlon's (2008) conative view of blame is perhaps the most notable example. I discuss this view in further detail in Section 1.2.2.

In Section 1.2, I offer a rough taxonomy of explicitly nonreactive varieties of blame. Here I focus on cognitive and conative accounts as nonreactive paradigms. In Section 1.3, I examine whether certain accounts of blame that are more difficult to categorize – quality of will accounts and functionalist accounts – ought to be characterized as reactive or nonreactive. I conclude that the negative reactive attitudes play a sufficiently central role for the majority of these accounts to give rise to the problem of blame, and thus they are best characterized as reactive.

Finally, in Section 1.4, I turn to explicating the problem of blame itself. Once we recognize that the most vexing skeptical challenges to blame concern reactive blame and its attendant harms, a helpful analogy to a more familiar problem arises. This more familiar problem is *the problem of punishment*, and I argue that attempts to resolve this problem are instructive for understanding the problem of blame. In particular, attempts to resolve the problem of punishment help to explicate two clear desiderata for resolving the problem of blame, desiderata that if met should satisfy even the most skeptical blame curmudgeon. I devote the remainder of Part I to arguing that both of these desiderata can ultimately be met by a plausible account of reactive blame.

1.1 Reactive Blame

As noted earlier, part of the difficulty in articulating the problem of blame is the fact that there is little consensus about what the target concept actually *is*. Furthermore, there are significant methodological disagreements about how we ought to approach theorizing about blame in the first place. While some adopt a method akin to traditional conceptual analysis, others take paradigm instances of blame to be the best starting point, while still others think that we should begin by analyzing the work we want blame to do for us in our moral lives and offer an account that can make sense of blame's functional role.

For now, I will largely set these methodological differences aside, though I will return to them in Part II. In the next three sections, my goal is only to provide a rough taxonomy of the varieties of blame currently on offer, and a clearer method for distinguishing reactive blame from its less harmful counterparts. To that end, I will carve up the terrain along one central fault line: accounts of blame that take the negative reactive attitudes to play some central role, and those that do not. Those that fall under the former category are the varieties of blame I will call *reactive blame*, the kind of blame that the hard problem of blame is actually a problem for.

I will have a great deal to say about the positive components of reactive blame in the following chapters, and so wish to avoid any substantial commitments just yet. A full blown account of reactive blame (or, for that matter, any account of blame) should tell us something about the *object* of blame (what blame responds to), the *content* of blame (what, if any, propositional content is involved in blaming), what kinds of *responses* count as genuine blaming responses (does blame require some kind of communicative expression, or does private blame count?), and what the *aims* of blame are (what kinds of valuable or evolutionarily useful things does blame do for creatures like us?). I will discuss all of these features of reactive blame in substantial detail in Chapters 2–4. Here only a few preliminary remarks are in order for the task of initially distinguishing reactive blame from nonreactive varieties more generally.

First, it is important to note that I will be casting the net of reactive blame quite broadly. What I call reactive accounts will encompass a wide range of views sometimes characterized as *Strawsonian* in spirit, due to the central role played by the negative reactive attitudes that feature so prominently in P. F. Strawson's (1962) *Freedom and Resentment*. While nearly every other feature of blame may differ across reactive accounts of blame, what they all have in common is some kind of central role for these affective attitudes. But which attitudes? This question will feature prominently in the discussion of blame and the negative reactive attitudes in Chapter 3, but for now the reader can assume *at minimum* the relevant attitudes will be the varieties of moral anger: resentment, indignation, and guilt.

What do I mean when I say that these moral emotions play a *central* role in reactive accounts of blame? I take confusion about this question to have motivated a significant amount of criticism directed toward reactive accounts thus far. So, for the remainder of this section, I will attempt to clarify three possible answers. While I take the first answer to be the most widespread, I think it is also the least charitable way of construing the kind of centrality that is granted to the negative reactive attitudes for reactive blame. I also take this construal to give rise to much of the criticism just mentioned. As such, I will offer two alternatives that I think proponents of reactive accounts of blame can and should endorse instead.

1.1.1   Reactive Essentialism

What all reactive accounts of blame have in common is that the negative reactive attitudes play *some* central role in making sense of what blame is.

But the way that we understand the degree of centrality can make a significant difference when it comes to the plausibility of a particular reactive account of blame. Here I will characterize three main options for understanding this role that have coalesced in the literature thus far: (1) reactive essentialism, (2) functional reactivity, and (3) canonical reactivity.

The first option, which I will call *reactive essentialism*, is perhaps the most natural way of understanding reactive blame. It is also the one that opponents of reactive blame have called the most attention to. Reactive essentialism is the view that some experience or expression of the negative reactive attitudes is a *necessary* feature of blame. Thus, an instance of apparent blame will count as genuine only if it is accompanied or characterized by the actual experience or expression of a negative reactive attitude.

I take this way of understanding reactive blame to be something of a straw man. While much ink has been spilled arguing that reactive blame so understood is descriptively implausible – it is subject to a wide array of counterexamples[3] – it is not at all clear that any proponents of reactive blame actually endorse reactive essentialism.[4] In fact, many of those who have defended accounts of explicitly reactive blame most vigorously have themselves acknowledged such counterexamples and weakened their views accordingly. R. Jay Wallace, for example, argues only that blame involves a *susceptibility* to the reactive emotions,[5] stating explicitly that "it is not required that we actually feel the relevant emotion in all the cases in which it would be appropriate to do so" (Wallace, 1994: 77). Wallace instead characterizes the connection between the reactive attitudes and blame as indirect and disjunctive. Blame is about holding one another to expectations we accept, and the reactive attitudes are constitutively linked to these expectations:

> . . . to hold someone to an expectation, I suggest, is to be susceptible to a certain range of emotions if the expectation is violated, or to believe that it would be appropriate for one to feel those emotions if the expectation is violated. (Wallace, 1994: 23)

I will discuss Wallace's view in much greater depth in Chapter 3, but here I wish to emphasize that even for Wallace – whose view is often taken to be a paradigm reactive account – the role played by the reactive attitudes is not an essential one. While susceptibility to the reactive attitudes is a *sufficient* condition for blame on Wallace's view, it is not a necessary one.

---

[3] See for example Sher (2006) and Scanlon (2008).
[4] Susan Wolf (2011) is perhaps one notable exception.   [5] See Wallace (1994: 12).

Rather, one might also hold someone to an expectation and blame them by meeting the second disjunct above, and simply believing that it *would* be appropriate for one to feel the reactive attitudes in a given circumstance.[6]

Wallace is not the only proponent of reactive blame to avoid commitment to reactive essentialism.[7] In fact, this kind of reactive essentialism is quite difficult to find clear examples of.[8] Nor do I see any clear reason for a proponent of reactive blame to accept reactive essentialism. There are alternative ways of understanding the central role that these attitudes play which are far more plausible. In what follows, I will set reactive essentialism aside, and focus instead on characterizing reactive blame in terms of one or both of these two alternatives.

1.1.2   Functional Reactivity

Angela Smith (2013) has recently offered an alternative to reactive essentialism, which I will here call *functional reactivity*. Smith is primarily interested in the role that moral protest plays in blame, arguing that registering one's moral protest is an essential feature of blame left out by many nonreactive accounts. She attempts to carve out a middle ground between "moral assessment" accounts of blame, and "moral sanction" accounts, taking blame to involve more than a mere negative judgment about its target's quality of will while still falling short of full blown punishing or sanctioning (Smith, 2013: 27).

Smith states the view as follows:

> To morally blame another, in my view, is to register in some significant way one's moral protest of that agent's treatment of oneself or others. (Smith, 2013: 29)

---

[6] Here my claim that Wallace does not endorse reactive essentialism might be puzzling to some, given Wallace's well-known criticism of nonreactive accounts like Scanlon's for "leaving the blame out of blame" (Wallace, 2011: 349). Wallace's criticism targets the fact that, on Scanlon's account, the negative reactive attitudes are at best only contingently related to blame. We could fully account for genuine blame on Scanlon's view without them. On Wallace's view we could not, though this need not entail the kind of strict reactive essentialism discussed here. As I will discuss later, Wallace and others can make sense of the centrality of the negative reactive attitudes without going so far as to claim that their experience or expression is a necessary condition for genuine instances of blame by appealing instead to *functional* or *canonical* reactivity.

[7] Even Strawson himself makes no explicit commitment to *this* degree of centrality for the reactive attitudes, despite the important role he takes these attitudes to play in constituting our blaming and responsibility-related practices more broadly.

[8] As noted earlier, Wolf might be one exception and goes so far as to say that "liability to feel angry emotions and to form angry attitudes appears to be an inevitable feature of allowing oneself to be not just physically but emotionally vulnerable to other people" (Wolf, 2011: 337).

While registering such protest "need not take the form of a Strawsonian reactive attitude," Smith acknowledges that explicitly Strawsonian accounts do *come closest* to capturing the element of moral protest that she does take to be essential. Understood as a form of moral protest, Smith then takes the function of blame to be twofold. First, blame registers the fact that the victim did not deserve a certain kind of treatment by "*challenging* the moral claim implicit in the wrongdoer's action" (Smith, 2013: 43). Second, blame "prompts moral recognition and acknowledgement of this fact on the part of the wrongdoer and/or others in the moral community" (Smith, 2013: 43). And resentment and indignation are *very common* ways of protesting the conduct of others and meeting these two aims. However, these negative reactive attitudes are not the *only* means of doing so. It is possible, for example, to challenge and prompt recognition of such conduct "dispassionately," sometimes by merely modifying our attitudes, intentions, and expectations of one another (Smith, 2013: 45).

The fact that the negative reactive attitudes are not a necessary feature of moral protest rules out reactive essentialism for Smith. However, Smith's account of blame still has a significantly reactive feel, and she ultimately concludes:

> Of all of the traditional and contemporary accounts of blame on offer, it seems to me that the Strawsonian account comes closest to capturing this crucial aspect of these distinctively moral responses, which perhaps explains why his view has had such staying power. To the extent that it fails, it is only in placing too much emphasis on just one – albeit one very important – set of emotional reactions as the sine qua non of moral protest. (Smith, 2013: 48)

Here an alternative to reactive essentialism begins to emerge. Rather than taking the negative reactive attitudes as an *essential* feature of reactive blame, we might more charitably understand the centrality of the negative reactive attitudes to blame in something like Smith's terms. While these attitudes are not strictly necessary, they are often the *best*, or at least *the most common* means we have of meeting and sustaining the aims of blame. Call this understanding of the way in which the negative reactive attitudes are central to reactive blame *functional reactivity*.

On Smith's view, the aims of blame directly involve moral protest, but one need not be committed to this detail in order to embrace functional reactivity. Here I simply take Smith's view to be instructive in elucidating a plausible alternative to reactive essentialism.

1.1.3 Canonical Reactivity

Functional reactivity is not the only alternative to reactive essentialism. Victoria McGeer has also recently applied Jackson and Pettit's (1995) appeal to canonical features of a kind to blame, and in doing so, sketched an additional alternative. Canonical features are those features that have criterial significance, in that they "account for our interests in identifying a kind as such, even though things belonging to the kind do not invariably manifest the feature in question" (McGeer, 2013: 168). Canonical features are more than mere characteristic or typical features of a kind, but also fall short from counting as essential or necessary. McGeer suggests that the negative reactive attitudes are precisely this kind of feature of blame. I will call McGeer's method of characterizing the centrality of the negative reactive attitudes to blame *canonical reactivity*.

This proposal for understanding the centrality of the negative reactive attitudes arises in the context of McGeer's attempt to resolve a tension similar to the one at issue for what I have been calling the hard problem of blame – blame seems to be an important and valuable way of responding to wrongdoing, yet often has an angry, punitive edge that seems difficult to justify. McGeer argues that the project of resolving this tension and thus "civilizing blame" is subject to two constraints. First, she finds attempts to simply abandon reactive, angry blame problematic, arguing that a *psychologically realistic* account of blame must be an account of the reactive variety, "taking blame to be a phenomenon that displays the negative profile (warts and all) that is typically associated with [it]" (McGeer, 2013: 163).[9] Further, any attempt to civilize blame can only meet a second *normative constraint* by explaining precisely how this "unsavory" kind of blame "can still do valuable normative work so long as it is constrained by social and institutional practices that support its more constructive features" (McGeer, 2013: 163). For McGeer, it is precisely the negative reactive attitudes, understood as a canonical feature of blame, which do this valuable normative work.

I will discuss McGeer's view in further detail in Chapter 4, and here I wish to focus only on her characterization of the negative reactive attitudes as canonical features of blame. This characterization presents yet another plausible way of understanding the central role that the negative reactive attitudes might play for reactive blame while avoiding full blown reactive essentialism. McGeer's account is similar to the one sketched by Smith in that it takes the functional role of blame to be an important starting point. However, her own view of the functional role of blame differs in that McGeer is primarily concerned with blame as a

---

[9] As discussed earlier, I am in significant agreement with McGeer on this point.

psychological kind, taking a naturalistic, evolutionary approach to under-standing its aims.

According to McGeer, blame involves both backward and forward-looking elements of appraisal. In regard to the former, blame is triggered by various events only insofar as they are coded or perceived as situations of a certain emotion-inducing type, namely as norm transgressions (McGeer, 2013: 171). In regard to the forward-looking element, blame disposes us to behave in ways that at one point had an overall tendency to enhance individual fitness in ancestral popula-tions by promoting large-scale human cooperation (McGeer, 2013: 171). On McGeer's account, the psychological feature that plays both these forward- and backward-looking roles is *moral anger*. Moral anger is the psychological state that *typically* plays the causal role of blame in creatures like us, and the unpleasant emotional character of this state is *not incidental* (McGeer, 2013: 169). While it is possible to blame dispassionately without moral anger (and thus reactive essen-tialism is false), such instances of blame are in some sense *defective* on McGeer's account. They lack a *canonical feature* of blame, namely the negative reactive attitudes that constitute the varieties of moral anger.

But how ought we to understand the distinction between canonical features, and other kinds of features? Here McGeer is also instructive. She distinguishes between features of a kind that are essential or constitutive, those that are merely "kind-associated," and those that are canonical. Essential features are, again, those necessary to a genuine instance of the kind, whereas mere kind-associated features are "features whose contingent association with the phenomenon in question is of no criterial signifi-cance" (McGeer, 2013: 168). The ability to fly, for example, is a kind-associated feature of birds. While many members of the kind have this feature, it does not figure in how we demarcate the bounds of the kind itself. The ability to fly is a contingent feature of birds, and not the sort of thing we appeal to in order to distinguish birds from non-birds, or to understand the kind of thing birds are.[10]

Canonical features, in contrast, are those that *do* have criterial signifi-cance. They are the very features that

> ... account for our interest in identifying the kind as such, even though things belonging to the kind do not invariably manifest the feature in question. (McGeer, 2013: 168)

---

[10] Perhaps Smith's account might best be characterized as one for with the negative reactive attitudes are merely "kind-associated," while the fact that they are the *best* kind-associated features for sustaining the functional role of blame is what renders this account a functionally reactive one. Thanks to Neal Tognazzini for suggesting this point.

Canonical features therefore represent a middle ground between mere kind-associated features and features that are essential. Genuine members of the kind can lack a canonical feature, but we could not make sense of the kind itself without such features. Here McGeer's use of the kind "heart" as an example is instructive:

> Whether natural or artificial, hearts are canonically the kind of things that pump blood. A heart deserves to be called a heart only so far as it is a thing of *that* (instrumental) kind. But, of course, this doesn't mean that all hearts are able to pump blood. Things of that kind sometimes malfunction. (McGeer, 2013: 168)

Just as hearts are canonically the kinds of things that pump blood, blame is canonically the kind of thing that involves moral anger. Yet, just as a heart that has stopped beating is still heart, so too might a dispassionate instance of blame still count as genuine blame. However, like the stopped heart, such an instance of blame would be defective in some sense. Blame is *the kind of thing* that usually involves moral anger, and this negative reactive attitude serves as a canonical feature.

I take both functional reactivity and canonical reactivity to represent plausible ways of understanding the way in which the negative reactive attitudes are central to reactive blame. Here I will not take a stand on which of these alternatives to reactive essentialism I am inclined to endorse. Nor is it clear that these two characterizations should necessarily be treated as distinct options. It is worth emphasizing that the appeal to the functional role of blame is an important feature of each way of understanding the centrality of the negative reactive attitudes for reactive blame, and that one might easily combine a normative approach to understanding this role like Smith's with a naturalistic, evolutionary approach to understanding it like McGeer's.[11]

In what follows, I assume only that reactive essentialism is an uncharitable way of characterizing reactive accounts of blame. Critics are correct to point out that counterexamples involving apparently genuine yet dispassionate instances of blame abound, but incorrect to dismiss reactive blame because of them. There are other plausible ways of construing the central role of the negative reactive attitudes for reactive blame that need not characterize these emotions as necessary or essential. In what follows,

---

[11] In fact, this will largely be my approach in Chapter 4.

I invite the reader to think of the role of these attitudes, especially moral anger, in terms of either *functional reactivity*, or *canonical reactivity*.

I will use these two ways of thinking about centrality to distinguish reactive accounts of blame from their nonreactive counterparts. As we will see in Section 1.3, it is not always clear whether an account of blame is nonreactive or reactive to a degree relevant to the problem of blame. And this is especially true once we have abandoned reactive essentialism as a way of characterizing the latter. In what follows, I will use the disjunction of functional and canonical reactivity as a test for the degree of reactivity needed to give rise to the problem of blame. If an account takes the negative reactive attitudes to be necessary to explaining or sustaining the functional role of blame, or to distinguishing blame as a genuine kind in the first place, then it is an account of *reactive blame* in need of defense from the problem of blame.

I turn now to a brief tour through two explicitly nonreactive alternatives to reactive blame, accounts that seem to easily avoid the problem of blame and worries about permissibility.

1.2 The Varieties of Nonreactive Blame

Work on blame has thus far occurred across a wide range of philosophical subdisciplines, and as such has not yet lent itself to anything like a canonical taxonomy. One noteworthy exception in recent work has been Justin Coates and Neal Tognazzini's (2013) clear and informative attempt to carve out the various areas of the terrain in their introduction to *Blame: Its Nature and Norms*. In this section, I will largely borrow from their chosen method of categorization, with a few noteworthy departures that I think help to better sharpen the distinction between reactive and nonreactive blame in particular.

Coates and Tognazzini carve up the terrain of blame in terms of four main categories: cognitive accounts, conative accounts, Strawsonian accounts, and functional accounts. Strawsonian accounts correspond straightforwardly to what I have here been calling reactive blame, as accounts that explicitly take the negative reactive attitudes to play some central role. Here I will set Strawsonian accounts aside and focus on the two main categories of paradigmatically nonreactive blame: cognitive accounts and conative accounts. I will then turn in Section 1.3 to discussion of accounts that are a bit more difficult to characterize as reactive or nonreactive, and offer some suggestions for how we ought to make this distinction in light of the discussion of functional and canonical reactivity.

1.2.1 Cognitive Accounts of Blame

If reactive blame occupies one extreme on the spectrum of the potential harms of blame, *cognitive accounts* lie at the other. Cognitive accounts are those that take blame to be some kind of *evaluative judgment*, where the content of this judgment varies. For example, some cognitive accounts take the content of the evaluative judgment involved in blame to be a kind of negative mark on one's "moral ledger" (Zimmerman, 1988: 38).[12] This kind of view was proposed by J. J. C. Smart (1961), who characterized blame as similar to dispraise in that it involves a *grading* judgment of its target as a thing of a certain kind.[13] However, for Smart blame goes beyond mere dispraise in that this evaluative judgment has some additional significance. It implies that its object is responsible for their action or character.

Other cognitive accounts take blame to involve an aretaic judgment, or as Gary Watson puts it, to see the conduct at issue "as a poor exercise of human evaluative capacities, as characteristic of someone who cares little about standards of excellence in human affairs" (Watson, 2004: 265). While Watson does not take this kind of cognitive blame – the kind associated with what he calls the *attributability* face of responsibility – to be the only kind of blame, it is itself a robust cognitive alternative to reactive blame.

What the variety of cognitive accounts have in common is that *some* evaluative judgment is not only necessary, but also sufficient for blame. Further, these accounts make no mention of the reactive attitudes. The varieties of moral anger play *no* role in blame on a straightforwardly cognitive account, though they may turn out to be merely contingently associated with the relevant evaluative judgment. Thus, cognitive accounts constitute perhaps the clearest example of straightforwardly nonreactive blame.

However, not all evaluative judgments are normatively equal. This is especially clear when we consider evaluative judgments about one's *quality of will*. Judgments about quality of will seem to have a special normative force, and are importantly distinct from other kinds of negative evaluative judgments, say about one's awful cooking or bad driving. Quality of will *matters more to us*, and judgments about it flag ways in which someone has "dropped below some standard that we accept (or perhaps that we think

---

[12] For similar views, we might classify as "ledger" views; see Glover (1970) and Haji (1998).
[13] See also Schlick (1939).

they should accept), whether of excellence, morality, or respectful relationships" (Coates and Tognazzini, 2013: 9). We care about such judgments in ways that we simply do not care about what others think about our cooking or our driving, even (and perhaps *especially*!) if they are never communicated to us.

Views that take blame to be constituted by an evaluative judgment of ill will are often categorized as cognitive accounts. However, for my current purposes things are not so clear cut. Because judgments of ill will have special significance and force for us, they are precisely the kind of judgments that tend to trigger the negative reactive attitudes. Whether or not such views end up counting as reactive or nonreactive will depend on the details (namely whether or not the negative reactive attitudes turn out to be an essential, functionally necessary, or canonical feature of blame), and as such I will treat them separately in Section 1.3. Before dealing with these thornier issues, it will be first helpful to get a clear picture of the other paradigmatic variety of nonreactive blame, conative blame.

1.2.2   *Conative Accounts of Blame*

In addition to cognitive accounts, *conative accounts* represent perhaps the most fully developed and plausible alternative to reactive blame. Among the most prominent defenders of conative accounts of blame are George Sher (2006) and T. M. Scanlon (2008). Conative accounts follow cognitive accounts in taking some kind of evaluative belief or judgment to be central to blame, but depart from these more minimal accounts in that the relevant belief is not sufficient. Conative accounts take some corresponding change to the blamer's motivation – their desires, attitudes, or other dispositions to behave in certain ways – to also be necessary. Here I will focus on Sher and Scanlon's accounts as the two most fully developed conative accounts currently on offer.

According to Sher's conative account, blame is a belief–desire pair. The belief in question is that the target of blame has acted badly or has a bad character, while the corresponding desire is the desire that the target *had not* acted badly, or *had not* had a bad character (Sher, 2006: 112). In regard to the belief component, Sher clarifies that "bad acts" refer to "morally defective acts that render agents blameworthy" (Sher, 2006: 9). So, the belief component looks to be simply a judgment that the target of blame has a character or has committed some wrong conduct for which they are blameworthy. It is then the desire component of the core pair that allows this account to avoid vicious circularity by further elucidating what the blameworthy are worthy *of* – namely, whatever reactions are made appropriate by the overall pair.

This core belief–desire pair composes the first "tier" of Sher's account of blame, with some class of blame-related behavioral and attitudinal dispositions forming the second tier (Sher, 2006: 138). According to Sher, it is the desire component of the core belief–desire pair that explains the relevant behavioral and attitudinal dispositions:

> [T]he obvious way to invoke D [the desire that the target of blame had not had a bad character or acted badly which makes up the desire component of the belief-desire core of blame] to account for our disposition to become angry at those we blame is to assimilate that anger to the other negative feelings that we have when we see that we cannot get what we want. Just as obviously, the way to invoke D to account for our disposition to display hostility toward those we blame is to see our hostile behavior as a natural expression of our negative feelings toward them. (Sher, 2006: 104–105)

Sher's key insight is that there is something motivational at the heart of our blaming reactions. His view has the advantages of allowing for a significant degree of variation across our actual blaming responses and explaining why the negative reactive attitudes are not necessary to blame.[14] In regard to the latter, consider a particularly close relationship with a friend or loved one. In this case, the belief that she is blameworthy paired with a desire that she had not wronged you might dispose you to other responses than hostile negative reactive attitudes. Hoping to maintain the relationship you might instead be disposed to calmly confront her, and communicate information about the kind of amends or apology that would be needed to reconcile fully. Many have criticized Sher's claim that the core belief–desire pair he identifies is sufficient to explain a wide enough range of apparent instances of blame, or even that it is necessary to do so.[15] Here I do not wish to assess the overall plausibility of Sher's conative view of blame, but merely to note it as a robust conative alternative to reactive blame.

Perhaps, the most richly developed and defended alternative to reactive blame is another conative account, the account developed over the past several decades by T. M. Scanlon (1988, 1998, 2008). Scanlon (2008) explicitly proposes an account of blame that he takes to satisfy four main desiderata, namely to explain: (1) the difference between blame and mere

---

[14] This core belief–desire pair remains constant across all agents and contexts, but will make different reactions appropriate depending on the relationship between the blamer, wrongdoer, and victim.

[15] For persuasive arguments to this end, see Smith (2013).

objective stigma or *moral outcome luck*; (2) the relation between blame and *wrongness*; (3) the *significance* of blame and why blame matters to us; and (4) the *ethics* of blame (who can be the target of blame, who has standing to blame, and why we should blame).[16]

According to Scanlon, to *be blameworthy* entails that something about your attitudes toward others *impairs* the relationship that they can have with you. This notion of impairment is central to Scanlon's account of blame, and it arises out of his account of the standards constitutive of our interpersonal relationships (Scanlon, 2008: 131–138). These relationships are constituted by the *reasons* one takes themselves to have for treating others in certain ways, and corresponding *dispositions* to feel and act in certain ways. Nondefective interpersonal relationships should be mutual or reciprocal and governed by certain normative standards and ideals. The relevant kind of normative ideal is simply whatever must be true in order for an individual to have a relationship of the relevant kind; how they should behave ideally; and what attitudes they should have ideally relevant to that kind.

On Scanlon's view, different kinds of relationships can, and in fact sometimes do, have radically different normative ideals. The conditions that must be met in order for me to be a term in an interpersonal romantic relationship will be drastically different from the kinds of ideal attitudes, dispositions, and expectations needed to engage in a relationship between colleagues. These normative ideals set the standards for a kind of relationship, and also restrict what might count as a genuine interpersonal relationship of the relevant kind. While on Scanlon's view there will be a wide array of kinds here, not just any relation will count. One-off or grue-like[17] relations (say between people who see each other in the hallway in passing on Tuesdays) will not count, because there is no apparent normative ideal relevant to them. Finally, on Scanlon's view most of our interpersonal relationships are *contingent* and *conditional*.[18] Maintaining them often depends on several factors that can lie outside of one party's control, and

---

[16] See Scanlon (2008), chapter 4.

[17] "Grue-like" relations, like grue-like predicates, would be those that are very poorly *entrenched*. In the past, we have not projected many hypotheses involving them or relations coextensive to them. In other words, they are the kind of relations that we do not often (or ever) find ourselves in need of in order to make useful explanatory or inductive claims, and they are likely to be massively or randomly disjunctive. They are relations that do not "hang together" in any apparent way. For further discussion see Goodman's (1955) account of grue-like predicates.

[18] One notable exception is *the moral relationship* that Scanlon posits between all moral-reasons-responsive agents in order to avoid the objection that his view cannot make sense of blaming strangers. See Scanlon (2008: 139–152).

they can be *ended*. Often relationships come to end due to an impairment. But they can also be ended blamelessly and without impairment, such as when two friends simply drift apart.

Like blameworthiness, actively blaming someone is closely related to the normative ideals of our interpersonal relationships and what it means to impair them. On Scanlon's view, an interpersonal relationship is *impaired* when one party, while standing in the relevant relation to another person, holds attitudes toward that person that are ruled out by the standards (normative ideals) of that relationship, thus making it appropriate for the other party to have attitudes other than those that the relationship normally involves. This notion of impairment is not all or nothing – most of our interpersonal relationships can continue in an impaired form. A bad friend, for example, might still be considered a genuine friend (Scanlon, 2008: 131–138). When a relationship has been impaired in the relevant sense, it is appropriate *to blame* the party who has caused the impairment. Scanlon explicitly defines what it means to blame someone as having two features: (1) a judgment that the target of blame is *blameworthy* (as stated earlier, the belief that they have impaired the relevant relationship); and (2) to take the relationship with the target of blame to be *modified* in a way that this judgment renders appropriate.

Here the notion of *modification* still needs to be elucidated, and it is this feature that renders Scanlon's account of blame a conative one. Scanlon uses the example of Joe, a disappointing friend, to articulate some of our options for modification:

> Suppose I learn that at a party last week some acquaintances were talking about me, and making some cruel jokes at my expense. I further learnt that my close friend Joe was that party, and that rather than coming to my defense or adopting a stony silence, he was laughing heartily and even contributed a few barbs, revealing some embarrassing facts about me that I had told him in confidence. This raises some question about my relationship with Joe. ... Possible responses, on my part, to what Joe has done fall into three general categories. First, I might consider whether I should continue to regard Joe as a friend. An answer to this question is a judgment about the meaning of Joe's action – about what it shows about his attitude toward me, considered in relation to the requirements of friendship, and about the significance of that attitude for our relationship. Second, I might revise my attitude toward Joe in the way that this judgment holds appropriate. I might, for example, cease to value spending time with him in the way one does with a friend, and I might revise my intentions to confide in him and to encourage him to confide in me. Third, I might complain to Joe about his conduct, demand an explanation or justification, or indicate in some other way that I no longer see him as a friend. (Scanlon, 2008: 129–130)

While Scanlon takes it to be a merit of his account that it allows for a wide array of relationship-modifying responses to count as blaming responses, this example highlights a few noteworthy possibilities. First, and perhaps most minimally, modification might involve simply altering your judgments and attitudes about the nature of your relationship with the target of blame. A betrayal like Joe's might lead you to view him as more of an acquaintance than a friend. In doing so, you might change your intentions toward Joe, and adjust your expectations of him in the future. For example, you may no longer intend to spend substantial amounts of time with him, or to confide in him. Or, you may abandon the expectation that he will keep any future confidences, or defend you against slander from others.

Whatever the attitudinal revision, this first kind of modification need not entail any overt behavior or speech that communicates the modification of your relationship. If the target of blame is not particularly observant, then it is compatible with Scanlon's view that this kind of blaming modification might occur without any uptake from that target. In practice, it does seem that blame is sometimes "silent" in this way, and so one virtue of Scanlon's account is that it has the resources to make sense of this kind of *private* blame.

But blame is often public, and does in fact aim at some form of uptake from its target. On Scanlon's account revising not only our attitudes but also our *dispositions* can mark a modification to a relationship to both the blamer and target of blame. Returning to Joe, my previous disposition to feel happiness when good things happen to Joe may weaken. Likewise, I might adjust or completely abandon my disposition to defend him when others speak poorly of him, to prioritize spending time with him, or to help him when he is in need. It is not clear how fine grained we ought to be in characterizing these kinds of dispositions, but in Scanlonian terms we might think of many of them under the umbrella of a certain kind of *withdrawal*. Perhaps, one of the most widespread ways in which we blame others we judge to be blameworthy is to mark the impairment they have caused by taking a step back from them. We withdraw, and adjust many of the ways that we were previously disposed to engage with them.

This second kind of modification is far more likely to receive uptake and be noticed by blame's target. It is difficult for someone engaged in a genuine friendship not to notice when a friend withdraws or distances themselves. But it is still not the most overt way of marking the fact that an impairment has caused a particular relationship to be modified. Scanlon also acknowledges that we sometimes *express* our judgment that a relationship has been impaired with an explicit complaint, demand for explanation, apology, or justification, or by pairing any of the above with an expression of resentment or indignation. However, this final possible means of modification has an entirely contingent relation to blame. While we *can* mark modifications to our relationships in response to a judgment of impairment in ways involving the reactive attitudes, we need not do so:

> The account of blame that I offer is like Strawson's in seeing human relationships as the foundations of blame. But it differs from his view in placing emphasis on the expectations, intentions, and other attitudes that constitute these relationships rather than on moral emotions such as resentment and indignation. (Scanlon, 2008: 128)

On Scanlon's view, then, the negative reactive attitudes are neither an essential, functionally necessary, nor canonical feature of blame. As such Scanlon's account is explicitly nonreactive, and constitutes perhaps one of the most fully developed alternatives to reactive blame.

1.3   Quality of Will and Functional Accounts

While some accounts of blame are obviously reactive (for example, Strawson and Wallace's accounts), and others are clearly nonreactive (for example, Sher and Scanlon's accounts) some views are more difficult to place on either side of the fault line of reactivity. This is especially true of one subset of views often taken to be a kind of cognitive account – *quality of will accounts*. It is also true for accounts that take the functional role or aims of blame as their methodological starting point, a family of views that Coates and Tognazzini categorize as *functional accounts* of blame. Quality of will and functional accounts often attribute *some* important role to the negative reactive attitudes, but it is not always clear whether this role is central enough to give rise to the problem of blame.

While attempting to characterize all of the varieties of blame currently on offer along the fault line of reactivity is well beyond my current purposes, it may be helpful to treat at least one prominent version of each of these kinds of accounts as test cases. And with the distinction between reactive essentialism, functional reactivity, and canonical reactivity discussed in Section 1.1 now in hand, we have a clear method for doing so. In this section, I will take Pamela Hieronymi's (2004) quality of will account and Christopher Franklin's (2013) functional account as test cases, and assess the extent to which each of these views might be committed to reactive essentialism, functional reactivity, or canonical reactivity. Ultimately, it seems that both views are committed to at least one of the latter, and I conclude the section with some brief remarks on whether we ought to draw any broader tentative conclusions about the reactivity of quality of will and functional accounts more generally (I think that we should).

1.3.1 Quality of Will Accounts of Blame

As discussed earlier, *quality of will accounts* of blame are sometimes categorized loosely as cognitive accounts. Like cognitive accounts, quality of will accounts take blame to involve a particular kind of evaluative judgment. However, unlike evaluative judgments about one's moral "ledger," or aretaic character, judgments about quality of will seem to matter to us in ways that feel distinctly *forceful*. And that is due in large part to the apparent connection between our beliefs about the quality of one's will and the negative reactive attitudes. The question, then, of characterizing such views as reactive or nonreactive will hang on what the view takes this connection to amount to. If the negative reactive attitudes are an *essential* feature of our evaluative judgments about one's quality of will, if they are necessary for such judgments to fulfill the *functional role* of blame, or if they are *canonical* features of such judgments, then the view in question will count as a reactive account of blame and one for which the problem of blame is in fact a problem. If not, then while the view might acknowledge that the negative reactive attitudes can (or even that they often contingently do) accompany our judgments about quality of will, then these views would be better characterized as nonreactive.

While there are a wide array of views that take an evaluative judgment about one's quality of will to feature significantly in blame,[19] here I will focus on Pamela Hieronymi's (2004) influential account in particular. According to Hieronymi, blame is an evaluative judgment of ill will or disregard. Hieronymi's account is especially instructive for examining the centrality of the negative reactive attitudes for quality of will views, as she is explicitly interested in the *force* of blame, and whether or not such force could be subject to what she calls *the target charge of unfairness* (Hieronymi, 2004: 115).

The target charge of unfairness is the claim that the characteristic force of blame is unfair in certain conditions, namely when either: (1) the target

---

[19] For a helpful taxonomy of the wide array of views of blame that take quality of will to be a central component, see Shoemaker (2015).

of blame could not have done otherwise and gotten themselves off the moral hook; (2) they did not have the ability to control their behavior in light of moral reasons; or (3) they did not play a sufficient role in becoming the kind of person that they are (Hieronymi, 2004: 116–118). Whether or not the target charge is true will depend on what the force of blame actually is, and on Hieronymi's view, the primary force of blame lies in the judgment of ill will that constitutes blame itself. Even though this judgment is descriptive "many truths are important to us," and it matters to us whether such judgments of ill will are true, or whether others think that they are true about us, because of the importance of our mutual regard for one another (Hieronymi, 2004: 122).

As noted in Section 1.2, judgments of ill will are important to us in ways that evaluative judgments about other features – for example, one's bad driving or cooking – are not. They are judgments about a kind of moral failure – their object has disregarded the worth or standing of a fellow person. According to Hieronymi, this is precisely what lends the evaluative judgment of ill will constitutive of blame its special force and significance. However, she argues that the target charge of unfairness does not apply to this particular kind of force, because the only thing that could render it unfair would be an absence of *object-focused reasons* for thinking that the judgment that gives rise to it is true.[20] According to Hieronymi, whether the target of blame could have done otherwise in a way that would get them off the moral hook or played a sufficient role in becoming the kind of person that they are is not relevant to whether an evaluative judgment that they have failed to regard others' moral worth or standing appropriately is fair. What matters is simply whether they have so failed. Barring any object-focused reasons to think that a judgment of ill will is false, we lack grounds for thinking that a corresponding instance of blame is unfair.

However, the special significance of evaluative judgments of ill will is not the *only* feature of blame that lends it its force that Hieronymi considers. She also notes that the disagreeable, adverse effects of the negative reactive attitudes that tend to correlate with such judgments sometimes lend blame some *further* force. However, according to Hieronymi the force of these attitudes is not located primarily in their affect, as the emotional aspect of these attitudes is largely involuntary.

---

[20] I discuss Hieronymi's distinction between object and attitude-focused reasons and how they might inform our understanding of what renders blame deserved in the basic sense further in Chapter 2. This distinction is also sometimes referred to using Parfit's (2001) terminology of "object-given" and "state-given" reasons, or in terms of epistemic versus pragmatic reasons (see also Reisner, 2009).

Instead, Hieronymi argues that the negative reactive attitudes lend blame an additional "multifaceted" force (Hieronymi, 2004: 133). While the affective component of these attitudes often serves to *mark* the significance of the evaluative judgment of ill regard at the heart of blame, their own force is itself derived largely from the significance of this judgment (Hieronymi, 2004: 133).

Whether or not Hieronymi's account is best characterized as reactive or nonreactive will depend on the nature of this significance-marking role.[21] Are the negative reactive attitudes *essential* to this role? Here the answer seems clearly no. Are the negative reactive attitudes *functionally necessary* to marking the significance of our judgments of ill will? This possibility seems far more plausible. Perhaps for creatures like us with the psychological makeup that we find ourselves with these unpleasant emotions are the only way to adequately mark this kind of significance.[22] Finally, do the negative reactive attitudes seem to be a canonical feature of blame on this view? Here I am unsure, but a case could certainly be made for thinking that we might have difficulty understanding blame as the kind of thing that involves judgments of ill will that have the special force that they do without their relation to the negative reactive attitudes.

So, while Hieronymi's account of blame is often characterized as a cognitive (and thus nonreactive) one, I think we have good reason to treat it as sufficiently reactive to give rise to worries about permissibility and the problem of blame. Hieronymi's account of blame is likely to find itself in the curmudgeon's crosshairs along with other more explicitly reactive accounts.

1.3.2   Functional Accounts of Blame

Another subset of views about blame that do not clearly lend themselves to the reactive or nonreactive distinction are *functional accounts*. Often such

---

[21] This question is also distinct from how Hieronymi herself would characterize the view. Because she takes great care to locate the source of blame's force in a set of judgments and not the reactive attitudes, it may be the case that she would push back on a reactive characterization in order to avoid breathing life back into the target charge of unfairness she so effectively defuses. However, my motivating reasons for getting a clearer picture of which accounts of blame we ought to consider reactive are different from Hieronymi's. While Hieronymi is careful to move away from appeals to reactivity to explain the force of blame and thus how it might inform any potential charges of *unfairness*, I am primarily concerned with the all-things-considered permissibility of blame. We may very well have good reason (and in fact I will argue in Chapter 2 that we do have such reasons) to view these potential threats to blame as distinct. And so while I ultimately think Hieronymi's view is sufficiently reactive to give rise to the problem of blame, this is not inconsistent with reasons to view it as nonreactive in distinct contexts where fairness is of primary concern.

[22] Such an account would be very similar to McGeer's (2013).

views have a *hybrid* feel to them, combining elements from cognitive, conative, and straightforwardly reactive accounts. What functional accounts have in common is the idea that *we should identify blame with its tasks*. Coates and Tognazzini characterize this kind of view in terms of the following methodology:

> ... we should figure out what *function* blame serves and then allow the particular context to determine which mental state or activity best serves that function, and so let context determine which way of responding counts as blame. (Coates and Tognazzini, 2013: 16)

Both Smith and McGeer's accounts might be characterized as functional accounts of blame, in that they both begin with an account of the aims of blame. Recall that for Smith, blame is a form of moral protest; and for McGeer, blame is *the kind of thing* triggered by perceived wrongdoing that in turns disposes creatures like us to behave in certain ways (McGeer, 2013: 171). As discussed in Section 1.1, I take Smith and McGeer's accounts of blame to each be instructive examples of plausible accounts of reactive blame that avoid commitment to reactive essentialism. In taking the role of the negative reactive attitudes to be the most paradigmatic means of achieving the aims of blame (in Smith's case), or to have criterial significance crucial to identifying the kind of thing that blame is (in McGeer's case), each view gives the negative reactive attitudes sufficient pride of place to give rise to the problem of blame curmudgeons are worried about. Will this be the case for other explicitly functionalist accounts of blame?

Whether a specific functionalist account of blame will best be characterized as reactive or not will ultimately depend on the details, in particular on how the aims of blame are characterized and the degree to which we need the negative reactive attitudes to sufficiently pursue or understand those aims. It may be helpful to note that I suspect most functionalist views will tend in the direction of reactivity, but here I will examine Christopher Franklin's (2013) *value account of blame* as a functionalist test case.

On Franklin's view, the aim of blame is to properly value the objects of moral value, and blame is "a mode of valuation required by the standards of value" (Franklin, 2013: 209). According to his preferred account of what it means *to value* something (as opposed to merely judging it valuable), valuing requires certain emotional and deliberative dispositions. Perhaps foremost among them is the disposition to protect and defend the objects one values. While Franklin avoids controversial commitments to an account of what the proper objects of moral value actually are, he takes it as a given that they will include human beings (Franklin, 2013: 213–216). When such objects suffer an instance of moral wrongdoing, Franklin takes this to have a specific kind of symbolic meaning – wrong actions express the wrongdoer's claim that the object wronged is not to be valued after all (Franklin, 2013: 218–223).

The role of blame in valuing the proper objects of moral value is to protect and defend these objects against such claims. And doing so requires more than mere expression of a judgment that the symbolic claim expressed by wrongdoing is false. Disagreeing is not defending, especially when it comes to claims as serious as the denial of one's value as a person.[23] Instead, Franklin argues that properly valuing persons and truly defending and protecting them from such claims requires a disposition to blame wrongdoers in just the sort of way colored by the negative reactive attitudes. Mere judgments, or the kinds of dispassionate modifications to other dispositions sufficient to blame on conative views like Scanlon's, will not be enough here. Franklin argues instead that what is required to fulfill the aims of blame and successfully protect and defend the proper objects of moral value when they are wronged is a disposition to experience and express the negative reactive attitudes (Franklin, 2013: 218–223).

In offering an account that takes dispositions to experience and express the negative reactive attitudes as crucial to achieving the aims of blame, it seems that Franklin's account is best characterized as a reactive one. While the negative reactive attitudes are not a necessary or essential feature of blame on this view, Franklin seems clearly to embrace at least some form of functional reactivity. Because the aims of blame cannot be met without the negative reactive attitudes on this account of blame, this view is also likely to end up in blame curmudgeons' crosshairs.

Before turning to the problem of blame itself, a few brief remarks on whether or not this examination of Hieronymi and Franklin's accounts as test cases for reactivity suggests any broader conclusions about quality of will and functionalist accounts in general might be helpful. For my part, I expect that most functionalist accounts of blame are likely to be reactive accounts. That is because such accounts often appeal in some way to the kinds of dispositions needed to act as strong *motivating forces* for achieving

---

[23] Franklin's view is, of course, more nuanced than this, in that he takes care to argue that proper valuing will often depend on a set of standards unique to the kind of thing being valued. When it comes to persons in particular, the negative reactive attitudes are crucial to upholding these standards. I will discuss these features of Franklin's view in greater detail in Chapter 4.

the aims of blame. While conceptually it may be possible for other dispositions to serve this kind of role, I take it to be instructive that Smith, McGeer, and Franklin all coalesce around dispositions involving the negative reactive attitudes as the paradigm for this kind of motivating force. As Joshua Greene notes, "when Nature needs to get a behavioral job done, it does it with intuition and emotion wherever it can" (Greene, 2010: 367).

When it comes to quality of will accounts, my expectations are similar. Hieronymi's account is not unique in taking the negative reactive attitudes to be not only closely correlated with evaluative judgments of ill will, but to perhaps have some tighter connection to them when it comes to our ability to mark their significance. And so it would not be surprising if the majority of quality of will accounts turn out to be reactive and subject to the problem of blame as well.

But what precisely is this problem? While I have characterized it broadly in terms of a kind of tension that arises between the value blame seems to have and the harm that it causes, I have not yet fully explicated the problem that blame curmudgeons and others inclined toward skepticism about blame are concerned with. Now that we have a clearer picture of the kind of blame that gives rise to worries about permissibility in the first place, we can now move on to the task of more clearly explicating the problem of blame itself.

1.4 The Problem of Blame

What I have here called *the problem of blame* concerns whether we should, all things considered, ever blame one another. Questions about normative adequacy are essentially *prescriptive* in nature. We want to know what we ought to do when it comes to attributions of blame. Are these attributions, their corresponding blaming practices, and the broader responsibility-related practices that depend on them ever justified and permissible to engage in?

As should now be evident, the many varieties of blame and the corresponding differences in the harm that can accompany blame complicate the task of assessing where the bar for establishing permissibility lies. For some accounts of blame, the bar seems relatively low. Returning to Scanlon's conative account, while some challenge the descriptive accuracy of his view (namely whether it fully captures the kinds of blame that appear to be central to our actual blaming practices), the bar for the permissibility of this kind of blame seems low. Because Scanlon does not take any affective response or expressive feature to be necessary to blame, his account is consistent with full-blown blaming practices that could involve little to no harm.[24] It is only when the variety of blame on offer accommodates the particularly unpleasant features of blame (as McGeer puts it, "warts and all") that the stakes are sufficiently high to give rise to the problem of blame. And reactive blame is precisely the kind of blame that raises the standards for permissibility the highest. But what, precisely, do these standards amount to? Here I will attempt to explicate them in terms of two desiderata for *normative adequacy*, making use of an analogy with a related problem concerning permissibility and harm when it comes to punishment.[25]

1.4.1   *Blame versus Punishment*

The first step to explicating the desiderata for a normatively adequate account of reactive blame is by noting an analogy with a similar and more familiar problem: *the problem of punishment*. Like reactive blame, punishment causes harm. The problem of punishment arises when we try to understand how and why it could be permissible to intentionally inflict the harms of punishment on wrongdoers, despite our standing pro tanto reasons not to cause harm to others.[26] Two possible solutions to the problem of punishment – deterrence and retributivism – can each serve to elucidate something about the desiderata for a normatively adequate account of reactive blame.

On one hand, deterrence theorists sometimes argue that it is permissible to intentionally cause harm via punishment because the reasons we have not to harm can be *outweighed* by some overwhelming good. In particular, the harms of punishment might reduce harm on a larger scale. On the other hand, retributivists sometimes argue that it is permissible to intentionally cause harm via punishment because the reasons we have not to harm are *defeated* in some cases, namely when the relevant harm entailed by punishment is deserved. When it comes to the permissibility of

---

[24] One might even think that it would be downright puzzling to demand arguments for establishing the permissibility of withdrawing from someone who has clearly manifested ill will toward you.

[25] I credit and thank Vargas (2013) for this helpful way of characterizing the relevant standard.

[26] Here, I assume that there are at least some moral reasons, that among them is a standing pro tanto reason not to cause harm, and that this reason often entails that we ought to refrain from certain kinds of harmful behaviors. While I wish to avoid any commitments regarding the nature of our moral reasons, I take it as a given that anyone who is at least agnostic about the permissibility of blame will be happy to accept these assumptions. Those who wish to deny the existence of moral reasons of any kind will take any success theories of moral responsibility or blame as a nonstarter, and thus will fall outside of the bounds of my target audience in this book.

punishment, we might therefore characterize a possible desideratum for a normatively adequate view of punishment in the following way:

> **Normative Adequacy(punishment):** we are justified in punishing if either (a) our reasons not to punish are outweighed because punishment entails some overwhelming good, or (b) our reasons not to punish are defeated because in at least some cases the harm entailed by punishment is deserved.

Might we say the same thing about the desiderata for a normatively adequate view of reactive blame? Here the corresponding standard would be that we are justified in blaming if either (a) our reasons not to blame are outweighed because reactive blame entails some overwhelming good; or (b) our reasons not to reactively blame are defeated because in at least some cases blame is deserved in the basic sense.

While this first pass is instructive, I do not think that it is ultimately correct. This is due to an important difference in the relation between (a) and (b) for punishment versus blame. In the case of punishment, deterrent and retributive strategies for establishing the permissibility of punishment are usually pursued independent of one another.[27] The desideratum for a normatively adequate account of punishment sketched earlier is in turn a disjunctive one. Punishment is permissible if *either* the deterrence theorist or retributivist gets things right. But this does not seem to be the case for reactive blame. Rather, when it comes to blame there is an underlying assumption that the value of blame could outweigh our reasons not to harm only if blame is *also* deserved in the basic sense, and that basic desert of blame could defeat our reasons not to harm only if the value of blame *also* outweighs our reasons not to harm.

To see this more clearly, consider first the way that whether or not the value of reactive blame outweighs our reasons not to harm is dependent on basic desert. Recall that, for example, on Franklin's functional account reactive blame is a necessary condition for valuing what we ought to value. If this is correct, then there is at least a prima facie case for thinking that the value of even reactive blame might outweigh the disvalue of its unpleasant and harmful features. When it comes to ranking the value of our various moral practices, properly valuing the objects of moral value themselves looks like the kind of thing that plausibly appears at the top of the list. But, even if this is correct then the following challenge is also plausible: the value of this practice (properly valuing the objects of moral

---

[27] This is, of course, an oversimplification in that one might also offer a *hybrid* account of punishment that incorporates both consequentialist and non-consequentialist considerations. See, for example, Hart (1968) and Scheid (1997).

value) will only be relevant to the *all things considered* normative adequacy of reactive blame insofar as reactive blame is also *deserved*.

If we want to know whether or not it is ever permissible to reactively blame, it is not enough to say that reactively blaming is good for us.[28] This is perhaps most obvious when considering the perspective of the unfortunate *targets* of reactive blame. Anyone who has ever been on the receiving end of misplaced resentment will agree that attempts to justify blame via appeal to the overall value of blame alone will be of little comfort. The harms of reactive blame raise the stakes. Reasons for thinking that the harms of reactive blame are outweighed by its value are not enough if we lack any further reason to think that those harms are also deserved. We must also have good reason for thinking that our standing reasons not to harm one another are *defeated* when it comes to reactive blame. What the intuitive impermissibility of misplaced reactive blame highlights is that appeals to value alone are insufficient to meet the relevant standard of normative adequacy without an accompanying defeater.[29]

On the other hand, might appeals to basic desert alone be enough to do the relevant justificatory work? Mere appeal to desert also appears insufficient to do the relevant justificatory work. Assume for the sake of argument that we do have a defeater to the harms of blame – some people are in fact deserving of blame for some of their actions in the basic sense. Those skeptical of the permissibility of blame might still reasonably push back against the claim that reactive blame is normatively adequate. Surely there are things we might do that, while deserved, would not be all-things-considered permissible. Hitler, for example, might have reasonably deserved to live out the remainder of this natural life in a torture chamber. Had he survived WWII, this fact about desert in itself would not be sufficient to justify the claim that it would be permissible for anyone to actually lock him up in one and throw away the key.[30]

---

[28] For articulation of a similar problem for revisionist views about free will, *the normativity anchoring problem*, see McCormick (2013). See also criticism of McKenna's account of the warrant of blame, his substantive desert thesis, in Chapter 2.

[29] While I take this point to be relatively uncontroversial for possible dissent, see Ciurria (2019). Ciurria argues that advancing intersectional feminist aims is sufficient to render blame apt, even if it is not deserved.

[30] Examples abound here, pick your favorite serial killer. There are also two possible readings of this claim. On the first reading, the claim is that it would not be permissible to lock him up. On the second reading, the claim is that even if this punishment is morally appropriate, no actual person would have standing to enact it. The point that desert does not on its own entail permissibility goes through on either reading. Thanks to Neal Tognazzini for pointing out this ambiguity.

The same can be said of reactive blame. Perhaps it turns out that the negative reactive attitudes are far more harmful to creatures like us psychologically speaking than we currently recognize. If we came to discover this fact, or that attributions of blame violate some other weightier moral considerations, then skepticism about the normative adequacy of this kind of blame would be reasonable despite the further fact that it is deserved in the basic sense. While the impermissibility of misplaced reactive blame suggests that basic desert is necessary for a normatively adequate account, further considerations like these suggest that it is not sufficient.

1.4.2   Two Desiderata for Normatively Adequate Reactive Blame

Defending the permissibility of reactive blame therefore requires meeting two desiderata for normative adequacy. One must defend both the claim that reactive blame is sometimes deserved in the basic sense, *and* the claim that the value of this kind of blame outweighs its corresponding harms. In order to meet blame skeptics on their own terms, a maximally persuasive argument for the permissibility of reactive blame should meet the following two desiderata for normative adequacy:

> **Normative Adequacy/value (NAV):** we are justified in blaming only if our reasons not to blame are *outweighed* because blame entails some overwhelming good.
> **Normative Adequacy/desert (NAD):** we are justified in blaming only if our reasons not to blame are *defeated* because in at least some cases blame is deserved in the basic sense.

I take each of these desiderata to be independent necessary conditions for establishing the permissibility of blame. Taken together, they are also jointly sufficient. Despite being unpleasant and even harmful, if reactive blame entails some overwhelming good for creatures like us *and* it is also deserved in the basic sense, then it is unclear what more skeptics about its permissibility might reasonably require.

Do we have any reason to think agents can be (and sometimes are) deserving of reactive blame in the basic sense, and that this kind of harmful blame is valuable? My goal in the next several chapters will be to systematically argue for affirmative answers to both of these questions.

1.5   Conclusion

Here I hope to have laid the groundwork for a defense of the permissibility of reactive blame. In light of the discussion in Section 1.1, we can proceed with a clearer sense of what reactive blame is, and why skeptical concerns target this variety of blame in particular. Section 1.2 serves to further distinguish between the kind of blame that gives rise to the problem of blame and those that do not by canvassing some of the most prominent accounts of explicitly nonreactive blame. Section 1.3 offers a demonstration of how we might deal with borderline cases, those that do not clearly lie on either side of the fault line of reactivity. Finally, in Section 1.4, I explicate the problem of blame itself. What standards of normative adequacy must be met in order to meet blame curmudgeons on their own terms? Here I argue that a plausible account of normatively adequate reactive blame must meet both a value-based desideratum (NAV), and a desert-based desideratum (NAD). I now turn to the prospects for an account of reactive blame to meet the latter.

CHAPTER 2

The Structure of Basic Desert

Consider a case of blame scapegoating. You and your colleague, Amy, have been tasked with an important project, one so important that your supervisor has made clear that your jobs and the jobs of others in your department depend on its successful completion. Unfortunately, the week before the project is due, Amy goes AWOL. Despite your best attempts to complete it on your own, there is just too much work for one person and you are unable to do so. You show up to work early on Monday, head hanging, prepared to break the bad news to your supervisor and colleagues. However, as you pull into the parking lot you see Amy's car. You breathe a sigh of relief that Amy is not, as you had feared, actually dead or seriously ill. You are curious to hear her explanation, and hopeful that whatever it turns out to be will gain sufficient sympathy from your supervisor to grant a brief extension so that you will be able to complete the project and save everyone's jobs after all.

You walk into the office hopefully and see that, as expected, Amy is there speaking earnestly with your supervisor. However, you do not expect the angry look that your supervisor directs at you as they see you walk into the office. They dismiss Amy, who walks by silently and without making eye contact. As you make your way toward your supervisor's office, they pick up the phone and hold up a hand, indicating that you should come back later. Your colleagues begin to filter in, and when they have all arrived your supervisor ends the phone call and emerges to make what looks to be a somber announcement.

As expected, your supervisor announces that the important project was not completed, and because of it several people will need to be laid off. To your great shock, they follow this with a further announcement that this failure is *your* fault – they have just completed an informative meeting with Amy, who despite reservations felt the need to share that you flat-out refused to help her with the workload over the course of the last week. Because of this, you and your coworker, Derek, will need to be let go.

Derek is furious, and primarily *at you*. He turns to you, shouts, "This is all your fault!" and storms out of the office. Dazed, you collect up your things and leave as well, noting Amy smirking in the corner as you go.

Do you *deserve* to be the object of Derek's blame in this case? Of course not. You are innocent, and whatever blame amounts to a plausible account of blame ought to accommodate the apparent truism that blaming the innocent is never deserved. But paradigmatic examples of failing to deserve blame, such as the example of blame scapegoating described here, are relatively cheap. It is far more difficult to specify the conditions under which an agent *is* deserving of blame, is deserving of blame *in the basic sense*, and furthermore *why* this is so.

To make this latter notion clearer, consider two variations on the aforementioned case. In both variations you are in fact the person who bailed on the project. In the first variation, assume that some success theory[1] of moral responsibility is correct, and when you knowingly and willingly choose to ignore your workload, you satisfy all of the necessary and sufficient conditions for responsibility according to this theory. Derek is aware of this, and blames and resents you for his firing *only* because you satisfy these conditions and he believes that you are blameworthy. In the second variation, assume that some brand of eliminativism about moral responsibility is correct. Again, Derek is aware of this fact, and firmly believes that no one is ever deserving of praise and blame in the basic sense. But, in this variation, your supervisor gives Derek an out. In order to forestall this kind of thing in the future and better promote productivity at the office, the supervisor announces the following policy: Whenever an employee fails to do an assigned task, their coworkers must actively blame them and hold them responsible, or someone (not the accused) will randomly be fired. In light of this, Derek chooses to blame you in the second variation despite his personal skepticism about blame, and *only because of the policy* and to safeguard his job. While there may be some sense in which Derek's blame is *justified* in this variation and you deserve this response – you are, for example, aware of the policy when you knowingly and willingly choose to ignore your workload, and thus seem as fair a target for its execution as anyone – it is intuitively *not* the basic sense. And while the first variation looks like a better candidate for an example of basic desert, it is far from obvious why this is so.

---

[1] By *success theory* I mean views that accept necessary and sufficient conditions for moral responsibility, which, taken together, human beings do sometimes satisfy in the actual world. Thus, on a success theory we are, at least sometimes, morally responsible for our actions.

In fact, it is notoriously difficult to articulate what basic desert of blame amounts to. This notion appears to be, as Michael McKenna (2012: 120) has put the point, "the elephant in the room" in discussions of free will, moral responsibility, and blame. However, appeals to basic desert (or lack thereof) are often wielded by philosophers in these debates. For example, one way of understanding the force of Derk Pereboom's Four Case Manipulation Argument is that it shows that determinism is incompatible with basic desert of moral praise and blame.[2] Thus, any brand of compatibilism will be unsatisfying if the agents who meet the proposed compatibilist conditions for responsibility still fail to deserve moral praise and blame in the basic sense.[3] Another instructive example is the role that basic desert plays in recent exchanges between eliminativists about moral responsibility (like Pereboom) and revisionists like Manuel Vargas.[4] One question central to the success of revisionism is whether or not this kind of view can justify our responsibility-related practices, in particular those that involve moral praising and blaming. These practices, as Pereboom and others claim, presuppose that agents do in fact sometimes deserve praise and blame in the *basic* sense.[5] And so revisionists, like compatibilists, must show that the account of responsibility they offer captures a form of agency capable of delivering basic desert, or they must justify further revisionism about the normative grounds for our blaming practices.[6]

The goal of this chapter is to attempt to capture the shape of the elephant, albeit roughly, and in a way that does not stack the deck against any of the particular disputants in these debates. I begin in Section 2.1 by identifying a number of relatively uncontroversial features that serve to provide a first step in distinguishing between basic and nonbasic desert. These features provide only a negative characterization of basic desert, but

---

[2] For the original presentation of this argument, see Pereboom (1995).
[3] However, Daniel Haas (2013) has recently argued that many Strawsonian compatibilists may not presuppose the same notion of basic desert that Pereboom saddles them with, and further that it is an open question whether or not they should. Haas also argues for a distinction between basic desert understood as fit and basic desert understood as merit. According to Haas' interpretation, the kind of basic desert Pereboom stipulates is at issue in the debate between compatibilists and incompatibilists is merit-based desert. But, Haas argues, there is also a robust notion of fit-based desert, which, although perhaps not basic in the non-comparative, pre-institutional sense, might still be a robust notion of basic desert. I discuss these distinctions further in Section 2.1, and here wish to point out that the fittingness account defended in what follows is intended to be the kind of desert Pereboom stipulates is at issue in these debates.
[4] See Pereboom (2001, 2005, 2007a, 2007b, 2009a, 2009b, 2014) and Vargas (2005, 2009, 2011, 2013).
[5] See Pereboom (2009b) and McKenna (2009).
[6] Thanks to Michael McKenna for suggesting the latter alternative.

restricting focus to basic desert of blame in particular suggests some further positive features. In Section 2.2, I turn to a particular attempt to offer a positive account of what makes agents deserving of blame offered recently by Michael McKenna. McKenna characterizes this account as a "substantive desert thesis," but I argue that we should not accept this account as a positive characterization of basic desert (McKenna, 2012: 141). However, understanding why is instructive regarding the distinction between basic and nonbasic desert, and also suggests an argument for a new analysis of basic desert of blame. In Section 2.3, I sketch this positive account, the *fittingness account*, and argue that it has two significant explanatory virtues. Finally, in Section 2.4, I address a familiar problem for analyses that appeal to fittingness in other domains – circularity. Here I offer some initial arguments for thinking that circularity does not pose as significant a threat to my fittingness account of basic desert of blame as one might initially assume.[7]

But isn't there something strange about trying to explicate basic desert? Doesn't the very fact that this brand of desert is *basic* preclude this kind of analysis? As McKenna puts the point:

> If a concept is basic, then it cannot be derived from other more basic concepts, or it cannot be exhaustively explained (noncircularly) in terms of them, or it cannot be reductively analyzed in terms of them. (McKenna, 2012: 121)

It is true that attempts to analyze a *conceptually* basic primitive would be misguided, but I see no reason to consider the notion of desert at issue to be basic in *that* sense. In practice, we often fall back on conceptual primitiveness only after a great deal of work analyzing a concept has failed, and the prospects for future success begin to look reasonably grim. But explicit attempts to analyze basic desert, especially basic desert of blame, are still largely underdeveloped. Perhaps the difficulty in explicating basic desert of blame arises largely from its close relation to a family of other normative concepts, including fairness, justification, appropriateness, fittingness, and correctness. At the end of the day, it may turn out that basic desert is best understood as *most* basic among these, but even so there might still be a great deal to say about basic desert. Here again McKenna puts the point nicely:

---

[7] A full-throated defense of the fittingness account of basic desert will require a more complete account of reactive blame, and so I return to questions about circularity in Chapter 4 once such an account has been offered.

> But [desert] can nevertheless be elucidated. What inferences are licensed by basic desert? What entails it, and what does it entail? What is the normative force of the claim that blame is deserved, and what sort of practical punch, so to speak, does deserved blame deliver? If that practical punch involves a harm, what does the harm amount to? What about considerations of proportionality between the wrong serving as the basis of blame and the activity of blaming? (McKenna, 2012: 121)

Even if basic desert does turn out to be a conceptual primitive, attempting to analyze it might still take us some ways toward *elucidating* basic desert, and toward answering some of the aforementioned questions. So, in what follows I will assume that basic desert is not in fact primitive in a sense that would make further analysis misguided.

2.1 Basic versus Nonbasic Desert

Perhaps the best way to get a foothold on what basic desert is begins with what basic desert is not. Most recent attempts to articulate the distinction between basic and nonbasic desert take Joel Feinberg's remarks on desert as a starting point:

> In respect to modes of treatment which persons can be said to deserve, then we can distinguish three kinds of conditions. There are those whose satisfaction confers eligibility ("eligibility conditions"), those whose satisfaction confers entitlement ("qualification conditions"), and those conditions not specified in any regulatory or procedural rules whose satisfaction confers worthiness or desert ("desert bases"). (Feinberg, 1970: 58)

Feinberg suggests that the distinction between different modes of desert depends in some way on the conditions whose satisfaction confers desert. According to Feinberg, basic desert is conferred only by the satisfaction of conditions "not specified in any regulatory or procedural rules." In other words, in order for the satisfaction of some conditions to confer basic desert, rather than nonbasic, they must be noncontractualist or noninstrumental. Here is how Pereboom puts the point regarding basic desert of blame in particular:

> The desert at issue here is basic in the sense that the agent, to be morally responsible, would deserve to be the recipient of the expression of such an attitude just because she has performed the action, given sensitivity to its moral status; not, for example, by virtue of consequentialist of contractualist considerations. (Pereboom, 2013: 189)

Feinberg's and Pereboom's remarks emphasize the importance of the relevant notion of a *desert base* in articulating the difference between basic and nonbasic desert. In what follows, I take a desert base to be whatever it is that agents are deserving in virtue of. Feinberg's and Pereboom's attempts to distinguish basic from nonbasic desert suggest that both kinds of desert have the same conceptual structure, and that the difference between the two depends on the nature of the relevant desert base. As a first pass, we can understand the conceptual structure of desert as a three-place relation involving an agent (A); an object – what it is that is deserved (X); and a base – what it is that X is deserved in virtue of (B):

(1)   A deserves X in virtue of B.[8]

What constitutes the difference between basic and nonbasic desert is the nature of the base, B. And initially we can at least specify what the relevant base *cannot* be like if it is to generate basic, rather than nonbasic, desert. Again borrowing from Feinberg and Pereboom, institutionally generated, instrumental, contractualist, and consequentialist bases are out. At best they generate only nonbasic desert.

This characterization of basic desert is still largely negative but can be further explicated by restricting the scope of the object of desert at issue. For my current purposes, the relevant object is blame. First, shifting attention to basic desert of blame highlights a shortcoming of characterizing the structure of basic desert in terms of (1). Understanding basic desert of blame in particular as merely a three-place relation is problematic because it fails to recognize a distinction between the subject of desert (in this case, an agent) and what it is that subject deserves blame *for*. When we ask whether an agent deserves blame, we do not, for example, ask whether she deserves blame in the same generalized way that we might ask whether people deserve respect. Rather, we want to know whether the agent in question deserves blame *for a particular action, quality of will, or character trait*. Structurally, then, when restricted to blame, basic desert is better understood as a four-place relation:

(2)   A deserves blame *for Y* in virtue of B.[9]

---

[8] Here I borrow from Roskies and Malle's (2013) helpful articulation of what they call the "conceptual structure" of basic desert.

[9] Why not a five-place relation: A deserves blame *from S* for Y in virtue of B? I take questions about *standing* to blame to be distinct from questions about basic desert. An agent might deserve blame in the basic sense, even though no actual agent has standing to actively blame them. Therefore, it would be a mistake, I think, to include the *blamer* as a relata in this analysis of basic desert of blame. Thanks to Neal Tognazzini for raising this question.

Given the relatively uncontroversial features of the distinction between basic and nonbasic desert that are identified earlier in this chapter, we should also exclude post-institutional, contractualist, consequentialist, and instrumental considerations as possible bases for basic desert of blame. But once the scope of basic desert is restricted to blame in particular, there is more to say about what the relevant desert bases *are*. In light of the fact that basic desert of blame has the structure identified in (2), it is natural to suppose that the kinds of things an agent can deserve blame in virtue of must be features of what it is she deserves blame *for*. The most plausible candidates for desert bases for basic desert of blame, then, will be the most plausible objects of blame itself: features of the agent's action, quality of will, or character traits.[10]

Though rarely made explicit, I take this characterization of basic desert of blame to be accepted by the majority of those interested in basic desert in the context of free will and moral responsibility.[11] It should therefore come as no great surprise that it is also relatively uninteresting. This characterization still leaves open, for example, questions about *which* features of an agent's action, quality of will, or character are candidate desert bases, and *why* these features, but not others, constitute bases for basic desert of blame.

It is not obvious how one might answer the former question without presupposing a substantive positive view of the conditions for moral responsibility, presuppositions I wish to avoid here. However, there is room to explore a version of the second question independent of such presuppositions. Though admittedly natural to suppose, are there any positive arguments in favor of taking only features of an agent's action, quality of will, or character to be the kinds of things agents can deserve

---

[10] In Section 2.3, I provide an argument for thinking that these features *should* be taken as the only kinds of things agents can deserve blame in the basic sense in virtue of. In Chapter 3, I go on to show that these features can function as the right kind of desert base for basic desert of blame, and in Chapter 4, I argue that we have at least some reason to think that our appraisals of these features are truth tracking. In this section, my goal is only to canvass the few widely agreed-upon features that those interested in basic desert often *do* appeal to in order to distinguish basic from nonbasic desert. Nor is this particular list intended to be an exhaustive way of characterizing the relevant features. Something like the capacity for reasons-responsiveness, for example, might ultimately be included in the specific features of the causal mechanism for an agent's action that we ultimately decide are part of the relevant desert base.

[11] See, for example, Pereboom (2001, 2009b, 2013, 2014). This notion of basic desert also appears to be what Galen Strawson (2002: 442) has in mind when he talks about agents being "truly and without qualification deserving of praise and blame or reward or punishment." McKenna (2012: 126) also seems to accept this characterization of basic desert of blame, though he claims that as specified it is "too lean to assess." I agree that *as specified* it is too lean, but I think that there is more to be said about genuinely basic desert and develop this view in Section 2.2.

blame in the basic sense in virtue of? Examining where one positive attempt to explicate desert of blame goes wrong suggests that there are.

2.2 Substantive Desert Theses and the Wrong Kind of Reasons

In this section, I take Michael McKenna's (2012) proposal for a substantive desert thesis as a case study. Though I will argue that McKenna's characterization does not provide an adequate account of desert of blame in the basic sense, understanding why is instructive.[12] In particular, it suggests a positive argument for thinking that the appropriate bases for basic desert of blame should be restricted only to facts about the agent being blamed and her action.

McKenna offers the following substantive desert thesis for blame (for simplicity, call it SDT):

> It is a noninstrumental good that, as a response to the meaning expressed in an agent's blameworthy act, that agent experiences the harms of others communicating in their altered patterns of interpersonal relations their moral demands, expectations, and disapproval. Because this is a noninstrumental good, it is permissible to blame one who is blameworthy. (McKenna, 2012: 141)

McKenna does not initially commit himself to SDT, but rather proposes it as a desert thesis consistent with his conversational theory of moral responsibility and blame. Here it is beyond my current purposes to dive too deeply into McKenna's rich conversational view, but ultimately he tentatively accepts SDT as the best account of the warrant of blame and identifies three reasons for thinking that the harms of blame according to the conversational theory are in fact noninstrumentally good. First, on McKenna's view, the harms of blame involve "adversely affecting a distinctive class of welfare interests," those that concern "unfettered exercising of capacities to engage in social intercourse and maintain friendships, freedom from interference in one's personal life, and a sustained level of emotional stability" (2012: 167). McKenna argues that these harms are therefore noninstrumentally good because (1) on the conversational model of blame, sensitivity to them requires or reveals that the agent being blamed is committed to membership in the moral community; (2) subjecting a wrongdoer to these harms reveals a commitment to morality on

---

[12] McKenna himself does not explicitly call this a *basic* desert thesis. Here I am not interested in offering an objection to McKenna's overall view, only in whether or not his desert thesis *should* be understood as a basic desert thesis (and arguing that it should not be).

the part of the person doing the blaming; and (3) the conversational process that these harms play an integral part in is itself noninstrumentally valuable (2012: 167–171). In McKenna's view, it is therefore permissible for members of a shared moral community to blame one another because it is good to do so, and it is good to do so because our blaming practices are a constitutive feature of a conversational activity that is noninstrumentally valuable.

McKenna himself acknowledges that one might deny that the goods at issue here are in fact noninstrumentally valuable (2012: 170). This is an interesting question and one that deserves further attention, but here I will grant that they are. More relevant to the topic at hand is his characterization of these considerations as providing a plausible account of the *warrant* for blame. In light of this characterization, how should we understand SDT? Can SDT provide a robust, positive explication of basic desert of blame? Or is it instead a thesis about what *justifies* blame, in regard to either particular attributions or our blaming practices more generally?

The answer seems clearly to be the latter. In order to see why, consider SDT in light of the structure of basic desert of blame identified by (2). What, in particular, does McKenna have in mind as candidate desert bases? SDT suggests the following: An agent deserves blame for a particular action or feature of her character in virtue of *the noninstrumental value of the conversational activity constituted by our blaming practices*. But then, given the uncontroversial features of basic desert identified in Section 2.1, SDT is at best a nonbasic desert thesis. Even granting that the value of the conversational activity McKenna is interested in is noninstrumental, the desert base identified in SDT is itself consequentialist. According to SDT, agents deserve blame because of the value of this conversational activity (noninstrumental or otherwise), and *not* in virtue of the features of their action or character that they are being blamed *for*.

The key point to emphasize here is that while McKenna's desert thesis might be plausible as an account of the warrant or *justification* for blame,[13] it is not a plausible account of *desert* of blame in the basic sense. And identifying this distinction is vastly helpful in teasing apart the conceptual space between the two closely related notions of justification and desert. SDT would ground what agents deserve blame in virtue of in facts about the value of blaming them – namely, that doing so is a constitutive feature of noninstrumentally valuable conversational activity. But this is clearly *the wrong kind of reason*.

---

[13] Or perhaps even a kind of forensic evidence in support of the claim that there is some noninstrumental good in harming a person by blaming her. Thanks to McKenna for suggesting this further possibility.

Bearing this point out requires a brief aside regarding the nature of blame itself, and reactive blame in particular. For my current purposes, what I am ultimately interested in are basic desert of reactive blame and whether an account of reactive blame can successfully meet the desert-based desideratum for normative adequacy (NAD). Narrowing our focus to basic desert of reactive blame in particular allows us to see *why* desert theses such as SDT would ground basic desert of blame in the wrong kind of reasons.

Recall that the key feature of reactive blame is its affective component – the negative reactive attitudes play some central role in this kind of blaming as either an essential feature, a feature necessary to understanding and meeting the functional role of blame, or as a canonical feature. Given that the varieties of moral anger play this central role for reactive blame, there is a clear analogy to draw between the *reasons* for having these negative reactive attitudes and the reasons for having other affectively colored attitudes.[14] And a great deal of work has already been done articulating the kinds of reasons that are appropriate or *fitting* for having such attitudes.[15] Consider the classic example of admiration. One might have any number of reasons for admiring a particular object, but a distinction can be made between the kinds of reasons that might make admiration *fitting* or appropriate and those that do not. This distinction has been widely characterized in terms of the right versus wrong kinds of reasons for a given attitude, and it is often highlighted via the use of examples of the wrong kinds of reasons. Here is a familiar example: consider a world in which an evil demon has set things up such that those who do not admire the demon will suffer some sort of hideous punishment, though the demon himself possesses no admirable qualities. In such a world, you obviously have a reason to admire the demon – failing to do so will land you with a hideous punishment. But this reason is *of the wrong kind*. While the fact that you have a reason to admire the demon in this case might, all else being equal, *justify* your admiration, there is a clear sense in which your admiration is not fitting or appropriate.

---

[14] Zac Cogley (2013: 206) argues for a link between a similar kind of appraisal and a particular conception of moral responsibility he calls "fittingness accounts." While Cogley is explicitly concerned with the appropriateness of the blaming emotions themselves, not basic desert of blame, his account of the "core appraisal" of the blaming emotions might serve as an alternative to the account I defend here, though one that takes on board a number of substantive (and more controversial) commitments about the moral psychology of blame and the variety of distinct conceptions of moral responsibility that I wish to avoid here.

[15] See for example Brentano (1969), D'Arms and Jacobson (2000a, 2000b), Olson (2004), Rabinowicz and Rönnow-Rasmussen (2004, 2006), Suikkanen (2004), and Hieronymi (2005).

Here I wish to suggest another way of putting the point: the demon does not *deserve* your admiration. And we can extend this line of reasoning to particular instances of blame understood in terms of SDT. If McKenna is right and blame is constitutive of a noninstrumentally valuable conversational activity, then for each particular instance of blame, there is a *pro tanto* reason to take up the attitudes of moral anger and resentment. Furthermore, in the absence of further reasons that outweigh it, this reason might also plausibly *justify* a particular instance of blame. But if this reason is the *only* one in favor of taking up these attitudes in a particular case, then there is still a clear sense in which moral anger and resentment are *not fitting* or, in other words, *not deserved*.

In short, if we understand desert of blame in terms of SDT then particular attributions of blame look to be subject to a wrong kind of reasons problem. Given the assumption that blame is, at least in part, constituted by the negative reactive attitudes, it is reasonable to think that, like other affective attitudes, blame can be justified by both the right and wrong kind of reasons. But in cases in which the reasons to blame are of the wrong kind (as in instances of blame understood in terms of SDT), there is no reason to think that particular instances of blame, though justified, are also *deserved*. And, given the relatively uncontroversial negative features of basic desert of blame articulated in the previous section, there is a clear explanation why. According to SDT, the desert base for instances of blame will always be consequentialist.

If this is correct, then a closer look at why SDT falls short of a substantive basic desert thesis suggests a potentially fruitful positive characterization of basic desert, a *fittingness account:*[16]

(3)   A deserves X for Y in virtue of B, where B is only *the right kind of reason.*

---

[16] Here it may be helpful to contrast this account with two accounts of *blameworthiness* that have recently appealed to fittingness. First, David Shoemaker (2017: 508) offers *Fitting Response-Dependence about the Blameworthy:* "The blameworthy (in the realm of accountability) just is whatever merits anger (the angerworthy); that is, someone is blameworthy (and so accountable) for X if and only if, and in virtue of the fact that, she merits anger for X." Second, Pereboom (2020: 109) offers *Fitting Protest-Response-Dependence about the Blameworthy:* "The blameworthy (in the realm of accountability) just is whatever merits moral protest (the morally protestworthy); that is, someone is blameworthy (and so accountable) for X if, and only if, and in virtue of the fact that, she merits moral protest for X." While each of these accounts also appeals to fittingness, it is important to note that the target both Shoemaker and Pereboom attempt to analyze is *blameworthiness*, not basic desert. While Shoemaker and I seem to be in agreement about the importance of fittingness and moral anger for an analysis of blame, the fact that Shoemaker attempts to analyze blameworthiness in terms of fit renders worries about circularity more serious for his fittingness

But then what do the *right* kind of reasons look like? Here one might object that a fittingness account of basic desert of blame is unhelpful unless the notion of fit can provide some further traction in identifying what kinds of desert bases do make blame genuinely fitting or deserved. For now, I will set this question aside but will return to it in Chapter 3. And, even if we could not explicitly identify the right kind of reasons to blame, drawing the analogy between blame and other affective attitudes is still vastly helpful in articulating the distinction between basic and nonbasic desert of blame. At the very least, it provides further content to the largely negative character of basic desert discussed in the previous section. However, understanding basic desert as fit *can* take us a step further in articulating a positive account of basic desert. In particular, a fittingness account has at least two powerful explanatory virtues. First, it suggests a positive argument for taking only features of the agent being blamed and her action as appropriate bases for basic desert. Second, it is particularly well suited to explain the conceptual distinction between basic desert of blame and the closely related normative concepts of justification and fairness.

2.3 Virtues of the Fittingness Account

Section 2.1 identified one of the only widely agreed upon assumptions about what the appropriate bases for basic desert of blame are: features of the agent and her action. In this section, I argue that the fittingness account of basic desert of blame has the unique potential to explain *why* the appropriate bases for basic desert of blame should be restricted to these features. This argument appeals again to an analogy between blame and the right kind of reasons for other affective attitudes. Furthermore, the fittingness account has the additional explanatory virtue of allowing us to distinguish between basic desert of blame, justification, and fairness. Taken together, these arguments provide good reason to take the fittingness account of basic desert of blame seriously.

account. I discuss worries about circularity further in Section 2.4, and again in Chapter 3. And, because Pereboom is explicitly pursuing a form of blame free from the negative reactive attitudes, whatever "merits protest" will be distinct from the fittingness account I am pursuing here. While Pereboom's account might be a fruitful view of blameworthiness for *nonreactive* accounts of blame, it will not be relevant to reactive blame.

2.3.1   Object-Focused Reasons to Blame

First, while the distinction between the wrong versus right kind of reasons
for holding a particular affective attitude seems intuitively clear,[17] it is
notoriously difficult to articulate what the *right* kind of reasons are for any
particular attitude. Consider again the example of admiration. Like examples of nonbasic desert, examples of the wrong kind reason for admiring an
object are cheap. If the fact that the demon will subject you to some
hideous punishment if you fail to admire it is the wrong kind of reason to
admire it (it may render your admiration justified, but it cannot render it
fitting or deserved), what would the right kind of reason look like? The
obvious answer is that *genuinely admirable properties* possessed by the
demon would provide the right kind of reason to admire it.[18]

One way to cash out this distinction further is to appeal to *object-focused*
versus *attitude-focused* reasons (or, in Parfit's (2001) terms, "object-given"
and "state-given" reasons).[19] Pamela Hieronymi provides a particularly
clear statement of the distinction:

> ... object-given or content-related [hereafter "object-focused"] reasons are
> provided by or have something to do with the object or content of the
> attitude, while state-given or attitude-related [hereafter "attitude-focused"]
> reasons are provided by or have something to do with the state or
> attitude itself. (Hieronymi, 2005: 441)[20]

Returning to the admiration example, the fact that you will be subject to a
hideous form of punishment if you fail to admire the demon provides an
attitude-focused reason to admire it. This reason might ultimately (again,
all else being equal) justify your admiration of the demon, but it is
irrelevant to whether the cognitive feature of your attitude (in this case

---

[17] Though some do in fact reject this distinction. See Rabinowicz and Rönnow-Rasmussen (2004).
[18] This initial proposal will likely flag the circularity worries mentioned at the outset of this chapter.
I initially address these worries in the following section with the goal of further defusing them in
Chapter 3.
[19] Here I intend to use this particular distinction largely as a heuristic. I suspect that a satisfying
application of the distinction in this particular context requires a much more fine-grained account
of the attitudes of moral anger and resentment, which I discuss further in later chapters. However,
even for those who reject this distinction, I think that the same line of argument can be run in terms
of epistemic and pragmatic reasons (though see Reisner (2009) for dissenting arguments). For those
who reject this *kind* of distinction altogether the fittingness account on offer will likely appear to be
a nonstarter, but given its theoretical usefulness across a wide array of philosophical topics I take a
full blown rejection of this kind of distinction to be a costly assumption to hang one's hat on.
[20] I also credit Hieronymi (2004) with offering a precursor to the fittingness account I develop here,
and for initially suggesting that this kind of distinction might be applied to blame and in
particular resentment.

the corresponding appraisal that the demon is admirable) is correct. On the other hand, an object-focused reason to admire the demon is precisely the kind of consideration that *does* (or at least could) count in favor of thinking that the relevant appraisal is correct. The fact that the demon does in fact possess some admirable feature would provide an object-focused reason for you to admire it. So, for those who accept this distinction, only object-focused reasons provide the right kind of reasons for a particular attitude.

Returning to blame, the distinction between object and attitude-focused reasons suggests a line of argument for thinking that only facts about the features of an agent and her action constitute the right kind of reasons to blame. Like admiration, blame plausibly has a cognitive component – some kind of evaluative belief or appraisal relevant to whether the agent is *blameworthy*.[21] And so, only considerations that count in favor of the correctness of this judgment will count as object-focused reasons to blame. Which considerations are those? While the answer to this will depend on one's preferred account of the nature of blame, the discussion of a wide array of varieties of blame in Chapter 1 suggests that *all* of these views take some feature of the target of blame's action, character, or quality of will to be relevant here. And so, on a fittingness account of blame, only facts about the features of an agent and her action constitute bases for basic desert of blame, because only these facts provide the right kind of reasons to adopt the relevant attitude. If this is correct, the fittingness account has the theoretical virtue of explaining *why* only features of the agent being blamed and her action constitute bases for basic desert of blame. These are the only considerations relevant to whether or not the evaluative appraisal central to blame is correct or not.

2.3.2 Desert, Justification, and Fairness

The fittingness account has the additional virtue of allowing us to explain the distinction between desert and the closely related concepts of justification and fairness. These concepts are often run together in matters related to blame and moral responsibility. Regarding justification, it is sometimes assumed (recall the examples of charges often lodged against revisionists and compatibilists discussed at the outset of this chapter) that

---

[21] I will discuss this feature further in Chapter 3, and offer a positive argument for embracing a cognitivist view of the negative reactive attitudes, whereby what unifies these attitudes as a kind is their shared propositional content.

the fact that blame is not deserved in the basic sense entails that our blaming practices or particular instances of blame cannot be justified. But this claim is rarely argued for, and the discussion of SDT in the previous section strongly suggests that these concepts are distinct. The fittingness account of basic desert of blame not only respects this conceptual distinction, but also provides an explanation for why it exists – basic desert of blame and the justification of blame are generated by *different kinds of reasons*. Perhaps what we are interested in or what we want desert to track for us is something more closely akin to *correctness*, not justification.[22] And thus restricting the bases for basic desert of blame to just those considerations that count in favor of correctness, as the fittingness account recommends, captures this intuition nicely.

What of fairness? It is less obvious that desert and fairness are normatively and conceptually distinct. However, Dana Nelkin (2013) has argued (I think persuasively) that desert is only one of multiple considerations that bears on the overall fairness of our treatment of one another. Further, there are at least some considerations that plausibly undermine desert but not fairness. Nelkin points out that if an agent has no control over her action, this intuitively disqualifies her from genuine desert of sanctions or adverse treatment (Nelkin, 2013: 122). But surely there is room to say that it could still be *fair* to sanction her if, for example, the procedure for doing so is fair in other ways. If we take blame to be a kind of unpleasant sanction, as reactive blame very well may be, then the fittingness account also suggests a potentially fruitful explanation for this distinction. Basic desert of reactive blame, on the fittingness account, is fairly narrow. The fact that an agent had no control over her action looks like a plausible candidate for a consideration that counts in favor of thinking that the appraisals of features of the agent and her action relevant to her blameworthiness are *false*. Whatever the necessary conditions for blameworthiness are, *some* degree of control over one's action must one of them. And so, the fittingness account of blame provides an explanation for why an agent who lacks control entirely cannot deserve reactive blame in the basic sense. But, importantly, the fittingness account also *leaves room* to say that, even so, it might be fair to blame her. If, for example, some version of eliminativism about moral responsibility is true, then perhaps all of us lack the kind of control necessary to be genuinely blameworthy all of the time. It might nonetheless be fair to go on blaming and sanctioning one another given

---

[22] Hieronymi (2004) also suggests that we take seriously the same kind of gap regarding the appropriateness of resentment.

that we are all subject to the same lack of control. None of this is to say that it *would* be fair to blame an agent who completely lacks control of her action, but it is a virtue of the fittingness account that it can accommodate the conceptual possibility that it would be. On the fittingness account of basic desert of blame offered here, this is again because basic desert and fairness might depend on different kinds of reasons.

2.4 Circularity

Taken together, the arguments in the previous section provide good reason to take the fittingness account seriously. However, there is a particularly troubling potential objection looming. Fittingness accounts in other domains often face charges of vicious circularity – the concept being analyzed in terms of fit appears somewhere in the explication of the fittingness relation itself. This claim is often lodged against fittingness (or "buck-passing") analyses of value. Is the fittingness account of basic desert of blame open to this kind of objection?

The severity of circularity objections to fittingness accounts often depends on the level of generality of the thing being analyzed. The more general the concept being analyzed in terms of fit, the more likely it is that this very concept will appear somewhere in the explication of the fittingness relation. Fittingness accounts of value, against which circularity objections are most often raised, look to be especially vulnerable to this kind of worry. If value is to be analyzed in terms of pro-attitudes that are fitting, then what makes certain pro-attitudes themselves fitting? Appeal to the fact that the fitting attitudes are those generated by object-focused reasons, or considerations that count in favor of thinking the appraisal "X is *valuable*" are correct, look viciously circular. We are left analyzing value in terms of a particular set of fitting pro-attitudes, but the fact that these pro-attitudes are fitting is grounded in the fact that the object of these attitudes is valuable. Is the fittingness account of basic desert of blame open to the same kind of objection?

Circularity worries about fittingness analyses often dissipate as the specificity of the thing being analyzed increases, and the fact that the fittingness account on offer is relatively specific – it is an attempt to explicate not only basic desert, but basic desert of *reactive blame* in particular – itself undermines the force of circularity worries here. However, in light of its force in other domains, this worry still constitutes a serious obstacle to motivating the fittingness account of basic desert of blame. In what remains here, I will suggest some strategies for how this potential objection might be addressed. I will also return the issue of circularity in Chapter 3, once the nature of reactive blame has been discussed more fully, and I have offered a positive account of the right kind of reasons to blame.

Applied to a fittingness account of basic desert of reactive blame, the circularity objection might have the following structure: (1) the fittingness account analyzes basic desert of blame in terms of the right kind of reasons to blame; (2) but what makes a reason to blame of the right kind is just the fact that the agent being blamed is blameworthy; so (3) the fittingness account recommends that we analyze blame in terms of blameworthiness, which is at best uninformative and at worst viciously circular.[23]

This initial formulation of the objection rests on a confusion about what is being analyzed. In this case, it is not blame itself, but *what it is in virtue of which blame is deserved in the basic sense* that is being analyzed in terms of fit. The circularity objection in its basic form would only be relevant to the fittingness account on offer if *basic desert* were being analyzed in terms of the right kind of reasons, and the right kind of reasons analyzed in terms of, for example, what is *deserved*. But that is not the proposal. The fittingness account does take basic desert to be analyzed in terms of the right kind of reasons, but on this account the right kind of reasons are analyzed in terms of whatever features of an agent and her action blameworthiness ultimately depends on. And so, this version of the circularity objection is not relevant to the fittingness account of basic desert of blame.

However, there is a version of the objection that is relevant. The proponent of this objection can and should press the point that the aforementioned response conveniently stops a step short in the analysis. How are we to analyze *blameworthiness*? For the fittingness account of blame to ultimately be informative and avoid the circularity worry, it must be possible to provide an account of blameworthiness that does not itself appeal to *desert*. Given that the examples used to motivate many accounts of blameworthiness do often appeal to intuitions about whether or not agents are deserving of blame, is it plausible to think that a successful account of blameworthiness can avoid such appeals?

On the view I have been sketching thus far, I see no reason to think that the truth-makers for beliefs about blameworthiness must themselves appeal to facts about basic desert. In fact, if we are to understand the role of the negative reactive attitudes for reactive blame in terms of functional

---

[23] I take this to be precisely the line of the objection that Shoemaker's (2017) Fitting Response-Dependence about the Blameworthy is especially vulnerable to.

or canonical reactivity in particular then it seems not only possible, but *likely* that the truth-makers for the relevant evaluative beliefs will be determined by facts about the aims of blame or blame's canonical features, and what these facts turn out to be will likely be an empirical question.[24] As noted earlier, I will have more to say about circularity after offering a more fully worked out positive view of what the right kind of reasons to reactively blame might look like in the next chapter. Here I hope simply to have defused some anticipated initial concerns about this kind of worry for fittingness views in general.

2.5 Conclusion

We now have in hand a proposal for what the shape of the elephant in the room looks like – basic desert of blame can be understood in terms of the fittingness of its affective component, the negative reactive attitudes, the fittingness of these attitudes (or the bases appropriate to basic desert of blame) can be analyzed in terms of the right kind of reasons, and there is at least no initial reason to think that a plausible account of the right kind of reasons will itself appeal to basic desert and thus fall subject to worries about vicious circularity. At the very least, the fittingness account helps to provide further content to characterizations of basic desert that have thus far been largely negative. At best, it is a novel and potentially fruitful positive analysis of basic desert of reactive blame in particular, one that has the powerful theoretical virtues of explaining not only why the only bases appropriate to basic desert of blame are features of the agent being blamed and her action, but also the distinction between desert and other closely related normative concepts such as justification and fairness.

---

[24] Here it may be helpful to make explicit the direction of fit between analyses of blameworthiness and basic desert that I am proposing. It is often assumed that blameworthiness is the explanandum, and basic desert appears somewhere in the explanans (even if basic desert itself turns out to be brute). But here I have been suggesting the opposite. What the fittingness account reveals is that we might fruitfully take the murky concept of basic desert as the relevant explanandum (we do, after all, seem to have much clearer intuitions about blameworthiness than basic desert) and blameworthiness to appear among the explanans.

Blame and the Reactive Attitudes

Chapter 2 suggests a potentially fruitful positive account of the structure of basic desert of blame, *the fittingness account*. According to this account, the desert base for basic desert of blame must track *the right kind of reasons*, where the right kind of reasons will be restricted to features of an agent, her action, or the quality of her will relevant to the conditions of blameworthiness, and will not include consequentialist or other purely forward-looking considerations. While the fittingness account is a significant step beyond mere negative characterizations of basic desert of blame, it will not take us far enough without a better understanding of what the right kind of reasons to blame actually are.

The goal of this chapter is to offer a tentative account of the right kind of reasons to blame. In Chapter 4, I will argue that this account can, when paired with the fittingness account of basic desert of blame, ultimately meet the normative challenges raised by blame curmudgeons. In other words, I will argue that this account can successfully meet both the value-based (NAV) and desert-based (NAD) desiderata for normative adequacy.

Mounting this argument will require a closer look at the reactive attitudes themselves. The fittingness account of basic desert laid out in the previous chapter grounds basic desert of reactive blame in facts about whatever it is that makes the reactive attitudes fitting. In order to gain any insight into what the right kind of reasons for these attitudes looks like we must therefore have a fairly sharpened picture of the relevant attitudes themselves. Which attitudes count here, and what characteristic features define this class and distinguish its tokens from other emotions? Finally, as noted at the end of Chapter 2, the fittingness account gives rise to a potential worry inherited by any sort of fittingness analysis – it must defuse worries about vicious circularity. In order to discharge this burden, we need a plausible proposal for how we might analyze *blameworthiness* without in turn appealing to desert. Here I will argue that a narrowly construed cognitivist view of the negative reactive attitudes suggests at least one possible way we might do so.

In this chapter, I survey three prominent reactive views of blame developed by P. F. Strawson (1962), R. Jay Wallace (1994), and David Shoemaker (2015). This survey is in no way intended to be an exhaustive tour through reactive accounts of blame, nor does it represent the varieties of reactive blame that I take to be most plausible.[1] I focus on these particular reactive accounts here for three reasons. First, Strawson and Wallace's views best highlight the important role that our interpersonal relationships and expectations play in understanding the reactive attitudes. Second, Wallace and Shoemaker's views highlight what I take to be the important but thus far much overlooked issue of whether we ought to embrace a cognitivist view of the reactive attitudes. Finally, these views represent three different options for how to understand the scope of which attitudes we ought to consider reactive in nature. While Wallace, for example, offers one of the most narrowly construed accounts, Shoemaker offers one of the most widely permissive, and Strawson's own account lies somewhere in the middle.

I begin in Section 3.1 with Strawson's initial characterization of the reactive attitudes and their relation to moral responsibility and blame. One worry often lodged against this kind of classic Strawsonian view is that it casts the net of which attitudes to count as genuinely reactive too widely. In Section 3.2, I turn to the far more narrowly construed account of the reactive attitudes offered by R. Jay Wallace. This narrow construal allows Wallace to more clearly articulate a unified view of the propositional content that these attitudes share, one that also seems to preserve what he takes to be the important depth or force of blame. In turn, Wallace's view suggests a first pass at understanding what the right kind of reasons to reactively blame might be. However, before fully articulating this account, it will be helpful to consider potential challenges to the cognitivist assumption that it depends on. While many accounts of the reactive attitudes make this assumption, there have thus far been no explicit arguments offered in its favor. In light of recent attempts to offer non-cognitivist alternative accounts of the reactive attitudes, a defense of this assumption looks to be in order. In Section 3.3, I offer some positive arguments in favor of cognitivism about the reactive attitudes. Here I take three recent arguments from David Shoemaker (2015) in favor of

---

[1] As will become clear in Chapter 4, my preferred account will also draw heavily on features of the accounts offered by Hieronymi (2004), Walker (2006), McGeer (2013), and Franklin (2013).

noncognitivism as my target, and argue that each offers no support for noncognitivism and in fact some appear to offer reason to embrace cognitivism.

Finally, in Section 3.4, I conclude with a proposal for the right kind of reasons to reactively blame. This proposal borrows heavily from Wallace's view, and the cognitivist arguments offered in Section 3.3. While I explicitly address the way that this account of the right kind of reasons can allow us to meet the desert-based desideratum for normative adequacy in Chapter 4, the proposal sketched here is sufficient to return to and defuse potential worries about circularity raised at the end of Chapter 2.

3.1   Strawsonian Blame

Strawson's (1962) discussion of the reactive attitudes arises in the context of adjudicating between those he calls "optimists" and "pessimists" about free will and moral responsibility. The former refers to consequentialist compatibilists who claim holding one another responsible can be justified by appealing to the good consequences of doing so. The latter refers to libertarian incompatibilists and hard determinists who claim that those who deserve to be held responsible must have a robust kind of metaphysical freedom that is incompatible with determinism. Strawson's take on this disagreement is that each party gets something right, and each gets something wrong. Optimists are correct that holding one another responsible does not depend on any exotic kind of freedom that would require the falsity of determinism, but they are wrong to think that the good consequences of holding one another responsible justify the practice of doing so. Pessimists are right to emphasize the latter about their optimistic opponents, but are wrong to think that we need any such justification in the first place. As Pamela Hieronymi puts it, Strawson would like to adjudicate the disagreement between these two camps by "convincing each side to stop talking one step earlier" (Hieronymi, 2020: 6). Strawson's key insight is that both are wrong in their assumption that our practice of holding one another responsible itself admits of any external justification. Rather, the practice has conceptual and explanatory priority. Instead of casting about for a consequence or type of freedom that might justify the practice, Strawson famously claims that we ought to begin instead with "the facts as we know them" and a closer look at the features of the practice as we find it (Strawson, 1962: 108).[2]

---

[2] All pagination from reprint of Strawson (1962) in Hieronymi (2020).

Strawson's methodological move of starting with the facts as we know them is what brings the importance of the reactive attitudes immediately to the foreground. What we find at the center of our actual practice of holding one another responsible is

> ... the very great importance that we attach to the attitudes and intentions towards us of other human beings, and the great extent to which our personal feelings and reactions depend upon, or involve, our beliefs about those attitudes and intentions. (Strawson, 1962: 111)

When we examine the facts as we know them, we see clearly that *quality of will* matters greatly to us. We care about the attitudes that others hold toward us, and the corresponding expectations regarding our own attitudes that arise in turn. Strawson gives us the following characterization of the attitudes we adopt in response to the quality of others' wills as

> ... the non-detached attitudes and reactions of people directly involved in transactions with one another ... the attitudes and reactions of offended parties and beneficiaries; of such things as gratitude, resentment, forgiveness, love, and hurt feelings. (Strawson, 1962: 111)

And, importantly, these attitudes arise only in the context of our *interpersonal relationship*s:

> We should think of the many different kinds of relationship which we can have with other people – as sharers of a common interest; as members of the same family; as colleagues, as friends; as lovers; as chance parties to an enormous range of transactions and encounters. Then we should think, in each of these connections in turn, and in others, of the kind of importance we attach to the attitudes and intentions towards us of those who stand in these relationships to us, and of the kinds of *reactive* attitudes and feelings to which we ourselves are prone. In general, we demand some degree of good will or regard on the part of those who stand in these relationships to us, though the forms we require it to take vary widely in different connections. The range and intensity of our *reactive* attitudes towards goodwill, its absence or its opposite vary no less widely. (Strawson, 1962: 112–113)

According to Strawson, part of what it means for me to be in an interpersonal relationship is for the quality of my will to matter to another person, and for theirs to matter to me in distinctive ways. And what it means for the quality of someone's will to matter to me is, at least in part, that I expect some degree of good will from them.[3] This expectation makes

---

[3] Though perhaps in some less intimate relationships, we more minimally expect only an absence of *ill will*.

corresponding demands on the other party to the relationship, demands that they also exhibit the relevant quality of will.[4] And this demand is itself constituted by a proneness to respond to the quality of the other person's will with the reactive attitudes. It is to be disposed to resent them when they fail to meet it. And when we actually *do* resent them in this kind of circumstance, we actively *blame* them.

The upshot here is that we are the kind of social creatures that find ourselves inexorably imbedded in a wide array of interpersonal relationships. What makes these relationships distinctively interpersonal is their corresponding expectations, demands, and the dispositions to respond reactively in regard to the quality of will manifested by each party in the relationship.

Strawson calls this general disposition to respond reactively to someone and see them as an appropriate term in an interpersonal relationship *the participant attitude*. In contrast, for those seen as excluded from "ordinary adult human relationships" we adopt *the objective attitude*:

> To adopt the objective attitude to another human being is to see him, perhaps, as an object of social policy; as a subject for what, in a wide range of sense, might be called treatment; as something certainly to be taken account, perhaps precautionary account, of; to be managed or handled or cured or trained; perhaps simply to be avoided, though *this* gerundive is not peculiar to cases of objectivity of attitude. (Strawson, 1962: 116)

The objective attitude can involve a variety of nonreactive emotions such as frustration, relief, sadness, or disappointment. While Strawson allows that we can sometimes deploy the objective attitude as a resource toward those who are otherwise appropriate targets of the participant attitude (for example, toward a patient in a clinical setting, or toward a difficult loved one as a "refuge" from "the strains of involvement"), we more naturally adopt it toward those who are not apt targets of the participant attitude in the first place (Strawson, 1962: 116). Such persons are *exempted* from our reactive responses, because the quality of their will does not (or at least should not) matter to us in the usual way characteristic of interpersonal relationships.[5]

---

[4] It is important to note that these expectations will vary widely depending on the nature of the interpersonal relationship itself.

[5] For a particularly insightful discussion of the distinction between Strawsonian excuses and exemptions, see Hieronymi (2020). While exempting conditions are those that render agents not apt targets of the reactive attitudes in general, excusing conditions are those that render otherwise appropriate targets excused in the circumstances because in fact their "will was not ill" (Hieronymi, 2020: 9).

We now have in hand the pieces needed to explicate a Strawsonian analysis of reactive blame and blameworthiness. As noted earlier, *to blame* someone is to judge that they have exhibited a poor quality of will relevant to the expectations that constitute a particular interpersonal relationship, and to adopt a reactive attitude toward them. One will be *blameworthy* on this view when they are in fact the *apt target* of the relevant reactive attitude.

What does this amount to? Here the details will depend on one's preferred analysis of the attitude itself, its affective component, and whether one takes the attitude to have any constitutive propositional content. Let us for now borrow from the discussion in Chapter 2 and assume a cognitivist view of the emotional component of the reactive attitudes.[6] On this kind of view, one will be blameworthy when the relevant reactive attitude is *fitting* – that is, when its evaluative propositional content is accurate. In Strawson's case this will be so when the target of blame has in fact exhibited *ill will* of the kind represented, and failed to meet an expectation constitutive of the relationship at issue.

For example, say that we are colleagues and one of the expectations constitutive of this particular interpersonal relationship is the expectation that we will save each other when the persistent and annoying used book buyer comes into the department office while we both are there working. If the irritating intruder happens upon you first, but I do not intervene, then we have at least a prima facie case that I have failed to meet this expectation, and as such it might be appropriate for you to blame me. Whether in fact it is appropriate – whether in fact I am *blameworthy* in this case – just depends on whether or not your evaluative representation of the quality of my will is accurate. If it turns out, for example, that I was on the phone with a sick relative in the hospital and that is the only reason for my failure, then the representation of ill will would not be accurate. But, if it turns out that I simply hid in my office to spite you (say, because of your own failure to show up for scheduled lunch plans earlier in the week), then this representation is accurate. My failure to save you *is* an instance of ill will on my part, and the fact that you are disposed to resent me in this circumstance is fitting as is your actual experience or expression of resentment. I am in fact *blameworthy*.

So, on Strawson's view, the right kind of reasons to blame will have something to do with facts about whether or not the target of blame has

---

[6] I defend my cognitive assumption explicitly in Section 3.3, though as an interpretive point I do not take Strawson himself to be explicitly committed to cognitivism.

exhibited some form of ill will (or at least an absence of good will). Whether or not this is the case will depend on the details of the relevant interpersonal relationship, and its corresponding demands and expectations. Instances of ill will (or lack of good will) will depend only on facts about these demands and expectations, and the target of blame's own attitudes in regard to them. As a first pass, this looks like a potentially plausible way of understanding the right kind of reasons to reactively blame, and one that does not seem to entail any vicious circularity for the corresponding analysis of blameworthiness if paired with the fittingness account of basic desert.

This picture is relatively straightforward in regard to resentment, but what of the other reactive attitudes Strawson mentions – attitudes such as gratitude, forgiveness, romantic love, and hurt feelings? It is not at all clear that each of these attitudes has its own distinctive propositional content, nor that the relevant content will share much (if anything) with that of the other reactive attitudes. This presents a significant problem for trying to account for *all* of the right kinds of reasons to blame on a reactive account like Strawson's, one that casts the net of the attitudes we should count as reactive fairly broadly. I turn now to a closer look at this problem as it is laid out initially by R. Jay Wallace, and how it motivates a narrower construal of the reactive attitudes such as Wallace's own.

3.2   Narrowing the Class of Reactive Attitudes

R. Jay Wallace combines the Strawsonian insights that (1) the reactive attitudes are central to our practice of holding one another responsible, and that (2) this practice is in some sense more fundamental than *being* responsible, with a Kantian approach to the kind of agency that renders these attitudes fair. However, he quickly departs from Strawson in his characterization of the reactive attitudes themselves, arguing that we ought to focus on a very narrow subset of the attitudes recognized by Strawson. Wallace notes that the broader that we cast our reactive net,

> ... the less plausible the claim becomes that holding people responsible is inextricably a part of this web of attitudes. The reason for this is that the inclusive interpretation of the reactive attitudes frustrates any attempt to provide an informative account of what *unifies* this set of emotions as a class. (Wallace, 1994: 11; emphasis my own)

While Wallace grants that a wide range of attitudes feature prominently in our interpersonal relationships, one of the primary burdens of a reactive account of blame and responsibility is to identify a subset of these attitudes sufficiently unified to be worthy of a single analysis. Another is to show that this class of attitudes really is a necessary, constitutive feature of our interpersonal relationships and practice of holding one another responsible. Here reactive accounts must walk a perilously fine edge. On the one hand, the need to establish the reactive attitudes as "inextricably" tied to our practice of holding responsible and our interpersonal relationships pushes in the direction of an inclusive, broad interpretation of which attitudes to consider. But, the more inclusive this picture becomes the more talk of the reactive attitudes as a theoretically useful, unified class is undercut.

3.2.1 *Wallace's Narrow Construal and Propositional Content*

This methodological dilemma is one that any reactive account of blame must address, and Wallace himself lands firmly on the side of a narrow construal:

> I therefore follow a different strategy for developing the Strawsonian approach. Instead of interpreting the reactive attitudes simply as those emotions implicated in interpersonal relations, I construe them more narrowly, taking the paradigms to be resentment, indignation, and guilt. Interpreting the reactive emotions in this narrow way permits us to understand how these emotions hang together as a class. (Wallace, 1994: 12)

Wallace is concerned that Strawson's broad construal of the reactive attitudes imparts a problematic "noncognitivist animus" to them (Wallace, 1994: 11). By restricting the class of emotions we are considering to only the varieties of moral anger, Wallace argues we can more easily identify the feature that unifies them as a genuine, non-grue-like kind – their *distinctive propositional object*. Here Wallace also makes the link between the reactive attitudes and our *expectations* even more explicit. When we restrict our focus to resentment, indignation, and guilt we see that the expectations that arise out of and partially constitute our interpersonal relationships are precisely the shared propositional object of these emotions.

As Wallace puts it, "Emotions that are constitutively linked to expectations, in this sense of holding someone to an expectation, are *the reactive attitudes*, as I will interpret them" (Wallace, 1994: 21; emphasis my own).[7]

---

[7] It is perhaps worth noting that Wallace is aware of the possibility that his reactive view of blame and moral responsibility turns out to be *revisionary* to some extent. While, like Strawson, he takes "the

He takes care to explicate the kinds of expectations at play here as *practical requirements* or prohibitions capable of linguistic formulation and being supported by practical reason, which are open to possible conflict (Wallace, 1994: 22–23).[8] Wallace formulates their connection to the reactive emotions disjunctively:

> ... to hold someone to an expectation, I suggested, is to be susceptible to a certain range of emotions if the expectation is violated, or to believe that it would be appropriate for one to feel those emotions if the expectation is violated. (Wallace, 1994: 23)

There are three different ways to meet this requirement and hold someone to an expectation: (1) by actually reacting with the attitudes of resentment, indignation, or guilt when one believes the relevant expectation has been violated, (2) by simply believing that it *would* be appropriate to so respond in cases where one believes the expectation to be violated, and (3) by *both* experiencing the reactive emotions and believing them to be appropriate to the given circumstance because an expectation has been violated (Wallace, 1994: 23).

The important role of *belief* in the previous characterization of the reactive attitudes and their relation to expectations brings us back to the explicitly cognitivist character of Wallace's reactive account. The belief *that a reactive emotion is appropriate* is not itself a necessary condition for holding one to an expectation, as one might hold someone to an expectation in the first case simply by experiencing resentment, indignation, or guilt because they believe *that the relevant expectation has been violated*. So while a belief about appropriateness is not necessary in order to hold someone responsible on this view, *some* belief is – the belief that an expectation has been violated. One must either believe that an expectation has been violated and feel the corresponding reactive emotions, *or* believe that it would be appropriate to respond to what one believes is a violation with the reactive emotions (or both). The upshot here is that this disjunctive feature of Wallace's view renders a belief about the appropriateness of a reactive attitudes sufficient, but not necessary, to holding someone to an

---

facts as we know them" regarding our practice of holding one another responsible to be in some sense fundamental, that does not exclude the possibility that we might ultimately conclude we should change the practice in substantial ways in light of a better understanding of those facts. Nor does he assume that this narrow construal of the reactive attitudes as paradigmatically the varieties of moral anger alone is the construal widely shared by the folk. Regardless, characterizing the reactive attitudes in this way is theoretically fruitful.

[8] Here Wallace (1994: 22) notes that they might be expressed as either an operator on sentences that describe kinds of actions in particular situations, or by imperatives.

expectation. The content of the distinctive propositional object of the reactive attitudes themselves – what these attitudes are *about* – is ultimately just the belief that an expectation has been violated.[9]

Turning back to responsibility and blame, *to hold someone morally responsible* on Wallace's view is "to hold the person to moral expectations that one accepts," where the relevant class of expectations is the class of distinctively moral practical requirements or prohibitions (Wallace, 1994: 63). According to Wallace, this class constitutes a special sphere within our ethical concepts, the normative sphere of moral rightness and wrongness. And we can use the term *obligation* to refer to this distinctively moral class of expectations understood as practical requirements (Wallace, 1994: 63–64).[10]

In turn, what it means *to blame* someone on this view is to hold them morally responsible, and thus to hold them to moral expectations (obligations) that one accepts. As discussed earlier, to hold someone to an expectation is just to feel or believe it appropriate to feel the reactive attitudes of resentment, indignation, or guilt because of a belief that the relevant expectation has been violated. The cognitive content here will be filled out by whatever practical requirements we "accept," namely those that end up constituting the sphere of moral rightness and wrongness.

3.2.2 *Preserving Depth*

In light of the importance of the evaluative and cognitivist character of this account of blame, one might naturally wonder whether the reactive attitudes themselves are really necessary. Wallace anticipates this question, and takes care to emphasize that our need for resentment, indignation, and guilt is twofold, even "given the punitive and potentially harmful aspect of these responses" (Wallace, 1994: 61). First, he makes the following critical remarks about blame without the reactive attitudes:

> Blame would be rendered superficial on this account, reduced to a way of describing what an agent has done, and perhaps registering a causal connection between the agent and the action so described. True moral blame,

---

[9] This feature of Wallace's view in particular is worth emphasizing here, as it will be directly relevant to my response to circularity worries in Section 3.4.

[10] Wallace (1994: 64) notes that this account "situates our practice of holding people morally responsible within a distinctive nexus of moral concepts, namely those of moral obligation, moral right, and moral wrong. This seems to be the context in which moral responsibility properly belongs." This idea of the proper place to situate moral responsibility and its attendant practices in our broader moral nexus is further developed in Wallace (2019).

by contrast, is a form of *deep assessment*, reflecting an attitude toward the agent who has acted wrongly that finds its natural expression in sanctioning behavior (avoidance, denunciation, reproach, censure, and the like). The reactive emotions are needed to explain this attitudinal aspect of *true* moral blame. (Wallace, 1994: 78; emphasis my own)

Wallace is firmly in the camp of those who take nonreactive accounts of blame to fail to sufficiently account for the distinctive significance of blame.[11] But further, these attitudes are essential to making sense of the special *depth* of our judgments of blameworthiness compared to other evaluative judgments about a person's actions. Take, for example, the fact that I am a terrible tennis player. Having made the mistake of asking me to be your partner, you would undoubtedly form an evaluative judgment about my performance on the court after our match, something along the lines of, "Wow, she really is garbage at tennis." While this evaluative judgment would of course have a negative flavor, taken in isolation it should not bother me much. After all, I am fully aware of how bad I am at tennis, and warned you when you insisted that you needed a partner. But were you to *hold me responsible* for my shoddy play in some way (perhaps you think I threw the game on purpose, to help your opponent cheat) matters are different. Your evaluative belief that I have violated a moral expectation that you accept (perhaps some kind of prohibition on cheating) has a distinctive depth that the mere evaluative judgment that I'm garbage at tennis does not.

   This distinctive depth seems to trace back in some way to *the conditions that make blame appropriate* – in other words, the conditions of blameworthiness. Those who drop the reactive attitudes from an account of blame are in a particularly difficult position to make sense of this difference. As Wallace points out, Scanlon's (2008) attempts to account for the fact that judgments of blameworthiness go beyond "mere description" will at best bottom out in appeal to whether this evaluative judgment is *justified*, namely whether it is directed at "features of a person that are open to assessment in terms of *reasons*" (Wallace, 1994: 80). But according to Wallace, appeal to justification for our judgments of blameworthiness that bottom out in whether the target features are open to assessment in terms of mere reasons still fails to set this kind of evaluation apart from other unwelcome judgments about things like one's aesthetic preferences or tennis skills. To look to reasons and justification alone is "to look in the

---

[11] For further discussion of this significance, see Chapter 1.

wrong place for the *force* of judgments of blame and responsibility" (Wallace, 1994: 81).

Where is the *right* place to look? For Wallace – and I think further for those who endorse a reactive account of blame in general – it is just in the conditions of fit for the reactive attitudes themselves. What renders these emotions appropriate, given their distinctive propositional objects? In Wallace's case, this will depend on whether an expectation that we actually accept has in fact been violated, and whether the target of blame possesses certain agential capacities needed for us to make sense of holding them to such expectations in the first place.[12]

3.2.3   *A First Pass at the Right Kind of Reasons*

Wallace's narrow, explicitly cognitivist construal of the reactive attitudes can now move us a step further toward an account of the right kind of reasons to reactively blame. On Wallace's view, the paradigmatic reactive attitudes are the personal, vicarious, and self-directed varieties of moral anger: resentment, indignation, and guilt. These emotions form a unified class because they share a distinctive propositional object: the violation of a moral expectation we accept.[13] When we believe that such a violation has occurred, and we either feel these emotions or believe it would be appropriate to feel them, then we hold the violator responsible. We actively blame the violator when we subject them to these reactive emotions, which are expressed by the various kinds of sanctioning behavior that the stance of holding one another responsible inclines us to. Finally, we determine whether someone is the appropriate target of blame, and thus blameworthy, by assessing whether or not the reactive emotions are fitting in the circumstance. And this just depends on whether a violation of a moral expectation we accept has in fact occurred.

For both Strawson and Wallace, the right kind of reason to reactively blame will have something to do with *the violation of an expectation*. Wallace's narrow approach of restricting the paradigmatic attitudes only to the varieties of moral anger helps sharpen the importance of the link between the reactive attitudes and expectations. And, his explicit

---

[12] The latter highlights a way in which Wallace's view is interestingly modular – it seems open as a coherent theoretical move to accept the reactive account of blame discussed here, yet reject the Kantian view of reflective self-control that Wallace himself pairs it with in order to make sense of how we determine who it is *fair* to hold responsible. Because much of the criticism of Wallace tends to fall on this Kantian component of the view, I will largely set it aside here.

[13] For Wallace, the violation of an obligation.

endorsement of cognitivism about these reactive emotions suggests an especially fruitful strategy for making sense of the right kind of reasons to blame. The plausible picture that begins to emerge is that the right kind of reason to blame will be facts about the violation of certain expectations that arise either as constitutive features of our interpersonal relationships (for Strawson) or the sphere of our moral obligations (for Wallace).[14] In either case what renders the reactive attitudes fitting will ultimately just be whether or not the relevant expectation has in fact been violated.

However, should we be so quick to follow Wallace in this explicit endorsement of cognitivism about the reactive attitudes? While questions about cognitivism are well worn in emotion theory, they have received surprisingly little attention in the context of blame and the reactive attitudes. As discussed previously, Wallace provides at least one consideration in favor of cognitivism – we are in need of an account of the shared propositional object of the reactive attitudes in order to make sense of the reactive attitudes themselves as a unified subset of our emotions. But what if we abandon the need for this kind of *monism* about the reactive attitudes? David Shoemaker (2015), for example, has recently offered substantive arguments in favor of a *pluralist* view of responsibility, reactive blame, and the emotions that constitute such blame. In light of these recent arguments, the assumption of cognitivism in regard to the reactive attitudes is in need of further defense. I turn now to the task of providing one. Those readers already fully on board with cognitivism may wish to skip ahead to Section 3.4.

3.3   The Case for Cognitivism

3.3.1   Shoemaker's Noncognitive Pluralism

David Shoemaker (2015) has recently defended a pluralistic tripartite theory of moral responsibility and blame, motivated by what he takes to be the fatal flaws of other reactive views. Shoemaker characterizes Strawson's original view as a *Pure Quality of Will* view, and takes an

---

[14] While I will adopt Wallace's narrow construal of the reactive attitudes in the view I defend below, I lean toward Strawson's emphasis on the importance of our interpersonal relationships in regard to which expectations matter here rather than Wallace's narrow construal of the relevant expectations to the sphere of our moral obligations.

affirmative answer to the following question as the primary desideratum for its success:

> Could a theory of responsibility appealing exclusively to quality of will do justice to the entire range of our responsibility responses in both their deployment and their suspension? (Shoemaker, 2015: 9)

Shoemaker takes a range of counterexamples involving exemptions identified by Gary Watson (2004) to show (he thinks decisively) that Strawson's own view cannot meet this desideratum.[15] There are no shortage of examples in the practice as we find it where we do in fact seem to exempt people (we suspend the reactive attitudes toward them *qua* agent) despite the fact that they obviously *do* exhibit a poor quality of will in some sense. In light of this, Shoemaker explores three main strands for refining Strawson's initial quality of will approach in ways that might meet Watson's challenge, which he characterizes as *Pure Quality of Judgment* views (hereafter PQJ's), *Pure Quality of Regard* views (hereafter PQR's), and *Pure Quality of Character* views (hereafter PQC's).

Shoemaker's take on the unifying feature of these three variations is that they each offer different interpretations of the term "will." This take is somewhat puzzling, though. What sets most of these views apart from Strawson seems rather to be a shift in focus *away* from the quality of our *wills* (in Strawsonian terms the attitudes we take toward others), and toward a more explicit focus on the quality of some other feature of our moral psychology. For example, the views Shoemaker categorizes as PQJ's focus on the target of blame's *judgment* (or lack thereof) about the worth of relevant *reasons* for their own actions and attitudes – those judgments that are properly *answerable* (Shoemaker, 2015: 10–11). For PQC's the focus shifts to some quality of the target of blame's *character*, specifically those features *attributable* to their deep self. Only PQR's seem to retain the Strawsonian focus on the target of blame's *attitudes*. Here Shoemaker cites McKenna's conversational view as a paradigm for *accountability*, emphasizing the quality of the target of blame's *regard* for others, understood as the "regard or concern one has for others (or oneself), and toward the relevance of moral considerations, as manifested in one's conduct" (McKenna, 2012: 59).

---

[15] For example, "a child can be malicious, a psychotic can be hostile, a sociopath indifferent, a person under great strain can be rude, a woman or man 'unfortunate in formative circumstances' can be cruel" (Watson, 2004: 228).

Here I do not wish to push the worry that characterizing this wide array of views as varieties of genuine *quality of will* accounts seems to stretch the notion of the kind of quality of will at issue in potentially misleading ways, only to note it. The important upshot about all of these views for Shoemaker is that while each can accommodate many of the counterexamples raised by Watson, he remains unconvinced that any can accommodate them all and account for the *entire range* of our responsibility responses. And, even if one of these views can be further refined to accommodate Watsonian exemptions, Shoemaker identifies a deeper worry. The problem is that the entire range of our responsibility responses includes a wide range of *ambivalent* responses to what Shoemaker calls marginal cases: cases in which our reactions are mixed, meaning that we seem to hold the target responsible in some ways but excuse them in others *at the same time*.

Monistic views of responsibility and blame – those that assume there is a single, univocal concept that we are trying to analyze – are saddled with an error theory about this ambivalence. They must identify and explain which response to marginal cases is getting things right, and which is in error. But Shoemaker thinks that this is itself a mistake. Rather, the lesson to be learned from our widespread ambivalence about a variety of different kinds of agency is that we should abandon the standard assumption of monism and instead embrace *pluralism* about responsibility and blame. What is going on in our response to marginal cases is that we are tracking the fact that the target is responsible in at least some way, but exempted in others.

Shoemaker focuses on our responses to several kinds of marginal cases – depression, scrupulosity, psychopathy, autism, intellectual disability, deprivation, and dementia – and argues that they each involve agents that meet the conditions for at least one of the three kinds of quality of will views discussed above (PQJ, PQC, or PQR), but are exempted from one or both of the other two. In light of this, Shoemaker proposes that there are in fact *three distinct sentimental syndromes* that respond to three distinct kinds of quality of will, which in turn reveal or determine the contours of three distinct kinds of responsibility (Shoemaker, 2015: 26).[16] The distinct kinds that he identifies are *answerability*, *attributability*, and *accountability*.

---

[16] Whether these three distinct sentimental syndromes "reveal" or "determine" the relevant kinds of responsibility would make a significant difference to the underlying ontology of Shoemaker's tripartite view. While he hopes to remain "officially neutral" about whether being responsible (the realist, or *B-tradition*) or holding responsible (the Strawsonian, or *H-tradition*) is more metaphysically fundamental, it is not obvious that one can move as easily between these two

First, attributability "consists in a structural expression relation between one's character and one's attitudes" (Shoemaker, 2015: 27). The emotions that compose the sentimental syndrome associated with attributability are admiration and disdain, and these emotions primarily target the quality of one's character. Shoemaker focuses in particular on the fittingness conditions for admiration, and argues that this reactive emotion will be appropriate when it responds to a privileged subset of psychic elements we take to be truly representative of agents, namely their *deep self.* On this view attributability responsibility maps closely onto the kind of responsibility identified by PQC views. Answerability, on the other hand, mirrors the focus of PQJ's. Shoemaker takes the emotional pair central to answerability's sentimental syndrome to be the pair of first-personal regret and admiration. Finally, accountability most closely resembles the kind of responsibility targeted by PQR views. It is the kind of responsibility that concerns our quality of regard, in other words our attitudes and intentions toward others. Accountability most closely resembles Strawson's own initial view, and is most closely associated with our responses to wrongdoing, slights, moral injury, and other norm violations. According to Shoemaker, the sentimental syndrome for accountability will be the varieties of moral anger and gratitude.

Shoemaker offers a sophisticated and nuanced pluralist account of reactive blame. His view is also the first to treat marginal cases seriously. Given the wide array of such cases and the powerful intuition of ambivalence that they generate, I take this to be a significant merit of Shoemaker's tripartite account. It is a feature of "the facts as we find them" that other reactive accounts cannot easily accommodate. However, in the remainder of this section, I wish to focus on another unique feature of Shoemaker's tripartite view – the fact that it is the only reactive account on offer to assume *noncognitivism* about the reactive attitudes themselves.

3.3.2 Motivating Noncognitivism?

Shoemaker broadly construes the class of reactive attitudes to be a subset of our sentiments that act as data points in our theorizing about blame and responsibility. He identifies two primary differences between the sentiments and the emotions more broadly, namely that the sentiments are

---

positions as Shoemaker himself seems to assume (Shoemaker, 2015: 20). I will discuss this issue further in Part II.

pan-cultural and *encapsulated from judgment*. Like other emotions, the sentiments have a "triple syndrome of feeling, thought, and action tendency" (Shoemaker, 2015: 21). But, when it comes to the sentiments in particular various aspects of the syndrome could be "missing or vary wildly from culture to culture" (Shoemaker, 2015: 21). The sentiments may differ across cultures, but we can still point to the instantiation of some roughly equivalent form of a sentiment universally across them.[17] This sets the sentiments apart from the broader class of emotions, which need not have the same cross-culturally distinguishable form. Finally, the sentiments are at least partially encapsulated from judgment. They have no constitutive propositional content.

Here I will focus on this assumption that the reactive attitudes are encapsulated from judgment, as it is what gives Shoemaker's tripartite view its uniquely noncognitivist flavor. Thus far there has been little real engagement between cognitivists and noncognitivists about the reactive attitudes specifically. Because Shoemaker offers explicit argument in favor of encapsulation, it seems a positive case for cognitivism is now called for.

Shoemaker cites three observable phenomena that motive noncognitivism about the reactive attitudes. First, appeal to encapsulation is needed to make sense of the fact that the reactive attitudes can be *stably recalcitrant*, or persist even in the face of contrary judgments.[18] Observation tells us that we sometimes continue to feel reactive emotions such as resentment even in light of the fact that we judge it unfitting in the circumstance. Consider, for example, my continued resentment of a friend for leaving me stranded at the airport for hours, even after I have learned that she had a flat tire. It would be odd to say that this judgment renders my emotion one of a different kind, when a more natural interpretation is that I continue to feel stubborn, recalcitrant resentment.

The second consideration in favor of taking the reactive attitudes to be encapsulated from judgment is the phenomenon of *unthinking action*. Here the idea is just that the reactive attitudes – especially the varieties of moral anger – can trigger immediate action tendencies unmediated by judgment whatsoever. For example, if you insult me in a deep way (perhaps you have accused me of being a Dallas Cowboys fan), I may feel

---

[17] Sentiments can therefore be contrasted with "culturally bound" emotions like, for example, Western existential angst (Shoemaker, 2015: 21). Here one would be hard pressed to pick out anything that looks remotely like an analogue in a variety of different cultures.

[18] For further discussion of recalcitrance, see D'Arms and Jacobson (2003).

a visceral impulse to punch you, despite the fact that I am fully aware that I should not do so. A cognitivist account of the reactive attitudes that takes some kind of propositional content to be constitutive or essential will have difficultly accommodating this phenomenon (Shoemaker, 2015: 22).

Finally, Shoemaker introduces the "*deliberative aspect* of the encapsulation of our sentiments from our judgments," which he takes to be especially relevant to the responsibility sentiments (Shoemaker, 2015: 23). Introspectively we often "projectively imagine ourselves into alternative scenarios" when deliberating about what to do, precisely so that we can try to discover "how we will *feel* about them" (Shoemaker, 2015: 23). The examples Shoemaker uses to identify this phenomenon are likely to resonate with many readers:

> When I am unsure if a joke I am considering telling is funny, I may imagine myself as a bystander to see whether I would be amused. When I am unsure if I should tell a particularly salacious anecdote at my friend's wedding, I may imagine how I would feel if my friend's parents were horrified by it. Or perhaps I am considering attending a party and I know that a guy who owes me a lot of money will attend. I may imagine running into him there to gauge my own reaction, in order to determine whether I ought to attend. (Shoemaker, 2015: 23)

Again, if our reactive attitudes have constitutive propositional content, then it is difficult to make sense of this projective activity. If this depiction is accurate, then it seems we are eliciting the relevant reactive emotions purely in response to a concrete counterfactual scenario. But the reason we need to do this in the first place seems to be that our *judgments* about the object of the relevant emotions have proved insufficient to elicit the emotion itself. When we project ourselves into these alternative scenarios, it seems at best that the propositional content is not *adding* anything. But if it is not, then why think such content is constitutive?

The upshot here is that Shoemaker, unlike other prominent defenders of reactive accounts of blame, offers at least some considerations explicitly in favor of noncognitivism about these attitudes. This argument depends heavily on the claim that each of the phenomena discussed earlier suggest that our reactive attitudes are encapsulated from judgment. According to Shoemaker, each phenomenon is difficult, if not impossible, to explain if these attitudes have some constitutive propositional content. However, I think that on this front Shoemaker is wrong. Rather than motivating noncognitivism, a more careful analysis of the comparative explanatory power of each view actually suggests a strong case for cognitivism.

3.3.3   Defending Cognitivism

In order to make a case for cognitivism, I will take each of the three phenomena just discussed in turn. Recall that Shoemaker draws a distinction between the *sentiments* (which he takes to be encapsulated from judgment) and our emotions more broadly, and assumes that the reactive attitudes are a subset of the former. But how strong is the case for thinking that the reactive attitudes are best characterized as a subset of our sentiments? In order to assess this claim, it will be helpful to first narrow the focus. In what follows, I will assume a narrow construal of the reactive attitudes akin to Wallace's. The motivation for this assumption is largely stipulative, in light of the overall goal of the project at hand.[19] As discussed at the outset of this chapter, resentment, indignation, and guilt are precisely the attitudes that give rise to the problem of blame in the first place. They represent the angry, harmful features of blame that raise the stakes when it comes to permissibility. While I am ultimately happy to allow that other attitudes might properly be called "reactive" in other contexts, at the end of the day their permissibility is not in need of immediate defense. If it turns out that Shoemaker is right to think that these other reactive attitudes are encapsulated from judgment, then so much the worse for a broad construal of the reactive attitudes also intended to make sense of this class of attitudes as a unified kind. In what follows, I set aside questions about encapsulation for other potentially reactive attitudes, and focus on the varieties of moral anger specifically.

3.3.3.1   Stable Recalcitrance and an Inverted Commas Defense
First, do we have good reason to think that resentment, indignation, and guilt are stably recalcitrant? Shoemaker supports this claim by gesturing toward the way that attempts to try to type-identify various other

---

[19] How is it that I can simply help myself to narrow construal? As discussed earlier, the problem of blame is clearly not a problem for *every* attitude that might be characterized as reactive, only those that are harmful, like the varieties of moral anger. If it turns out that, descriptively or psychologically speaking, Shoemaker is right and we ought to accept a much broader class of reactive attitudes, and that these other reactive attitudes are encapsulated from judgment, then so much the worse for a unified, univocal view of the reactive attitudes as a kind. In that case, my arguments here might best be construed as concerning only the *accountability* kind of responsibility and *reactive* blame, whereby this kind is genuinely distinct from other kinds of responsibility and blame. Regardless of how these questions shake out they will not undermine the arguments I offer here for taking a cognitivist view specifically of the varieties of *moral anger* to be more plausible than Shoemaker's noncognitivist alternative. So long as the varieties of moral anger are constitutive of *some* kind of reactive blame, the claim that we ought to be cognitivists about *that kind* (which will, of course, also be the harmful kind for which the problem of blame is a problem) goes through.

sentiments by some constitutive judgment fall prey to counterexamples. For example, Philippa Foot's proposal for taking the constitutive propositional content of pride to be a judgment about an achievement or status of one's own would rule out many apparent instances of pride as such (Foot, 1978: 20).[20] Shoemaker also points out that emotions that are *not* encapsulated from judgment (those that are "cognitively sharpened") seem to dissipate in the event that the relevant constitutive judgment does. In regard to resentment, he notes the following:

> If resentment is partially constituted by the judgment of having been wronged, then once one realizes one has not been wronged, what one feels is no longer resentment, *even if it is still anger.*[21] (Shoemaker, 2015: 22)

However, Shoemaker suggests that resentment does in fact persist in cases like this. And in light of this observation, he argues that we ought to conclude that resentment is best characterized as a sentiment that is encapsulated from judgment.

Returning to the cognitivist view of the reactive attitudes that I have been sketching thus far, resentment might have the following propositional content: *that an expectation has been violated*. But if Shoemaker is right about stable recalcitrance, then we sometimes continue to feel genuine resentment even after we have been presented with evidence and come to believe that in fact no such expectation has been violated. According to Shoemaker, what this phenomenon of recalcitrant resentment shows is that the propositional content at issue cannot be constitutive. We can experience genuine resentment without it.

Here there are at least two options for a cognitivist about the reactive attitudes to respond to Shoemaker's *recalcitrance challenge*. First, they might deny the psychological accuracy of the claim itself, and argue that in cases involving recalcitrance the resentment is merely apparent. While we may experience an attitude similar to resentment even after coming to realize that no expectation has been violated, we ought not to count it as a *genuine* instance of resentment.

While I myself find this response plausible, it will do little to move the needle with anyone who is not already inclined toward cognitivism about resentment. What sort of response could be persuasive? Here I think cognitivists can and should take a lesson from a similar dialectic regarding

---

[20] For example, the apparent pride one has in their favorite sports team when they win, or in the accomplishments of a child or loved one.
[21] Shoemaker cites D'Arms and Jacobson (2003: 143) here.

conceptual rationalism, and a strategy adopted by Michael Smith (1994) for defending this view against a structurally similar challenge posed by rational amoralists – *the amoralist challenge*.[22] Making this response salient will require a brief look at the context that it originally arises in. Conceptual rationalism[23] is the view that, at least conceptually speaking, our moral judgments entail reasons and such reasons carry with them corresponding motivation to act in accordance. So, for an agent to form a genuine moral judgement, "X is right," she must either have a corresponding motivation to X, or suffer some practical irrationality. One upshot of this view is that rational amoralism – instances in which a fully rational agent judges, "X is wrong," yet has no corresponding motivation to avoid X-ing – should be conceptually impossible.[24] However, not only do we have little trouble conceiving of such amoralists, many *actual* agents report their own experience of precisely this phenomenon.[25]

Like the first cognitivist response to recalcitrance suggested earlier, Smith notes that one option for defending conceptual rationalism against the amoralist challenge is to reject the phenomenon of rational amoralism as merely apparent. While amoralists may *seem* to judge that, "X is wrong," in fact they do not deploy the same shared concept as others who competently wield the concepts of RIGHTNESS and WRONGNESS. However, Smith himself points out that while rationalists will no doubt find this "inverted commas defense"[26] intuitive, it is also clearly question-begging. At this juncture, the only support for the claim that amoralists do not make genuine moral judgments that rationalists can appeal to is the fact that they lack any corresponding motivation. But this is precisely the plank of conceptual rationalism under fire from those who raise the amoralist challenge in the first place. So, while the inverted commas defense might have some explanatory power for rationalists within their own theory, it will do little to actually defuse challenges to the view based on the conceptual possibility of rational amoralists.

With this dialectic in mind, let us return to the challenge that Shoemaker claims recalcitrance poses for a cognitivist account of

---

[22] For the particular formulation of the challenge that Smith himself responds to see Brink (1986).

[23] At least as construed by Smith (1994). Here I am using the debate between Brink and Smith in particular as a heuristic that I think can inform our thinking about Shoemaker's parallel challenge to cognitivism, and wish to avoid any further descent into debates about internalism and externalism.

[24] See Smith (1994: 60–71).

[25] See, for example, the reflections of the famous killer Robert Harris, discussed by Gary Watson (2004).

[26] For further discussion of the inverted commas defense, see Hare (1952: 124–126, 163–165).

resentment. Cognitivists hoping to respond to Shoemaker will find themselves in precisely the same dialectical situation as conceptual rationalists in regard to the amoralist challenge. If they choose to appeal to an analogous inverted commas defense and argue that the recalcitrant "resentment" that Shoemaker notes is merely apparent, then this will obviously beg the question against noncognitivism. Simply assuming that genuine resentment requires some constitutive propositional content (and thus that genuine recalcitrant resentment is impossible) will do little to persuade anyone not already in the cognitivist camp.

Based on this first possible line of response, then, recalcitrance remains a problem for cognitivism. Given that the phenomenon Shoemaker characterizes as stable recalcitrance does seem powerfully intuitive, cognitivists would do well to offer a better defense against this challenge. Can they provide one? I think that they can, and that attending to the kind of strategy employed by conceptual rationalists might again be instructive.

Returning for a moment to the analogous dialectic, Smith goes on to point out that rationalists suffer no *comparative* question-begging disadvantage by denying some feature of rational amoralism as merely apparent. That is because, according to Smith, the amoralist challenge is *itself* question-begging. One will only find the conceptual plausibility of rational amoralists intuitive if they come to the table with the background assumption that genuine moral judgments require no corresponding motivation. And so rather than counting against conceptual rationalism, Smith points out that at best what the amoralist challenge leaves us with is a dialectical statement. What both rationalists and their opponents can and should agree on is that at least some actual human beings *report* the phenomenon described by the rationalist challenge. But, whether or not apparent amoralists *do* in fact exhibit all of the features asserted by the challenge[27] is precisely what the disagreement is about. As such, neither side can persuasively appeal to these features in a way that avoids begging the question against their opponent.

My view is that something very similar is going on when Shoemaker appeals to the phenomenon of recalcitrance to undermine cognitivism about the reactive attitudes. While those with noncognitivist background assumptions will find this description of the phenomenon at issue plausible, those with cognitivist background assumptions will not. They will be

---

[27] These features are threefold: (1) they make genuine moral judgments, (2) they lack *any* corresponding motivation to act in accordance with them, and (3) they suffer no practical irrationality.

as befuddled by the claim that recalcitrant "resentment" is the genuine article as intuitive rationalists will be about the rational amoralist's claims that they *really* understand that "X is wrong," yet feel no inclination whatsoever to avoid X-ing. And so, at best, I do not think that Shoemaker's appeals to recalcitrance can do much in the way of moving the needle in favor of noncognitivism. At best, we are also left with a dialectical stalemate.

While I take these considerations to be sufficient to defuse any dialectical power that Shoemaker's appeal to recalcitrance might have *against* cognitivism about the reactive attitudes, no one likes resigning themselves to a dialectical stalemate. Further, I claimed at the outset of this section that I would be making a case *for* cognitivism in this section. Diagnosis of a dialectical stalemate seems to fall well short of that. Can a cognitivist about resentment say anything further by way of *explaining* the phenomenon of apparent recalcitrance that Shoemaker highlights?

I think that a cognitivist can say more here, and in doing so can actually break the dialectical tie in favor of cognitivism. Again, what both parties – cognitivists and noncognitivists alike – should agree on is *the observable phenomenon as a data point.* Whether genuine recalcitrant resentment is possible or not, actual agents do in fact report experiencing attitudes that *seem* like recalcitrant resentment. Cognitivists should, at the very least, be able to explain this phenomenon. On the other hand, noncognitivists like Shoemaker should, at the very least, be able to explain why it *also* seems like resentment has some constitutive propositional content in other contexts. In other words, what the phenomenon of recalcitrance reveals is that both views – cognitivism and noncognitivism – about resentment will ultimately be saddled with *some* degree of error when it comes to our observations about the phenomenological experience of resentment. In order to break the dialectical tie what we need is an argument that one of these views is more *explanatorily powerful* than the other.

Once we have shifted our focus to the virtue of explanatory power, cognitivism seems clearly to have more to recommend itself than noncognitivism. In the context of resentment, this is especially clear when we focus on another phenomenon; both cognitivists and noncognitivists should agree on the apparent distinction between resentment as a specifically *moral* variety of anger, and anger more broadly. Cognitivists and noncognitivists alike should agree that while all instances of moral anger are instances of anger simpliciter, not all instances of anger are instances of *moral* anger. This distinction is necessary to make sense of recalcitrance in the first place.[28] But, if resentment is a sentiment fully encapsulated from judgment, then it is not at all clear how we might explain this distinction. Perhaps Shoemaker could appeal to some qualitative difference in the affective component of moral versus nonmoral anger, but any such appeal will be controversial at best. On the other hand, cognitivists have a ready explanation at hand – moral and nonmoral anger respond to *different objects*. They have distinct propositional content. But aside from dubious potential appeal to some qualitative difference there are no obvious resources in the offing for noncognitivists.

If this is correct, then what Shoemaker's focus on resentment and apparent recalcitrance reveals is not that that the phenomenon he identifies constitutes a damning counterexample to cognitivist accounts of resentment – rather, it is that what really matters in assessing the comparative theoretical advantages of these two views will be their *explanatory power*. While claims about intuitive recalcitrance ultimately land us in a dialectical stalemate, diagnosing the stalemate itself helps shed light on how to potentially move past it. And barring further noncognitivist arguments, it seems to me that the deck is stacked quite heavily in favor of cognitivism here, at least when it comes to resentment. Insofar as accommodating a genuine distinction between resentment and anger simpliciter is a desideratum, cognitivism has far more explanatory resources to do this distinction justice.

3.3.3.2   *Unthinking Action*

What of the phenomenon of *unthinking action*? Shoemaker points out, I think rightly, that we often exhibit the action tendency of moral anger – some form of retaliation – before or entirely without any corresponding judgment. Here Shoemaker uses drunken bar fights and instances of unreflective revenge as examples, and it seems there are no shortage of examples of this kind. If the reactive attitudes that comprise moral anger are not encapsulated from judgment, how can we make sense of this phenomenon? If, for example, the propositional content of resentment is the belief that an expectation has been violated, then why do we seem so often to lash out resentfully at others with little to no explicit thought about what it is we are lashing out *for*?

---

[28] Without the distinction between resentment and anger more broadly, it is not at all clear how a noncognitivist such as Shoemaker might make sense of what is *defective* about the lingering recalcitrant attitudes once we have come to believe that no expectation has been violated. But retaining recalcitrant genuine resentment at the cost of giving up resources for explaining why it is defective in some way seems a theoretical cost that noncognitivists should be unwilling to pay.

A cognitivist response here will echo the one laid out earlier. While Shoemaker asserts that instances of the phenomenon of unthinking action count as tokens of genuine resentment, this assertion puts the theoretical cart before the evidential horse. Whether or not this phenomenon will count as *genuine* resentment is precisely what the disagreement between cognitivists and noncognitivists *must resolve*, not a bit of uncontroversial data either side might appeal to evidentially. To treat the phenomenon as obviously demonstrative of one or the other of these two positions will beg the question against the opposing view, and such a move will land both cognitivists and noncognitivists back at the same dialectical stalemate discussed previously. So, Shoemaker's appeal to unthinking action does little to move the needle in favor of encapsulation and noncognitivism either.

There is again a more powerful response available to cognitivists. In fact, I myself am sympathetic to the phenomenological claim that examples of unthinking action like those Shoemaker cites seem to us, at least on some occasions, to be instances of resentment. However as with recalcitrance, cognitivists are better positioned to explain this as a distinct phenomenon more fully than noncognitivists. Even if we grant the claim that some unthinking actions seem to share the qualitative affective features of resentment, there is a clear *normative* distinction between instances of *unthinking* apparent resentment and *appropriate* resentment. The kinds of examples Shoemaker cites are precisely those we might use to highlight instances in which we think we *should not* resent their target. Insofar as we can, we think that we ought to mitigate such instances of apparent resentment as much as possible, and not merely because of the unfortunate consequences they often give rise to. If we grant that unthinking resentment counts as genuine resentment, then even noncognitivists will need to account for the fact that not all resentment is normatively of apiece.

Cognitivists have a clear explanation of this normative distinction in hand. The phenomenon of unthinking action is *defective* in the sense that *it is not even an instance of genuine resentment*. The fact that this phenomenon presents as phenomenologically similar to resentment absent its constitutive propositional content is precisely *why* we ought to mitigate the phenomenon insofar as we can. It is not merely that such instances are not fitting – sans the relevant content, they *cannot* be fitting.

Can noncognitivists account for this distinction? Perhaps they might appeal to the harmful consequences that unthinking resentment tends to have in order to explain the normative difference, but as noted earlier, the prospects for this kind of explanation to work for all (or even most!) instances of unthinking resentment look grim. And so, it seems that appeal to unthinking resentment at best leaves Shoemaker in another dialectical stalemate with cognitivists. And at worst it may actually provide another datum that cognitivists can highlight to demonstrate that cognitivism about the reactive attitudes has far more explanatory power than noncognitivism.

3.3.3.3   *Projective Imagination*

Finally, what conclusions should we draw from Shoemaker's insight that the reactive attitudes seem to involve a deliberative aspect of *projective imagination*? I find this to be the most intriguing of the considerations Shoemaker cites in favor of encapsulation. We certainly do sometimes engage in precisely the kind of projective exercise he identifies, imagining what we would feel like in certain circumstances in order to help determine what sorts of corresponding evaluative beliefs we ought to hold. But if we assume cognitivism about the reactive attitudes, and take such beliefs to comprise the constitutive propositional content of these emotions, then this activity of projective imagination does indeed seem puzzling. However, as with the preceding two phenomena, cognitivism has better resources to explain this phenomenon than noncognitivism.

To see why, assume for a moment that Shoemaker is correct and the reactive attitudes are encapsulated from judgment. If this were the case, the phenomenon of projective imagination would in fact be even *stranger* than if cognitivism about the reactive attitudes were true. Why think that our projectively imagined affective responses would suggest *anything* about a corresponding evaluative judgment, if in fact such responses are supposed to be encapsulated from judgment? In severing the link between resentment and judgment, it looks as though noncognitivism cuts far too deeply. Any attempts to cite a correlation between a particular affective response and corresponding evaluative judgment will be contingent at best. But worse, even if any such contingent correlation can be established, why think that there is any corresponding upshot for our practical deliberation? Once the reactive attitudes have been uncoupled from judgment, there is no clear reason to think that any contingent tie to a specific evaluative judgment will be sufficient to guide what one *should do* in the circumstance. And so, it seems that noncognitivism about the reactive attitudes should leave us deeply *suspicious* of the practical value of any exercises of projective imagination.

Not so for cognitivism. Cognitivists about the reactive attitudes again have a ready explanation of the phenomenon of projective imagination, and further can accommodate the valuable role Shoemaker himself identifies it playing in our practical deliberation. On the cognitivist view some evaluative judgments (according to the view I have been sketching thus far, the belief that an expectation has been violated) will be partly constitutive of the reactive attitudes. While we may not always experience the corresponding affective component,[29] it will provide at least some prima facie evidence that the relevant evaluative belief is correct. This evidence will of course be highly defeasible, and I will discuss the potential evidentiary role played by the reactive attitudes in far more detail in Chapter 4. Here the important upshot is that cognitivists' commitment to constitutive propositional content cements a connection of *some* kind between affectivity and evaluative judgment. Noncognitivists have no such resources. So, while I agree with Shoemaker that the phenomenon of projective imagination is one that might inform our views about whether the reactive attitudes are encapsulated, he seems here to draw precisely the wrong conclusion about this. Far from motivating non-cognitivism, projective imagination and any other phenomenon involving the reactive attitudes that we want to play a valuable role in practical deliberation actually provides substantial evidence for embracing cognitivism.

To sum up, I take the three phenomena Shoemaker offers in support of encapsulation to in fact suggest a strong positive case for *cognitivism*. At best, the way that Shoemaker attempts to wield these phenomena (as mere *intuitive* support or direct evidence for encapsulation) in favor of noncognitivism is question-begging. But further, at the explanatory level, it seems cognitivism is actually far better suited to not only accommodate, but *account for* all three of these phenomena. Given that cognitivism also enjoys the status of the standard default position on whether the reactive attitudes have constitutive propositional content, I therefore conclude that any burden to make a positive case for the view has been sufficiently dispatched. I will assume cognitivism about the reactive attitudes in what follows.

3.4 The Right Kind of Reasons to Blame

On a cognitivist account of reactive blame, what might the right kind of reasons to blame actually look like? First, let us take stock of the

---

[29] Given the assumption that reactive essentialism is false, and that we ought to understand the role of the reactive attitudes for blame in terms of either functional or canonical reactivity (see Chapter 1, Section 1.1).

components of the view I have been sketching thus far. In what remains, I will assume the fittingness account of basic desert of blame laid out in Chapter 2. This account arises in part out of my analysis of the problem of blame discussed in Chapter 1, and acknowledgment of the fact that the problem concerns *reactive blame* in particular. It is precisely this kind of angry, harmful blame that raises the stakes in regard to permissibility, and leads curmudgeons to question the normative adequacy of blame in the first place.

Once we have narrowed our focus to reactive blame, a new and potentially fruitful way of thinking about basic desert and the prospects for meeting the desert-based desideratum for normative adequacy suggests itself: *the fittingness account*. If the target of interest is reactive blame, then we might naturally borrow from the ways in which we already analyze a very desert-like feature of our more general affective attitudes. This is precisely what the fittingness account of basic desert of blame does, having the further promising features of distinguishing between desert and mere justification while also offering some explanation of *why* the widespread assumption that the proper desert bases for basic desert of blame should be restricted only to features of the agent or her action.

We are now finally in a position to say more about what those features might be and move beyond the strictly negative analyses of basic desert of blame that have dominated the literature thus far. By now the rough contours of a possible view of the right kind of reasons to blame should be apparent:

> **The right kind of reason to blame (RKR):** to deserve reactive blame in the basic sense is for reactive blame to be a fitting response to an agent. And, reactive blame is a fitting response to an agent just in case the agent's action or the quality of their will violated an expectation constitutive of one of their interpersonal relationships, and the blamer believes this is so.[30]

This proposal for the right kind of reasons to blame obviously requires a great deal of unpacking. First, this account of the right kind of reasons is inclusively disjunctive. A person will have the right kind of reason to blame if *either* some feature of the target's action, or the quality of their will violates an expectation constitutive of an interpersonal relationship to which they are a party, or both. The motivation for this disjunctive account is primarily that it leaves open substantive questions about the loci of the conditions for blameworthiness and moral responsibility. I see

---

[30] Thanks to Neal Tognazzini for helpful feedback on earlier formulations of RKR.

no reason to assume that reactive accounts of blame must follow the Strawsonian tradition of locating these conditions only in regard to an agent's quality of will.[31] Rather, I take this reactive account to be modular in that there is logical space to pair such an account of the right kind of reasons to blame with a wide variety of more fully developed accounts of the necessary and sufficient conditions for moral responsibility. The sorts of views I have in mind here are those explicitly concerned with identifying the *control condition* for responsibility, defined in terms of the relationship between some feature of the target of blame (for example, her deep self or capacity to recognize and respond to moral reasons) and her action.

In other words, while *basic* desert of reactive blame is grounded in the mere violation of a constitutive expectation, this account leaves open the possibility that a further degree of control might be required for desert simpliciter. To lay my own cards on the table, I find the view that the violation of a constitutive expectation does *all* of the desert-entailing work appealing. However, I anticipate that many will find this view radically deflationary. And, I do not wish to take the discussion too far afield by defending a deflationary view here, given that the primary task at hand is to defuse curmudgeonly skeptical worries about the permissibility of blame. Meeting this current goal need not (and furthermore probably should not, at least in a single manuscript!) require a positive account of basic desert of reactive blame, the nature of reactive blame, *and* a full blown account of the necessary and sufficient conditions for moral responsibility. For now, considerations of space require leaving these particular dots unconnected.

In short, it seems to me a merit of RKR that it avoids saddling itself with any obvious commitments regarding the control condition for moral responsibility, and I see no reason to think that it must do so.

3.4.1   *Extraneous Expectations and Interpersonal Relationships*

Turning to the feature of the account perhaps most in need of explication, what does it mean to say that an action or quality of will *violates an expectation constitutive of an interpersonal relationship*? Here it will be helpful to identify two related but importantly distinct issues:

(1)   Which *expectations* matter?
(2)   Which *relationships* will count as interpersonal in the relevant sense?

---

[31] And perhaps, in light of some of the worries raised by Shoemaker (2015), it should strive not to.

I will take each of these questions in turn. First, in regard to which expectations matter, we can begin by identifying a spectrum of possibilities. The extremes at each end have already been captured by the discussion of Wallace and Strawson in Section 3.2. One possibility is that we ought to construe the expectations relevant to basic desert of blame quite narrowly. More specifically, we might restrict them to some class of *normative expectations*. This extreme would closely resemble Wallace's position. According to Wallace, whether or not an agent is the appropriate target of the reactive attitudes will depend on whether they have violated an expectation *that we endorse*, where the expectations we endorse are those that constitute only our *obligations*, or as Wallace has more recently characterized things, *the moral nexus.*[32]

While this understanding of the expectations relevant to the right kind of reasons to blame has the advantage of tying these reasons tightly to other normative considerations, in my view it is ultimately too narrow. This is at least so in the context of settling questions about the permissibility of blame. The worries of blame curmudgeons clearly do not concern *only* instances of explicitly *moralized* reactive blame. In fact, they are likely *more* concerned about less morally loaded instances. The fundamental question about permissibility at issue raises questions not only about basic desert of blame for the clear (or even egregious) instances of wrongdoing that we are (unfortunately) sometimes confronted with. Perhaps even more pressing are questions about the permissibility of the more innocuous yet pervasively harmful instances of reactive blame that we direct at colleagues, friends, partners, and family members who let us down, even in cases where we would be hesitant to think that they have full-throatedly *wronged* us.

For this reason, I endorse a view of the expectations relevant to blame that leans toward a broader construal. This end of the spectrum is Strawsonian in spirit, acknowledging the wide variety of interpersonal relationships that give rise to reactive blame in our blaming practices as we find them.[33] We resent our friends and acquaintances when they spill our secrets or otherwise betray us, but also often resent those closest to us

---

[32] See Wallace (2019).

[33] Here it may be helpful to defuse a potential worry that there is a tension between this broad construal of the expectations relevant to blame and the narrow construal of the reactive attitudes that I endorse earlier in this chapter. While I think that we ought to narrow our view of the reactive attitudes relevant to reactive blame to the varieties of moral anger in order to thread the methodological needle noted by Wallace, this is of course compatible with a broad view of the contexts in which moral anger might be ultimately be appropriate.

for much lesser failures. Thus an account of the right kind of reasons to blame ought to respect the fact that the relevant expectations will vary widely, and involve a significant degree of *context-sensitivity*.

But, how much context-sensitivity? Here an initial worry emerges – might endorsing a broad Strawsonian view of the expectations relevant to the right kind of reasons to blame allow for *too much* to count as fitting, deserved reactive blame? While we may want to account for a wide range of blaming contexts, we do not want to do so at the cost of opening the blame floodgates entirely. If the account on offer yields the result that just *any* expectation will be relevant, then it will entail no shortage of obvious counterexamples, cases in which it might seem counterintuitive to say that the target of blame is deserving in the basic sense.

First, if the view I am here proposing does end up opening the blame floodgates in an obviously objectionable and deeply counterintuitive way, this might only motivate us back toward Wallace's end of the relevant expectation spectrum. Such a view would not deliver the groundwork needed in the next chapter for a full blown account of the permissibility of blame in *all* of the harmful guises and contexts that I think curmudgeons are worried about, but it might still constitute a significant victory against full blown skepticism.

However, I see no reason to retreat to this more circumspect position. Even on a broad Strawsonian construal of the kinds of expectations relevant to the right kind of reasons to blame that I wish to endorse, it will not be the case that just *any* expectation will do. To see why, consider a concrete example. Let us say that I expect my romantic partner to spare me any and all truths that might hurt me. The kinds of truths that fall under this umbrella will range from things like telling me that my new haircut is hideous to the fact that they no longer love me. The kind of expectation that I have in mind here would be a radical one, but not one radically different from the sorts of expectations we often find in the wide array of our actual interpersonal relationships. We often expect too much of one another, especially those we care about most. I will call such expectations *extraneous expectations*, as they are not even partly constitutive of the relationship in question. In many cases, extraneous expectations will not only be unnecessary to sustaining the relevant relationship, they may even be downright *damaging* to it. The above example seems clearly to be of the latter sort. Not only would the expectation to spare my feelings in this extreme way seem unnecessary to sustaining my romantic relationship, for this kind of relationship it is actually likely to undermine or even *destroy* it. The violation of this kind of extraneous expectation would not, therefore, count as the right kind of reason for me to blame my partner. If I blame my partner for violating this and only this expectation, then my blame would not be fitting in this context.

This example also serves to highlight precisely why we *should* embrace a view at the Strawsonian end of the spectrum, one that is heavily context-sensitive. While the expectation sketched previously would be extraneous to most (if not all!) romantic relationships, it might in fact be *constitutive* of other kinds of interpersonal relationships. Take our relationships with our colleagues and mere acquaintances. These less significant relationships are still robustly interpersonal. But in these contexts the expectation that the other person spare us truths that will hurt us seems far from extraneous. I *should* expect my colleagues to refrain from commenting on my new haircut if they think it is terrible, or revealing that they cannot stand my personality. Such an expectation is in fact constitutive of this less intimate kind of relationship. We sometimes *need* a certain degree of tactful dishonesty from our colleagues and mere acquaintances that we do not and should not expect from our closest loved ones.

There is of course a great deal more to say about extraneous versus nonextraneous expectations than I can do justice to here. The upshot, though, is that when it comes to the question of which expectations will be relevant to the right kind of reasons to blame I wish to endorse a broad Strawsonian view, but even this broad view will count *only non-extraneous* expectations as relevant. Determining which expectations are extraneous will depend on the details, and on identifying the sorts of expectations needed to sustain different types or tokens of our interpersonal relationships, versus those that are unnecessary or downright destructive.[34]

Finally, which kinds of relationships ought we to count as genuinely interpersonal? Our intuitions about whether an expectation is extraneous or constitutive to a particular type or token of relationship might be clear and obvious the closer we stick to the realm of the people we care about most, but don't matters become increasingly murky the farther out we move? For example, when a driver suddenly cuts me off in traffic for no apparent reason, I certainly *seem* to genuinely resent and blame them when I lay on the horn.[35] It seems we ought to be able to ask meaningful questions about the permissibility of this apparent instance of blame. Thus my account of the right kind of reasons to blame should have something to say about which facts could make the driver deserving of blame in the basic

[34] One possible avenue for cashing out the details might be Scanlon's (2008) work on this topic.
[35] I leave it to the reader's imagination to fill in other possible blaming responses here.

sense (or excuse them). But to describe my relationship with the driver – someone whom I have never and will never even meet – as *interpersonal* seems to stretch the conditions of felicitous usage. And without such a relationship, there is nothing to be said about which expectations are constitutive of it, and thus whether or not a non-extraneous expectation has been violated when the driver cuts me off.

This worry is important to note, but it is not a new worry about blame. It is simply an instance of a problem that all accounts of blame are confronted with: *the problem of the stranger.*[36] Insofar as we *do* think that it is sometimes appropriate to blame complete strangers to whom we stand in no obvious relation (and relatedly the dead and distant), can a given view of blame account for this? Here I have little new to add to this discussion, beyond gesturing to the persuasive answers I think others have already offered. Scanlon (2008: 139–152), for example, suggests that we stand in relation even to complete strangers as relata in *the moral relationship*, grounded in a kind of mutual concern we have for all other rational beings. While it is beyond my current purposes to assess the success of Scanlon's appeal to the moral relationship, here I wish only to flag that the problem at hand is not one unique to my account of the right kind of reasons to blame.

3.4.2   *Circularity Revisited*

With a positive account of the right kind of reasons to reactively blame now in hand, it is time to address the promissory note regarding circularity worries offered at the end of Chapter 2. Do such worries reemerge now that we have a clearer idea of what would actually render agents deserving of reactive blame in the basic sense according to the fittingness account?

I think not. Recall that for the fittingness account of basic desert potential circularity objections will target whether, in analyzing basic desert in terms of the right kind of reasons, the right kind of reasons must itself be analyzed in terms of what agents deserve in the basic sense. In Chapter 2, I offered some initial considerations that count against this worry, but now that I have articulated what the right kind of reasons actually *are* the worry can be defused more fully. If, as I propose here, the right kind of reasons to blame concern only beliefs about *non-extraneous expectations*, there is no reason to think basic desert will creep into our analysis of the relevant expectations. Again, the relevant kinds of

---

[36] For a helpful articulation of this problem, see Sher (2013).

expectations will be those constitutive of our genuinely interpersonal relationships, and while there may be relatively few comprehensive accounts of what such relationships amount to I am not aware of any that take the fulfillment of such expectations to involve the notion of desert, let along desert in the basic sense. Nor do I see any reason why an account of our interpersonal relationships and the expectations that constitute them would make any such appeal. And so, barring further argument for thinking that appeals to basic desert will somehow be required to fully analyze the expectations that ultimately constitute our wide array of interpersonal relationships, I will assume circularity worries for the view I propose have been sufficiently dispatched.

3.5 Conclusion

To sum up, I propose that we take seriously the following account of the right kind of reasons to blame: the right kind of reasons to blame are facts about whether or not the target of blame has in fact violated a non-extraneous expectation. We now have in hand a positive account of basic desert of reactive blame analyzed in terms of fittingness, whereby reactive blame is a fitting response to an agent just in case the blamer correctly believes that some feature of the target of blame's action or the quality of their will has violated this kind of expectation. While there is certainly much more interesting work to be done explicating the details of this account, I take the contours sketched here to provide ample substance to allow us to return to questions about permissibility and the problem of blame itself. Can this fittingness account of basic desert meet the desert-based desideratum for normative adequacy (NAD)? Can a narrowly construed cognitivist account of reactive blame meet the value-based desideratum (NAV)? In Chapter 4, I argue for affirmative answers to each of these questions.

Solving the Problem of Blame

As discussed in Chapter 1, the problem of blame concerns how it could be permissible to harm others by blaming them, given the variety of unpleasant attitudes and responses often associated with our blaming practices. Reactive blame puts these problematic features of blame front and center. Reactive blame is the *most* unpleasant kind of blame, and so any attempt to establish the normative adequacy of blame and fully defuse skeptical worries should address the permissibility of this kind of blame in particular.

In Chapter 1, I identified two desiderata for providing a normatively adequate account of reactive blame – a desert-based desideratum (NAD), and a value-based desideratum (NAV). With a positive account of basic desert of blame and a clearer articulation of the nature and scope of the relevant negative reactive attitudes in hand, we can now return to the problem itself. In this chapter, I offer arguments that both NAD and NAV can ultimately be met.

I begin in Section 4.1 with discussion of how reactive blame can meet the value-based desideratum (NAV). Here I argue that several accounts of reactive blame already on offer make a persuasive case for thinking that it plays a uniquely valuable role in the moral lives of creatures like us. In Sections 4.2 and 4.3, I take up the more formidable task of meeting the desert-based desideratum (NAD). In Section 4.2, I offer a parity of reasons argument for thinking that agents are – or at least can be – deserving of reactive blame in the basic sense. In Section 4.3, I argue that those who accept a perceptual model of the emotions have further reason to think that reactive blame is in fact sometimes deserved in the basic sense. If these arguments are correct, then we have good reason to think, contrary to the claims of blame curmudgeons, that even reactive blame is permissible and the problem of blame can be solved.

4.1   The Aims and Value of Blame

The account of the right kind of reasons to reactively blame proposed in Chapter 3 is compatible with a wide range of views about the potential value of blame. In this section, I will draw on arguments from Christopher Franklin (2013), Victoria McGeer (2013), and Margaret Urban Walker (2006) in order to argue that reactive blame is sufficiently valuable to meet NAV. According to the kind of hybrid account I have in mind, it makes sense for creatures like us to reactively blame because of the unique communicative role this kind of blame plays in valuing what we ought to value and sustaining the moral norms essential to our shared moral communities. Insofar as we wish to live in communities that value *any-thing*, reactive blame looks to play a critical role in doing so properly.

4.1.1   Valuing the Objects of Moral Value

Is there a plausible explanation for *why* creatures like us would make the kinds of unpleasant and affectively colored appraisals that constitute reactive blame? Christopher Franklin's (2013) "value account of blame," discussed briefly in Chapter 1, offers one plausible explanation: reactive blame is functionally necessary for valuing the proper objects of moral value. According to Franklin, free disvaluations of persons have a symbolic meaning, and instances of blame are needed to protect and defend the victims of such wrongdoing.[1]

This view depends on several substantive assumptions. First, it assumes that individual persons are intrinsically valuable, and thus the proper objects of moral value. While most will grant this assumption readily, it is far less obvious what actually *valuing* the objects of moral value amounts to. Franklin (2013: 214) suggests that valuing what we ought to value requires more than a mere judgment that a thing is valuable. On Franklin's view, valuing also requires certain emotional and deliberative dispositions. Norms governing these dispositions provide pro tanto reasons and arise in virtue of the nature of the object itself. Franklin assumes that the objects of moral value include humans, nature, and animals, but here I will restrict my focus only to individual persons and members of shared moral communities.

What do the relevant norms governing the dispositions required to properly value persons look like? Here Franklin first suggests the following:

---

[1]   For further discussion of the potential meaning or threat that blame carries, see Hieronymi (2004).

> To value persons is to be disposed to experience a range of emotions in response to how their lives go and to see certain considerations as reasons ... we must be disposed to experience and express blame in response to those who *freely* disvalue objects of moral value ... free actions function as, or express value judgments ... free disvaluations challenge the status of an object as valuable (or its degree of value) ... Blame (or guilt) serves both to acknowledge the wrongness of my action and to counteract my claim because it too plays an expressive role. (Franklin, 2013: 216–218)

According to Franklin, free disvaluations of persons have a symbolic meaning. Because they are actions performed for reasons, they are expressive of what we value and the degree to which we value it. When it comes to moral values in particular (especially the value of persons), the relevant norms require that we be disposed to *protect and defend* these objects of value.

In order to further elucidate what this disposition amounts to, let us consider an example similar to the one used by Franklin, a case in which I have freely insulted your romantic partner. First, it is important to note the sense in which the action in question (in this case my insulting your partner) is a *free* disvaluation. To avoid worries about circularity regarding the kind of freedom at issue, let us assume only that free disvaluations are those actions caused by an agents' own reasons, regardless of the source of those reasons.[2] Restricted in this way, free disvaluations will be all too familiar to human beings engaged in interpersonal relationships and broader moral communities. When I act in a way that freely disvalues someone, my action has a symbolic meaning. The reasons for my action are my own, and so when I act in this way, I express, both to myself and others, that I do not value (or do not value enough) the person in question.

Returning to the example, if I freely insult your partner, this expresses "a judgment about her worth," or a claim that "she is not to be valued" (Franklin, 2013: 218). In light of this symbolic meaning, the standards of valuing your partner as an object of moral value require that you protect and defend her by counteracting this claim. And on Franklin's view, a disposition to blame – and in precisely the way colored by moral anger – is essential to doing so. Reactive blame "responds to challenges to an object's

---

[2] So, free disvaluations are an agents' own in at least the most minimal compatibilist sense. While Franklin (2018) defends libertarian incompatibilism elsewhere, the value account of blame seems free from any such commitments. Here I will assume that Franklin's account of blame might be taken as modular, and leave open the possibility that free disvaluations could still be the result of manipulation and that we can freely disvalue others without having physically possible alternatives. In order to have the relevant symbolic meaning at issue here, it seems free disvaluations need only be a result of one's own reasons, regardless of the ultimate source of those reasons.

status issued in the free disvaluation and makes a case for its value"
(Franklin, 2013: 220). And it serves the role of protecting and defending
the person who has been freely disvalued in one or more of the following
ways:

> Blame (or guilt) serves both to acknowledge the wrongness of my action
> and to counteract my claim because it too plays an expressive role ... In
> particular you are standing up for your [partner] and defending her value in
> the face of a challenge, making clear that you value her and that my actions
> are inconsistent with her value. Moreover, by responding in this way, you
> are protecting your [partner's] value. You are making it clear to others that
> she is of value, and this is the first step in protecting her from further
> mistreatment ... and resist the subtle growth of contempt for her. You
> make it clear that you will not stand for or allow such treatment of her.
> (Franklin, 2013: 218)

On the other hand, *failure* to have the relevant disposition amounts to a
failure to "take her seriously, implying that what I did was 'no big deal'"
(Franklin, 2013: 218). Such failures also have significant symbolic meaning in that they

> ... involve you in a kind of complicity: your failure to act can be a form of
> acquiescence to the judgment expressed in the free disvaluation. To fail to
> stand up for the value also shows a failure of recognition: it is precisely our
> understanding of the importance of the object of value and the significance of
> the free disvaluation that moves us to experience and express blame. Moreover,
> to defend moral values involves expressing our condemnation of the act: by
> standing up and defending moral values we make it clear that we disagree with
> and will not stand for that kind of action. (Franklin, 2013: 220)

So, on Franklin's view, there is a clear explanation of why we blame.
A disposition to blame is essential to properly valuing the objects of moral
value. The standards of valuing persons as the objects of moral value in
particular require us to protect and defend them. Here it is important to
note, though, that Franklin does not take these standards of value to
require us to blame *in every instance* that we perceive a free disvaluation
of an object of moral value. Our moral lives are complicated and in at least
some cases our emotional attention will be required elsewhere. For example, if you are distracted because a loved one is desperately ill, then we
might not see it as a violation of the standards of value for you to fail to
blame a colleague for their rude treatment of another. The standards of
value require that we be genuinely *disposed* to blame, but not that we must
always respond to free disvaluations with an actual instance of reactive
blame (Franklin, 2013: 223). While widespread failures to be disposed to

blame would "fail to take seriously what is of value," our emotional limitations also temper our shared demands and expectations when it comes to protecting and defending each other as objects of moral value.[3]

4.1.2   Why the Negative Reactive Attitudes?

Do we really need *reactive blame* in order to properly value what we ought to value? On Franklin's view, we cannot protect and defend the objects of moral value adequately via alternative means, especially sanitized versions of blame that do not involve the negative reactive attitudes. Franklin himself defends this claim primarily by arguing that sadness (the nonreactive analogue of moral anger) cannot serve the same function as the varieties of moral anger, and by appealing to his own experience of value remarking that ". . . it is precisely because people value things so much that they are likely to become especially exercised when these objects of value are freely disvalued" (Franklin, 2013: 221).

But there is more to say here. Franklin's symbolic account can be bolstered further by attending to the psychological fact that affective blame is a *costly signal*. In offering a naturalistic account of blame as a psychological–moral kind, Victoria McGeer (2013: 169) points out that emotions in general are "motivational drivers in human beings, reliably and involuntarily priming certain action tendencies," and the negative reactive attitudes are no exception. Anger specifically is often characterized as a basic emotion in that it appears to be cross-culturally shared, innately programmed, rapid and involuntary, and relevant to individual survival. According to the evolutionary story, McGeer proposes that it is triggered by the perception of some kind of norm violation; this sensitivity to perceived norm violations helps us track the attitudes that others manifest in their behaviors; and we take these attitudes to be helpful and reliable indicators of patterns of behavior (McGeer, 2013: 174).

McGeer is skeptical about the psychological possibility for creatures like us to even engage in the process of blaming without the negative reactive attitudes, but she grants for the sake of argument that it is conceptually possible. Even so, McGeer argues further that the negative reactive attitudes constitute a uniquely powerful form of communication for creatures like us (McGeer, 2013: 181). First, they are *attention grabbers*. They draw our attention to the person, attitude, and behavior that triggers them, to the person who is experiencing them, and to our own behavior. In drawing

---

[3] I return to troubling issues regarding widespread failure and other kinds of failure in Section 4.1.3.

our attention both to our own emotional reactivity and the reactivity of others, the negative reactive attitudes thus draw us into an exchange about the meaning of our behavior, the nature of our mutual expectations, and of our shared moral norms. These attitudes, like other basic emotions, "make salient for us the communicative contents of what they convey" (McGeer, 2013: 181–182).

Second, McGeer points out that from an evolutionary and game-theoretic point of view, the varieties of moral anger are *hard to fake* (McGeer, 2013: 182). Because they are hard to generate in conditions where one does not actually perceive an injury or violation, attitudes like resentment, indignation, and guilt are uniquely effective ways to communicate how sincerely blamers believe that the target of blame has committed a violation, and also how sincere targets are on the receiving end of things. Feigned indignation and guilt are easy to spot. All of us are familiar with the difference between a genuinely indignant or guilty person and the faker (except perhaps in cases where we are dealing with a particularly good actor or a psychopath). The genuinely indignant person, for example, is flustered. Perhaps they raise their voice, or their face reddens, or at the very least they scowl in the way characteristic of those experiencing a flash of anger. The genuinely guilty person might slump their shoulders, turn their eyes downward, or even begin to cry. The greater the reaction the more strongly our attention is grabbed, and the more strongly we are encouraged to take seriously the gravity of the triggering violation. While it is *possible* to fake any of these responses, doing so convincingly or for an extended period of time is difficult. This is in large part because these emotions and their corresponding behavioral responses are not normally under our voluntary control. Because faking them is so cognitively costly, the varieties of moral anger have a special evidentiary and meaning-imparting role in our communication with one another (McGeer, 2013: 181–182).

To sum up, McGeer makes a strong empirical case for thinking that if the aims of blame have the sort of symbolic, communicative aims that Franklin suggests, then the varieties of moral anger are in fact the best candidate attitudes to achieve these aims. They are a uniquely effective means for human beings to protect and defend the proper objects of value given that they are such costly signals. And so, insofar as we care about properly valuing persons (and perhaps other proper objects of value), there is a strong case for thinking that the value-based desideratum for normative adequacy (NAV) can be met. If McGeer and Franklin are right, then reactive blame is something that we *need* in order to properly value anything at all. I turn now to one further consideration in favor of this claim, as it pertains to the way that we value others as members of shared moral communities in particular.

4.1.3 Failure to Blame, Shared Moral Communities, and Moral Norms

Before turning to the desert-based desideratum for normative adequacy, some reflection on *failures* to blame might serve to further strengthen the arguments that the value-based desideratum can be met. Such failures impact our interpersonal relationships, the authority of our moral norms, and the stability of our shared moral community in ways that give us even more reason to value reactive blame in particular.

To this end, Margaret Urban Walker makes the following remarks about the aims of resentment specifically:

> ... the "aim" of resentment is, ideally, to activate protective, reassuring, or defensive responses in some individuals, or in a community that can affirm that the victim is within the scope of that community's protective responsibilities, or that the resenter is in fact competent in grasping and applying the community's shared moral norms. (Walker, 2006: 135)

This characterization of the aim of resentment shares Franklin's emphasis on blame's protective role, without making any substantive commitments about the standards for properly valuing the objects of moral value. Walker is primarily concerned with offering an account of moral repair, where norm violations and corresponding blaming responses to those violations are what put us in a position that calls for repair in the first place. But, on Walker's view, blame is not just a response to norm violations. Our blaming practices actually support and sustain our moral norms.[4] This is because failure to blame in instances where we perceive the violation of a moral norm both undermines the authority of the relevant norm, and can also bring into question the victim's status as a genuine member of the corresponding moral community.

To see why, consider a toy case:

> *Philosophy club:* You are an undergraduate interested in philosophy and decide to join the philosophy club, and you happen to be their first woman member. Part of the mission statement of the club is to pursue philosophical inquiry into questions about diversity in a welcoming and supportive space. You are thrilled, because normative questions about how we ought to

---

[4] See also McGeer (2019).

try to promote gender and racial inclusivity and equity is something that you are passionate about.

The first few meetings of the club go well. At the start of every meeting the secretary reads the bylaws (which include a statement on the club's commitment to diversity and inclusivity), and everyone is friendly and respectful of your contributions to the discussion. You discuss Singer's drowning child and our obligations to the poor, and then Norcross's tortured puppies in Fred's basement and whether or not it is permissible to eat factory farmed meat. But then something changes when you suggest reading something on feminist approaches to ethics for the next meeting. The Vice President of the club sneers in response and shouts (in front of everyone), "That's not real philosophy, I knew you were an idiot!" You look frantically at the President and other members of the club, but they all remain silent. Most look out the window, or at their feet, but a few actually stare back at you with hostility. You become so uncomfortable that eventually you get up and leave.

After the meeting you try to chalk the outburst up to one bad egg. Surely someone will speak up on your behalf about how such exchanges violate the bylaws of the club by the time the club meets next. But at the next meeting everyone acts as if nothing has happened. Afterwards you feel even worse than before. No one says a word about it at the meeting after that, either. Or the next. Soon after, you quit the club.

Here *Philosophy Club* serves as a toy case for a particular moral community with shared expectations. Some of these expectations are governed by norms that have a special authority – they are moral norms. Moral norms differ from mere conventional norms in a variety of ways.[5] Moral norms (like the norm that we should not harm others) are more serious, are independent of authority, and their content concerns the welfare of others. Conventional norms (like the norm that you should raise your hand before you speak) are less serious, do not retain their force when a relevant authority gives permission to violate them, and their content concerns group or societal attitudes of approval and disapproval. Because of their dependence on authority, mere conventional norms plausibly retain their limited force as standing expectations even when violations go unaddressed, so long as the relevant authority has not granted permission to violate them further. In other words, they can admit exceptions without significant damage to the norm itself. But because moral norms are both more serious and authority independent, unaddressed violations *can* serve to damage them significantly. Moral norms involve expectations of how

---

[5] For further discussion of the framework of models of the moral/conventional distinction, see Smetana (1983), Turiel (1983), Turiel et al. (1987), and Turiel and Smetana (1984).

members of the community they apply to will act, and expectations of how moral authorities will respond to violations. But because of their serious-ness and authority independence, they also involve expectations of how *other members of the community* will respond to violations. Widespread failures to acknowledge the violation of moral norms by the members of a shared moral community can directly challenge the authority of the norm itself, or challenge the status of the victim as a member.

First, significant or repeated failures can suggest that the norm does not really have much moral authority after all. This is one plausible explana-tion of what is going on in *Philosophy Club* if we stipulate further that the club has had a long history of such outbursts before your membership (perhaps it is no coincidence that women do not stick around). This suggests that members of the club do not really expect each other to behave in the relevant way captured by the norm. While they pay lip service to diversity and inclusion, their lack of response to violations suggests that these norms do not have genuine *moral* authority in this particular community.

Second, consider a version of *Philosophy Club* in which the Vice President's outburst is a one-off. If the other members of the club do in fact expect their fellow members to behave in accordance with norms governing a commitment to diversity and inclusion, then their failure to blame the Vice President actually *damages* the relevant norm, and might also cause further injury to the victim. The Vice President has clearly violated this moral norm with his outburst, falling dismally short of what we would expect from members of a community that values diversity and inclusion in their treatment of one another. In failing to blame him, the other members of the club would then damage the authority of this norm. They will at the very least have lower expectations regarding their fellows' behavior in the future.

Finally, consider another variation of *Philosophy Club* in which a more senior member of the club has already made similar suggestions for discussing feminist philosophy, but was not met with the same reaction. In this case, it seems that what failure to blame communicates is that *you* are not really a member of this particular moral community. Paying dues or listing one's name on a group roster is sufficient for membership in some groups, but not shared moral communities. In order to be a member of a shared moral community, it is essential that the norms governing our expectations of one another are in fact widely shared. This explains why it is no great surprise that you stop attending meetings once you realize that no one is going to blame the Vice President for his outburst. It would certainly be understandable to take this failure to blame to communicate to you (and others) that you are not really a full-fledged member of the community that you thought you were.

The upshot here is that reflection on failures to blame suggests further reason to think that blame plays an uniquely valuable role for us in our moral lives, and thus that NAV can be met. If McGeer's insight about the negative reactive attitudes' status as costly signals are correct, then reactive blame in particular is the variety of blame uniquely suited to play these roles. I therefore conclude that NAV can be met.

However, NAV is not the primary source of skeptical worries about blame. Even skeptics, I think, are often willing to grant that reactive blame serves some – perhaps even many – valuable functions for us in our moral lives. What I take to be of primary concern to skeptics is rather NAD, the desert-based desideratum for normative adequacy. It is doubts about the prospects for reactive blame to meet *this* desideratum that largely motivate the problem of blame. The remainder of this chapter will focus on positive arguments for thinking that, on the fittingness account of reactive blame, NAD can in fact be met. We have good reason to think that agents are sometimes deserving of reactive blame in the basic sense. If this is correct, then given the overwhelming value of blame discussed in this section, it is not at all clear what reasonable worries from blame curmudgeons might remain. We will have good reason to think that the problem of blame can in fact be resolved.

4.2 The Parity of Reasons Argument

Elsewhere I have argued that there are epistemically relevant similarities between some of the paradigmatic moral judgments that play an important evidentiary role in our moral theorizing, and some of our judgments about moral responsibility.[6] This similarity relation can be used to ground a pair of *parity of reasons* arguments that the epistemic status of these two classes of judgments should stand or fall together. I argue that some of our judgments about moral responsibility should in fact inherit the same privileged epistemic status that we take their moral counterparts to have. While the original formulation of this line of argument was explicitly intended to defend a methodological assumption about the role that some intuitions can and should play in theorizing about moral responsibility, the relevant features of the class of responsibility judgments discussed are

---

[6] See McCormick (2015).

shared by instances of reactive blame. So, here I will present and defend a version of this argument for the claim that the propositional content of reactive blame, barring defeaters, can be correct. And if this is right, then we have good reason to think that we can be deserving of blame in the basic sense, and that NAD can be met.

4.2.1   The Structure of Parity of Reasons Arguments

First, it will help to say a bit about the general form of parity of reasons arguments, and differentiate between the two different versions that I will appeal to later.[7] Parity of reasons arguments are often intended to either bolster or undermine the metaphysical or epistemological status of a particular set of claims (X-claims) via appeal to the fact that they share some metaphysically or epistemically relevant features with another set of claims (Y-claims).[8] Whether the argument is intended to bolster or undermine the status of the X-claims depends on how we weigh our reasons for taking each set of claims to have the status that they do. The proponent of a parity of reasons argument must first establish that the apparently problematic features of the X-claims are in fact shared by the Y-claims and then argue that, by parity of reasons, the epistemological credentials of these two sets of claims should stand or fall together. On one version of this argument, a *companions in guilt* (CIG) argument, we might argue that our reasons for taking the X-claims to be problematic outweigh our reasons for taking the Y-claims to be uncontroversial, and conclude that the Y-claims should thus inherit the same problematic status as the X-claims. Alternatively, if we take our reasons for previously accepting the uncontroversial status of the Y-claims to outweigh our reasons for taking the X-claims to be problematic, this instead gives us reason to confer the same uncontroversial status to the X-claims that we do the Y-claims. Call this version of a parity of reasons argument a *companions in innocence* (CII) argument.

Here I will use a combined parity of reasons strategy and offer both a CII argument and a CIG argument in support of the claim that fitting appraisals of an agent as the target of the negative reactive attitudes have a privileged epistemic status. Paired with the fittingness account of basic desert defended in Chapter 2, we are therefore justified in believing that

---

[7] This discussion draws heavily on Hallvard Lillehammer's (2007) helpful analysis of the scope of this argumentative strategy as traditionally employed in defense of ethical objectivity.

[8] In what follows, I will restrict myself to epistemological varieties of parity of reasons arguments.

agents are sometimes deserving of reactive blame in the basic sense, and that NAD can be met.

The first crucial feature of this argumentative strategy is to establish that some class of unproblematic Y-claims really do share an epistemically relevant feature of the X-claims in question. Both CII and CIG arguments depend on this similarity claim. But, as many have noted, similarity is notoriously tricky – "everything is similar to everything else in some respect or other" (Lillehammer, 2007: 13).[9] In offering a parity of reasons argument, one must take care to establish that the similarity appealed to not only holds, but is in fact *relevant* to the epistemic status of the particular class of claims in question. So, I will begin with what I take to be an epistemically relevant similarity between some of our paradigmatic moral judgments (hereafter referred to as *M-claims*),[10] and appraisals of an agent as the appropriate target of the negative reactive attitudes (hereafter referred to as blame claims, or *B-claims*).

4.2.2   Establishing the Similarity Relation

The first step in offering a parity of reasons argument for the claim that we are justified in believing that B-claims have an epistemically privileged status is to establish an epistemically relevant similarity between these claims and another class of judgments that we already take to have this status. Here I will focus on a subset of our moral judgments, M-claims, and the features that best explain why we take these judgments (but not others) to play a defeasible evidentiary role in our moral theorizing. Barring defeaters we assume that we are justified in believing that M-claims are correct. I will attempt to make these features explicit using a series of examples. Consider first the following case:

> *Timmy the Toddler:* Timmy is a toddler. One day his older brother, Jimmy, is left in charge of Timmy. Jimmy really enjoys torturing Timmy, and not in the colloquial sense that usually applies to siblings. For example, Jimmy enjoys tying Timmy up and burning him with lit cigarettes.

When asked whether or not they think what Jimmy does to Timmy is *wrong*, *bad*, or *harmful*, I take it as an uncontroversial data point that most (if not all) normally functioning adults judge that it is. Furthermore, I take it that most (if not all) moral philosophers take this widespread judgment

[9] See also Lewis (1973).
[10] I will say more about *which* moral judgments belong to this class in the next subsection.

about Timmy's case to be correct and philosophically relevant.[11] It is just the sort of case that we, in practice, expect our moral theories to respect. Here what I mean by "respect" can be cashed out in a number of different ways. First, all else being equal we would be very suspicious of any moral theory that yields the wrong result in Timmy's case, the result that what Jimmy does is *not* wrong, bad, or harmful. To the extent that we value counterexamples in ethics, a theory which entails that Jimmy's action has no negative moral valence looks to be about as clear a counterexample as one can find. So, as our moral methodology currently stands, failure to respect the judgment that Jimmy's act of burning Timmy with lit cigarettes for fun is wrong, bad, or harmful counts against a theory. Second, all else being equal we would consider it a merit of a theory if it not only yields the right results in Timmy's case, but also goes some way toward explaining *why* what Jimmy does is wrong, bad, or harmful. Again, as our moral methodology currently stands, it counts in favor of a theory if it has the tools to explain the judgment that what Jimmy does to Timmy is wrong.

The upshot here is that judgments generated by Timmy's case look to be paradigmatic of the kind of judgment that we take to have a privileged epistemic status in our moral theorizing as it stands. These judgments do in fact play an (albeit defeasible) evidentiary role.[12] Furthermore, Timmy's case is in no way unique, and there are countless other cases like it we might identify as generating judgments which share this status.

However, not *all* cases generate moral judgments which have this status. Take, for example, the following case:

> *Charlie the Chicken:* Charlie is a chicken. One day the farmer who is his caretaker, Old McDonald, gathers some of the eggs that Charlie has recently laid. Old McDonald really enjoys eating omelets, and one day he prepares and eats one made with Charlie's freshly laid eggs.

This case and Timmy's case are structurally similar. However, we do not take judgments generated by Charlie's case to have the same epistemic

---

[11] Insofar as we take such judgments to ever get things right – here I set aside metaethical error theories.

[12] Another way to think of the role that this kind of paradigmatic judgment plays and the sense in which the privileged epistemic status of this kind of judgment is defeasible is to consider the role that this kind of judgment plays in service of reflective equilibrium. The judgment that what Jimmy does is wrong, bad, or harmful looks like a paradigmatic example of the kind of judgment that will compose the class of intuitions that we start with on one end of this process. We may of course end up giving up some (or even all) of these judgments in light of conflicts with principles at the other end, and this is one sense in which the status of these paradigmatic judgments might be considered defeasible.

status that those generated by Timmy's do. To help elucidate this point, consider the relation between judgments generated by Timmy's case, judgments generated by Charlie's case, and the following two moral principles:

TORTURE: torturing people for fun is wrong.
VEGANISM: consuming animal products is wrong.

In addition to the way in which we expect a moral theory to respect the widespread judgment generated by Timmy's case, we might also cite the judgment that Jimmy's act is wrong, bad, or harmful as providing some direct support for Torture. Or, we might use this judgment as a premise, or support for a premise, in an argument intended to establish Torture. Either of these is, in practice, a respectable methodological move to make. However, the same cannot be said for judgments generated by Charlie's case. Presenting someone who does not already assent to Veganism with Charlie's case will not help motivate the principle further. Nor would it provide any non-question-begging support in an argument for Veganism or for premises in an argument for Veganism. At the very least, such an appeal would not be persuasive. It is highly unlikely that anyone who does not already assent to the principle that consuming animal products is wrong will be moved by judgments about Charlie's case to accept Veganism. So, though structurally similar, judgments generated by Charlie's case do not play the same methodological role that judgments generated by Timmy's do. At least as things currently stand, they do not have the same privileged epistemic status that Timmy-type judgments do. And this difference cannot be explained by appeal to structural differences between the two cases that elicit these judgments.

So, what features of Timmy-type judgments and Charlie-type judgments might account for this apparent difference in their epistemic status? Why, ceteris paribus, should an ethical theory respect the former, but not the latter?

It looks as though the best explanation for this difference depends on two features in particular. The first is the degree to which judgments generated by each of these cases are *convergent*. Judgments about Charlie's case do not converge in the same way that those generated by Timmy's do. There is likely to be a great deal of disagreement among normal adults about whether what Old McDonald does is wrong, bad, harmful, or morally neutral. And this disagreement will likely depend on a variety of independent considerations, not features of the case itself. Given the importance that we often attribute (implicitly or explicitly) to convergence in other domains, it is reasonable to conclude that the high level of convergence of judgments about Timmy's case explains, at least in part, the privileged epistemic status that these judgments have in our moral theorizing. Judgments about Charlie's case do not enjoy this level of convergence, and so this difference can provide a plausible explanation, again at least in part, for the comparatively controversial epistemic status of Charlie-type judgments.

However, appeal to this difference in convergence is inadequate to the task of fully explaining the epistemic difference between these two kinds of judgments. This can be seen by restricting the class of individuals whose judgments we are interested in to only those whose judgments about Charlie's case *do* converge. Consider those who agree that what Old McDonald does *is* wrong, bad, or harmful, and a world in which only individuals in this restricted class exist. Call this possible world *Vegan Apocalypse*. Let us assume that the restricted class of individuals who exist in *Vegan Apocalypse* is made up entirely of normal adult human beings. They are not psychopaths or suffering from any other psychological or neurological deficiency that might render them incapable of forming genuine moral judgments. In *Vegan Apocalypse*, judgments about Charlie-type cases converge to the same extent that Timmy-type cases do in the actual world. If the different epistemic status of Timmy-type judgments and Charlie-type judgments can be explained fully by convergence alone, then, in the world we are considering, these judgments should share the same epistemic status. But surely they do not. If a neutral party were to come into existence in *Vegan Apocalypse*, then presenting them with Charlie's case alone would be unlikely to motivate the general principle, Veganism. But Timmy's case would still plausibly motivate Torture. So, we are in need of some feature in addition to convergence to adequately explain the different epistemological statuses of these two kinds of judgments.

I think that the following, in addition to convergence, provides the best explanation for this difference: there is a *qualitative* difference between these two kinds of judgments that is epistemically relevant. Even if we restrict our consideration to those whose judgments about Charlie's case converge, they are likely to have qualitatively different responses to Timmy's case and Charlie's case. They will be *horrified* by Timmy's case and feel certain that Jimmy's act is wrong, bad, or harmful. Timmy's case is, in an important sense, *more concrete* than Charlie's in that it elicits a strong affective response on the part of individuals presented with it. More specifically, we react to Timmy's case with some degree of moral anger, indignation, or resentment. Furthermore, this affective reaction to Timmy's case best explains *why*, at least introspectively, we feel certain that our judgment about Timmy's case is correct. Judgments about Charlie's case do not share this feature. Even among those who judge that what Old McDonald does is wrong, it is doubtful that their affective response (if there is one) to his eating the omelet is anywhere near on par with their response to what Jimmy does to Timmy. The fact that Charlie's case fails to elicit the same kind of affective response that Timmy's does best explains why we are less certain that our judgment about this case is correct.[13] It also helps to explain why attempts to support a principle like Veganism with Charlie's case are likely to be met with something like the incredulous stare. Perhaps a case describing, in graphic detail, the suffering imposed on particular animals as a result of the human consumption of animal products would provide such support.[14] But one thing is clear – Charlie's case will not.

So, it looks as though when we go about the business of moral theorizing we let some of our judgments about cases (like Timmy-type judgments) but not others (like Charlie-type judgments) move us toward certain conclusions. And we assume that our moral theories should, *ceteris paribus*, respect some of these judgments (like Timmy-type judgments) but not others (like Charlie-type judgments) because, barring defeaters, we take the belief that these judgments are correct to be justified. Here I hope to have made plausible the claim that a combination of *convergence* and *affectivity* best explain why we take the former (Timmy-type judgments) to have a privileged epistemic status in our moral theorizing. Barring obvious defeaters we assume that widely convergent moral judgments accompanied

---

[13] Here one might object that the explanation goes in the other direction – our relative lack of certainty is actually the best explanation for why we do not feel the same kind of affective response to Charlie's case as Timmy's. While addressing this worry might ultimately bottom out in appeal to intuition (for my part, it seems clear that the presence and absence of affectivity plays at least some directly relevant epistemic role in the credence I am willing to lend each of these claims), there are at least two further considerations in favor of thinking that the explanation works in the direction that I claim here. First, it would be odd for certainty to play a more basic explanatory role than affectivity in this context when it is difficult to find other examples in which it does so. Perhaps my own background intuitions are impeding my own ability to conceive of relevant examples, though. To that end, even if we can point to other instances in which certainty seems to generate or lend credence to affective (and especially *angry*) responses, those who find the inverse explanatory direction intuitive might also find the arguments in Section 4.3 persuasive in motivating the explanatory direction that I endorse.

[14] If so, I take it that the affective response to *these* sorts of cases will also play a prominent role in explaining their privileged status. So much the better for my argument here.

by some variety of moral anger (hereafter *M*-claims) get things right. And attributions of *reactive* blame share exactly these features.

Before turning to the parity of reasons argument, it will be helpful to acknowledge and respond to an obvious potential objection: while we have good reason to think that widespread convergence might be a truth-relevant feature of our judgments, the same cannot be said for highly affective judgments. Certainly, the same is not said of the influence of convergence and affectivity in other domains, for example in mathematics.[15] For those not moved by *Vegan Apocalypse*,[16] are there any other considerations in support of the claim that the affective component of these judgments is a necessary feature of the best explanation for why we take them to be truth-sensitive?

In fact, there are. Perhaps most persuasive is empirical support for the claim that affectivity plays an essential enabling role in generating ordinary moral judgments. Data generated by studies on psychopaths and others with emotional processing deficits, for example, suggest that people with such deficits have difficulty applying moral criteria.[17] In light of this data, strictly rationalist views of our moral psychology like those of Kohlberg (1969) and Piaget (1965 [1932]) have fallen largely out of favor. In their place, views that take our moral judgments to be (at least in part) the product of intuition or affective reactions, such as Haidt's (2001) and Nichols' (2002), have recently garnered support. While this empirical work does not provide *direct* truth-relevant support for the epistemic relevance of the affective component of these judgments, it does provide such support indirectly. If affect plays a necessary enabling role in generating competent[18] moral judgments, then it is reasonable to suppose that affect-free moral judgments are deficient. Insofar as we have reason to think any of our moral judgments are correct, those accompanied by an affective response such as moral anger are the best candidates.

These considerations suggest that there are at least some truth-relevant considerations in support of the affective feature of our epistemically privileged M-claims. B-claims share these features. So, M-claims and B-

---

[15] Thanks to an anonymous referee for suggesting this point and for raising this potential objection.
[16] As I anticipate, some vegan readers might not be.
[17] For example, see Blair (1995), Blair et al. (1997), and Nichols (2004).
[18] Here "competent" is intended to convey only that the judgments in question are produced *in the normal sort of way*, namely that the normal psychological processes that generate these judgments are not being biased or distorted. For further argument that even making the distinction between moral and conventional transgressions depends on a typical cognitive apparatus that generates an emotional response to the perceived pain of others, see Blair (1995).

claims share an epistemically relevant feature. If this is correct, and M-claims do in fact have the privileged epistemic status I have claimed, then there are two corresponding parity of reasons arguments for extending this status to B-claims.

4.2.3   Companions in Innocence

I begin with the CII argument. This argument starts from the initial assumption that B-claims (appraisals of reactive blame) are epistemically problematic or controversial. In order to situate this argument in the broader context of the permissibility of blame, this assumption will be a particularly strong one. Those who wish to argue that blame is never permissible based on the claim that blame is never deserved in the basic sense conclude that we have *no* good reason to think that appraisals of reactive blame are ever true. In order to meet blame curmudgeons on their own terms, I will therefore begin by granting this skeptical assumption about the epistemic status of B-claims. My argument then proceeds as follows:

1.   B-claims are epistemically problematic – we have no reason to think that they are ever true. (skeptical assumption)
2.   M-claims have a privileged epistemic status in our moral theorizing – barring defeaters we are justified in believing that they are true.
3.   B-claims share the epistemically relevant features of the M-claims that best explain their privileged status.[19]
4.   Our reasons for accepting (2) outweigh our reasons for accepting (1).
5.   Therefore, by parity of reasons, we should extend the same privileged epistemic status of M-claims to B-claims.[20]

If this is correct then, like M-claims, barring defeaters we are justified in believing that B-claims are true. So, we are justified in believing that at

---

[19]   I am here assuming that these features are relevant to the epistemic status of both kinds of judgments. For further argument in support of this assumption, see McCormick (2015) where I discuss a number of potential objections to the original formulations of the CIG and CII arguments.

[20]   This formulation of the argument (and the CIG argument later) as an indirect proof is intended to specifically target and reject a skeptical assumption that B-claims are epistemically problematic. Neal Tognazzini has suggested (in correspondence) that it might also be framed as the following inconsistent triad: (1) B-claims are epistemically problematic, (2) M-claims have privileged epistemic status in our moral theorizing, in virtue of feature F, and (3) B-claims also have feature F. I am happy to take this alternative formulation on board, and suspect it may be an even more effective way to motivate the argument in broader contexts where rejecting blame curmudgeons' skepticism is not the primary goal.

least some attributions of reactive blame are getting things right – their constitutive propositional content is accurate. According to the account of the right kind of reasons to blame offered in Chapter 3, this entails that we are justified in believing that the target of blame's action or the quality of her will has in fact violated a non-extraneous expectation. And, assuming the fittingness account of basic desert, this in turn entails that we *do*, contra skeptics, have at least some reason for thinking that agents are deserving of blame in the basic sense. And so, we have at least some reason for thinking that reactive blame meets NAD and is permissible.

One obvious place to push back against the CII argument might be to challenge (3) above, by rejecting the similarity relation between M-claims and B-claims. While M-claims and B-claims are, by stipulation, similar in the regards to their affective component, it is not obvious that the B-claims are similarly convergent.

What does it mean to say that some of our B-claims are convergent? In the case of M-claims, convergence simply tracks widespread agreement. Here one might argue that B-claims are *never* truly convergent because appraisals that an agent is the appropriate target of reactive blame are context dependent in a way that moral judgments are not. Perhaps, for example, B-claims depend on particular features of the subject making the appraisal and their circumstances. The worry then is that this context dependence leaves no room for the kind of convergence that is epistemically relevant to the privileged status of M-claims. The possibility of widespread agreement is out because no two subjects can make the same appraisal for B-claims.

There are at least two considerations that undermine arguments for this kind of disanalogy between M-claims and B-claims. First, we have a growing body of empirical data in experimental philosophy that shows ordinary folk do in fact display widespread agreement in their attributions of moral responsibility, especially when it comes to blame and in cases that prime concreteness and an affective response involving the negative reactive attitudes (Nichols & Knobe, 2007: 670).[21] Second, even if B-claims

---

[21] In the concrete condition, 72 percent of subjects judged that the subject described, Bill, was fully morally responsible for murdering his wife in the case described. See also Nahmias et al. (2006, 2007) for a variety of cases that generated agreement in more than 80 percent of subjects. Furthermore, the claim here is not that all, or even most, of our attributions of blame have the same degree of convergence as M-claims. All that is needed for the argument to go through is that at least some of our attributions do. This is sufficient to establish that we have reason to think that at least some of our appraisals of agents as the appropriate targets of the negative reactive attitudes are correct, and so on the fittingness view of basic desert we have at least some reason to think agents can be deserving of blame in the basic sense.

do depend in part on contextual features of the subject making the appraisal and her circumstances, this need not in itself undermine the prospects for such claims to be widely convergent. This is because there is a widespread assumption of *invariance* in work on moral responsibility and blameworthiness (Knobe & Doris, 2010).[22] If this assumption is correct, then the appraisals tracked by B-claims must be at least counterfactually convergent. They are such that *if* an agent *were* to find themselves in the same circumstances as the subject making a B-claim appraisal, then they *would* make the same appraisal. Those who wish to deny that at least some B-claims enjoy this kind of convergence will be left in the uncomfortable position of rejecting invariance and denying that the same conditions for blameworthiness apply for agents that find themselves in the same circumstances. Therefore, I take it we can assume with little additional cost that at least some B-claims are convergent to an extent that is in fact similar to M-claims.

Would the CII argument go through even without a plausible account of basic desert of blame like the fittingness account to pair it with? Here it is worth considering one final worry: if so, the CII argument would prove too much in generating the conclusion that blame is deserved *regardless* of what basic desert of blame amounts to. This would be a troubling result, but the CII argument does not entail it. First, as it is formulated the CII argument establishes only that we should extend the same privileged epistemic status of M-claims to B-claims. Second, recall that B-claims are *appraisals of agents as the appropriate target of the negative reactive attitudes.* As such, the CII argument on its own establishes only that appraisals of agents as the appropriate target of the negative reactive attitudes should have the same privileged epistemic status as M-claims. This does not entail that claims that such appropriate targets *deserve blame in the basic sense* unless paired with the fittingness account of basic desert. And so, worries that the argument proves too much can be set aside.

4.2.4 Companions in Guilt

For those who remain unconvinced by the CII argument, there is a second parity of reasons argument in favor of extending a privileged epistemic

---

[22] Knobe and Doris in fact are among the minority who argue *against* the assumption of invariance, which is the assumption that there is a single set of criteria for moral responsibility (and blameworthiness in particular) that applies in all cases. Invariance is motivated largely by concerns that if our criteria did vary based on situational features, then this would significantly undermine the fairness of our responsibility-related practices. For a defense of invariance against Knobe and Doris, see Warmke (2011).

status to our B-claims, a CIG argument. If we wish to maintain some version of the skeptical assumption that our B-claims are epistemically problematic (we have *no* good reason to think that they are ever true), then, by parity of reasons, we ought to extend this skepticism to our M-claims. But this would be deeply problematic. It would entail giving up the privileged epistemic status of Timmy-type judgments in our moral theorizing more broadly. In fact, depending on one's reason for skepticism about the truth of our B-claims, it may even entail that Timmy-type judgments have a particularly *problematic* epistemic status while Charlie-type judgments do not. Not only would this result be radically revisionary, it would largely undermine our methods of moral theorizing as they currently stand. If nothing else, judgments about cases like Timmy's serve to constrain our moral theories. Of course, they do not constitute indefeasible evidence. But they are the closest thing to evidence that we have in this domain, and we do in fact treat them as such. In light of these considerations, it is not at all clear how we might proceed without them.

The CIG argument can be formalized as follows:

1. B-claims are epistemically problematic – we have no reason to think that they are ever true. (skeptical assumption)
2. M-claims have an unproblematic epistemic status in our moral theorizing.
3. The features of M-claims that best explain their epistemic status in our moral theorizing are shared by B-claims.
4. Our reasons for accepting (1) outweigh our reasons for accepting (2).
5. Therefore, we should extend the same *problematic* epistemic status of B-claims to M-claims.

But again, this conclusion would have serious negative consequences for our moral methodology as it currently stands. It would entail that we have no reason to think that M-claims are ever true, and thus there is no reason to respect them in our moral theorizing. But surely this cannot be right.

I take this line of argument to function as a *practical* reductio of (1). Accepting skepticism about B-claims and reactive blame would, by parity of reasons, leave us in the uncomfortable position of (at best) taking Timmy-type judgments and Charlie-type judgments to be on par epistemically or (at worst) taking Timmy-type judgments to be especially problematic. I take this to be a cost to our moral theorizing high enough to entail that our reasons to avoid it will outweigh any independent worries about the epistemic status of B-claims. And so, we have at least some practical reason to reject claims that we have no good reason to think that agents are ever deserving of reactive blame in the basic sense.

To sum up, I take this pair of parity of reasons arguments to provide sufficient reason to think reactive blame can meet NAD. If one is willing to grant that M-claims have a privileged epistemic status in our moral theorizing, then the CII argument establishes that, by parity of reasons, we should extend this status to B-claims. There is reason to think that at least some of our appraisals that an agent is the appropriate target of the negative reactive attitudes are correct, and thus for thinking that agents can be deserving of reactive blame in the basic sense. Furthermore, those unwilling to accept the conclusion of the CII argument must confront the CIG argument. If we accept the skeptical assumption about the truth of our B-claims, then, by parity of reasons, our moral methodology is in need of radical overhaul. So, we have at least some practical reason to reject skepticism about the permissibility of blame, at least the variety generated by skepticism about basic desert.

Before concluding this section, a few remarks on what kind of justification the CII and CIG arguments provide for the permissibility of blame are worth noting. Taken together, I think that this pair or parity of reasons arguments justifies rejection of the skeptical assumption that our appraisals of reactive blame are never correct. Thus, this pair of arguments provide support for the claim that NAD *can* be met if we assume that the fittingness account of basic desert is also plausible. But there are important differences worth noting regarding the conclusions of the CII and CIG independently.[23]

The CII argument entails that there are some truth-relevant considerations in favor of thinking that our blaming appraisals are reliably correct. And so, if successful, the CII argument (paired, again, with the fittingness account of basic desert) provides *direct* evidence that NAD can be met. This argument offers support for the claim that agents are in fact sometimes deserving of blame in the basic sense. The CIG argument, on the other hand, entails that we have strong pragmatic reasons to at least proceed with caution when it comes to skepticism about the accuracy of our attributions of reactive blame. Thus, the CIG argument provides support only for the conclusion that we *should*, practically speaking, be wary of this kind of skepticism. Insofar as we think we should believe that

---

[23] For further discussion of the two distinct kinds of justification discussed here, see McCormick (2014), and for further discussion of how they pertain to arguments like the CII and CIG in particular, see McCormick (2015).

Timmy-type judgments are true, we should also believe that, barring defeaters, at least some targets of reactive blame are deserving in the basic sense. The fact that the CIG argument deals only in pragmatic reasons weakens its corresponding conclusion in comparison to the CII argument. Thus, while I take both arguments to be relevant to assessing NAD and solving the problem of blame, the CII argument is the stronger of the two. Only the CII argument provides direct evidence for thinking that agents can be deserving of reactive blame in the basic sense.

4.3 Perceptual Models and the Evidentiary Status of the Negative Reactive Attitudes

For those unconvinced by either of the parity of reasons arguments offered previously, there is an alternative route for supporting the claim that some agents are in fact the appropriate targets of the negative reactive attitudes, and thus that we have good reason to think that agents can be deserving of blame in the basic sense. This strategy emphasizes the fact that the negative reactive attitudes are a subset of our emotions, and because the emotions are perceptions of values, they can play a similar epistemic role to that of our perceptual experiences.[24] Perceptual experiences represent nonevaluative properties of the world, and emotional experiences represent evaluative properties. We take perceptual experiences to provide direct (though defeasible) evidence that the content of their nonevaluative representation is correct. Likewise, we might take the emotions to provide direct (though defeasible) evidence that the content of their evaluative representation is correct. If so, then barring defeaters we are justified in believing that our appraisals of agents as appropriate targets of the negative reactive attitudes are correct when they are accompanied by the corresponding emotional experiences. And so, on the fittingness account, the experience of the negative reactive attitudes provides at least defeasible evidence that an agent is deserving of blame in the basic sense.

Perceptual models of the emotions have been developed, criticized, and defended elsewhere, and it is beyond my current purposes to provide an exhaustive defense of them here. Rather, in Section 4.3.1, I will focus my attention on a particular objection to perceptual models that identifies a purported epistemologically relevant difference between our perceptual experiences and our emotional experiences. I find this objection to

---

[24] See Elgin (1996, 2008), Döring (2003), Johnson (2001), de Sousa (1987), Prinz (2004), Roberts (2003), Tappolet (2000), and Zagzebski (2004).

perceptual models of *some* emotions persuasive, but in Section 4.3.2, I argue that a subset of our emotions – those emotional experiences corresponding to explicitly moral evaluative beliefs – can still provide indirect evidence for the truth of those beliefs. And the negative reactive attitudes are precisely this kind of emotion.

4.3.1 *A Problem for Perceptual Models*

According to supporters of perceptual models, there is an analogy between our perceptual experiences and our emotional experiences, with sensory experiences taken as paradigms of the former. Both sensory and emotional experiences possess phenomenal properties, are essentially perspectival, are passive responses typically caused by features of the subject's environment, and are not themselves judgments or beliefs (they can occur independent of such cognitive states).[25] Furthermore, they are both representational states with naïve propositional content – they tell us about and thus represent the external world in a way that is subject to conditions of correctness. While these experiences are not themselves beliefs they are *like* beliefs in that they are "accurate when the associated propositions which form their content are true" (Brady, 2011: 136).

However, unlike paradigmatic sensory experiences, the emotions are also *intentional* in that they are about or directed at features of the world that constitute their target, and involve an a*ppraisal* of that target (Brady, 2011: 136). When you fear the shark swimming near your surfboard, for example, the shark is the target of this emotion and you represent the shark in an evaluative way – it is dangerous! The upshot of perceptual models of the emotions is that the similarity between sensory and emotional experiences is sufficient to allow the latter to play the same defeasible evidentiary role in justifying their corresponding evaluative beliefs that sensory experiences have in justifying our nonevaluative beliefs. Insofar as my sensory experience of a laptop in front of me is sufficient to justify my belief that there is a laptop in front of me, so too my fear justifies my evaluative belief that the shark is dangerous.

This of course is not always the case. Just as our sensory experiences can be generated in unfavorable circumstances, so too can our emotional experiences. If, for example, I have just taken some LSD this would be an obvious defeater to the normal evidentiary status of my sensory

[25] For a helpful summary of the similarities between sensory experience and emotional experience, see Brady (2011: 136–137).

experiences. This is precisely where the similarity between sensory and emotional experience often comes under fire. While the relevant defeaters to the evidentiary status of our sensory experiences will be relatively uncontroversial and caused by clearly atypical circumstances, examples of defeaters to the evidentiary status of the emotions are more widespread. Our experience of *recalcitrant* emotions constitutes an especially problematic example.

As discussed in Chapter 3, recalcitrant emotions are those that persist despite the fact that they seem clearly *irrational* in some way (for example, when we are afraid of a harmless spider or jealous in circumstances when we know there is no reason to be). This phenomenon suggests that emotions must respond to features of the world that constitute *reasons* to have the corresponding emotional experience. When we know that no such reasons are present, we can challenge the rationality of the emotion. However, this kind of rational criticism would make little sense for perceptual experiences. The properties of the laptop in front of me, for example, do not themselves constitute any reasons for me to have a visual experience.[26] If I fail to have such an experience while the laptop is in front of me (or, more analogous to recalcitrant emotions, if I begin to have visual perceptions of things that are not there), then something has gone wrong, but this failure is not a rational one. On the other hand, when I continue to fear the whale shark swimming beneath me even once I have realized that it is truly harmless, this is a rational failure.

This suggests an important difference between our emotional experiences and our perceptual experiences. Perceptual experiences provide direct evidence that, barring defeaters, the way they represent the world is correct. Upon having such an experience, we are not – in typical circumstances – motivated to search for further reasons, supporting the correctness of the representation. But emotional experiences do call out for further reasons. While recalcitrant emotions are perhaps the best example of the way emotional experiences are sensitive to reasons, they are not the only instances. Even in typical circumstances with no obvious defeaters, we often look for further reasons to think the appraisal of an emotional experience is correct. If I spot my significant other interacting flirtatiously with a stranger and feel jealous we would not think it inappropriate for me to look for further reasons supporting the appraisal that there is some infidelity going on. But we do not, in typical circumstances, require

---

[26] These properties might constitute *other* kinds of reasons, though. For example, the battery being almost out of power might constitute a reason to plug it in to charge.

further reasons for thinking that our perceptual experiences are accurate representations. We would think it odd for me to continue to look for further reasons for thinking there is a laptop in front of me once I have had the relevant visual perception in normal circumstances. Unlike our emotional experiences, our perceptual experiences just *are* sufficient reason for thinking that the corresponding representation is correct.

There is also a further motivational disanalogy between perceptual experiences and emotional experiences that bolsters the idea that the latter cause us to look for reasons but are not themselves direct evidence. This is the difference in how our attention is governed by each kind of experience. Unlike perceptual experiences, emotional experiences automatically and reflexively direct and focus our attention to stimuli that is evolutionarily important, such as stimuli that is dangerous. Emotional objects "hold sway" over us in a way that perceptual objects do not, persisting and dominating our attention in a way that makes it difficult to shift elsewhere (Brady, 2011: 141). This "attentional persistence" is a fast and dirty way of enabling us to discover reasons that might bear on the accuracy of the relevant representation, and it is a further "evaluative system" which acts as

> ... a "check and balance" on our relatively indiscriminate emotional-appraisal system, so as to ensure that emotional appearance really does match evaluative reality. (Brady, 2011: 141)

The fact that emotional experiences grab and hold our attention in a way perceptual experiences do not therefore further suggests that emotional experiences are not conclusive in the same way that perceptual experiences are. In typical circumstances, there is no need to look for further supporting evidence that a perceptual representation is correct – we assume that it is because the perception itself has already provided us with sufficient justificatory reasons for believing this is so. But the fact that emotional experiences have the attentional persistence that they do suggests that they themselves do not provide sufficient justificatory reasons for believing that the corresponding appraisal is correct.

So, it looks like the evidentiary status of perceptual and emotional experiences are actually quite different. One kind of experience (perceptual experience) *is* a justificatory reason for believing a nonevaluative appraisal is correct, and so such experiences provide direct evidence for the truth of the relevant belief. But the other kind of experience (emotional experience) cannot do the same direct justificatory work. In what follows, I will grant that these differences are epistemically relevant, but argue that the differences just cited serve to highlight the valuable *indirect* justificatory work that at least some of our emotional experiences can provide.

4.3.2   *Indirect Evidence and the Negative Reactive Attitudes*

Given the differences between perceptual and emotional experiences discussed in Section 4.3.1, we might draw the following conclusion about the evidentiary status of the latter: we should not take our emotional experiences to provide any additional justification for our evaluative beliefs.[27] Unlike perceptual experiences, our emotional experiences lose any apparent direct justificatory power as soon as we discover *other* reasons for thinking their element of appraisal is correct.[28] So, while emotional experiences motivate us to seek out justificatory reasons, taking these experiences themselves as reasons would be double counting. They cannot directly justify the evaluative beliefs they correspond to.

While I think that this conclusion about the *direct* evidentiary status of emotional experiences is correct, I do not think that that is the full story on their evidentiary status. The discussion thus far overlooks the fact that emotional experiences are not all of a piece – there are *different kinds* of emotional experiences. Importantly, some of our emotional experiences are distinctively *moral*, while others clearly lack this feature. While neither moral nor nonmoral emotional experiences can provide direct justification for the evaluative beliefs they correspond to, here I will argue that *moral* emotional experiences (including resentment, indignation, and guilt) can provide   strong   *indirect*   justification   for   their   corresponding evaluative beliefs.

First, it is instructive to look more closely at the kinds of examples used to motivate the claim that emotional experiences are *not* direct evidence for the truth of their corresponding evaluative beliefs. Consider the following examples concerning the emotional experiences of fear and suspicion:

> For instance, the fact that the large dog has sharp teeth, a short temper, is off its lead, and is advancing rapidly towards me are all good reasons for me to believe that it is dangerous. Or, take another example, the fact that Jones keeps changing his story under questioning, refuses to meet his interlocutor's eyes, and stands to gain financially from testifying against the defendant are all good reasons to believe that he is untrustworthy as a witness for the prosecution. In each case, the considerations in question are the

---

[27] Brady (2011) draws precisely this conclusion.
[28] For example, if we see that the shark swimming below us has a hammer-shaped head.

nonevaluative features of the object or event which seem directly relevant to the correct ascription of the evaluative property; they are precisely the kinds of considerations that we seek out when assessing the accuracy of our initial emotional appraisals. So should we be tempted to add to these considerations the respective facts that we are afraid of the dog or that we feel that Jones is untrustworthy? In other words, is it plausible to maintain that our emotional perceptions of the dog and of Jones are *additional* reasons to believe or judge that the dog is dangerous and that Jones is trustworthy? The answer to both of these questions is "no." (Brady, 2011: 142–143)

Here the relevant emotion and evaluative judgment pairs are fear and the appraisal that the dog is dangerous, and suspicion and the appraisal that Jones is untrustworthy. Brady is surely correct that the reasons he cites for thinking each appraisal is correct (the dog's sharp teeth, Jones' furtive behavior) are of the right kind to constitute direct evidence or justification for the corresponding evaluative beliefs. The emotional experiences of fear and suspicion in these examples do respond, at least in part, to these reasons. But Brady goes on to claim further that the emotions themselves provide *no* additional justificatory reasons for these evaluative beliefs. Interestingly, in motivating this claim, he largely sets suspicion aside and focuses on the example of fear. The problem with taking fear itself to provide justificatory reasons for thinking the dog is dangerous is that the fact that the dog is dangerous is also a reason that the emotional experience of fear responds *to* (Brady, 2011: 143). And so, to count the emotional experience of fear as an additional reason would be to suppose that fear is capable of justifying itself, which of course would commit us to a vicious justificatory circle (Brady, 2011: 143).

But why focus exclusively on fear? Brady does go on to list "insulting," "disgusting," and "amusing" as further examples of evaluative concepts best understood along sentimentalist lines – whether these judgments are correct depends on whether their corresponding emotional responses are fitting or appropriate, namely whether they themselves respond to the right kind of reasons. If this is the correct analysis, then it would of course be a mistake to then try to count the emotions themselves as further reasons for thinking the evaluative judgment is correct. To do so would render the relevant justificatory account viciously circular. At best, these emotions direct our attention toward the relevant justificatory reasons, but they cannot themselves provide such reasons.

However, not *all* of our emotional experiences and corresponding evaluative judgments are alike. The evaluative judgments that Brady focuses on – "dangerous," "insulting," "disgusting," and "amusing" – all look to be *nonmoral* evaluative judgments. While they represent the world as having certain evaluative features, these features are either evolutionarily significant (as in the case of "dangerous") or conventionally significant (as in the case of "insulting," "disgusting," and "amusing"). As such, nonevaluative facts about the features of the world relevant to human survival or the conventional norms we have established for ourselves provide the *full story* regarding whether the corresponding appraisal is correct. If we know all the relevant nonevaluative facts about the dog, for example, then we need no further reasons to justify our belief that the dog is dangerous. But, at least some of our evaluative beliefs cannot be fully justified by appeal to purely nonevaluative facts.[29] Returning to Jones, take "Jones is untrustworthy" as an example. Even if we know all the nonevaluative facts about Jones that Brady lists, it is still *an open question* whether Jones is untrustworthy in a way that it is not open to ask further whether the dog is dangerous. This is, after all, precisely why it is so difficult for prosecutors to decide on who to use as a witness. Even if all of the reason-constituting nonevaluative facts are there for thinking a potential witness is trustworthy, members of the jury will nonetheless need to *feel* that he is in order to take this evaluative belief as conclusive. While Brady may be correct in concluding that some emotional experiences cannot provide additional justificatory reasons for their appraisals, this is not the case for others. Our straightforwardly *moral* evaluative beliefs are still subject to an open question of their veracity even when all the nonmoral facts are in. And what this question calls for is precisely the kind of reason-constituting emotional experience that Brady denies could play this evidentiary role.

Which evaluative beliefs are subject to this open question condition? While it is far beyond my current purposes to try to provide a full account here perhaps the most obvious example will be our appraisals that some feature of the world (specifically an action) is "wrong," "unjust," or "unfair." Another plausible candidate will be our appraisals of the *intentions* of other agents – whether we represent their actions as "expressing ill will" toward ourselves our others. Even a full picture of the nonevaluative facts will leave the truth of these appraisals open to us in interesting ways.

---

[29] Here I have in mind something akin to Moore's (1903) Open Question Argument, though I hope to avoid further commitment to moral judgments being *sui generis*. The insight here is intended to reflect only something unique about our moral psychology when it comes to the credence we lend to nonmoral versus moral evaluative appraisals, given full knowledge of the relevant nonevaluative facts. If, however, fully motivating this argument does turn out to require taking on board the assumption that moral evaluative appraisals are *sui generis*, then I find this commitment no more costly than most commitments in metaethics.

And in all these cases, the corresponding emotional experience will be some variety of *moral anger*. For wrongness, injustice, or unfairness, the relevant accompanying emotional experience looks to be moral anger simpliciter. In the case of ill will, the relevant accompanying emotional experience will be resentment, indignation, or guilt. Here what I want to suggest is that without these corresponding emotional experiences we are left with a sense that our appraisals of wrongness, injustice, unfairness, resentment, indignation, or guilt are *still inconclusive*, even if we have full nonevaluative information about the circumstances. When it comes to appraisals like these, taking our emotional experiences to provide *additional justificatory reasons* in support of the correctness of our evaluative beliefs does not constitute double counting. There is an important sense in which we *need* this particular kind of moral emotional experience, epistemologically speaking.

But what sense is this? As noted earlier, it would be a mistake to think that these emotional experiences constitute *direct* evidence for the correctness of the corresponding moral evaluative beliefs. Even if the double counting worry can be defused, to claim that these emotions provide direct evidence would in fact be viciously circular. But these emotional experiences need not *be* reasons in order for them to have significant justificatory power.

Consider an analogy to a simple nonevaluative belief, "There is buried treasure on the beach." There are a variety of considerations that might justify this belief, and some of them provide direct evidence. For example, while sunbathing you might come across a Spanish doubloon, or find yourself subject to the testimony of the person who buried it. But there are also considerations that provide *indirect* evidence for the truth of the belief that there is buried treasure. Perhaps, Goonies style, you come across a historically substantiated treasure map that indicates it is there, and when you take a metal detector to the location where X marks the spot, the device goes off. While this of course would not provide direct or conclusive evidence that there is buried treasure on the beach, it would certainly provide *some* justification for the belief that it is there. In such circumstances, we would think it reasonable for you to take the time to come back with a shovel.

The metal detector is not itself reason constituting, but the conclusion I wish to draw here is that some of our emotional experiences – those corresponding to moral evaluative beliefs in particular – function in precisely the same way. While they do not provide direct evidence for thinking that their corresponding appraisals are correct, they do provide *some* justification for these corresponding beliefs. While emotions like resentment, indignation, and guilt do not themselves constitute reasons for thinking that an action is wrong, they still have significant indirect justificatory power. Much like the metal detector, this subset of our emotional experiences function as *reason detectors*. While they do not provide direct evidence that the corresponding evaluative belief is correct, they do provide evidence that *there are reasons around*, reasons that themselves would provide direct evidence if we can unearth them.

The upshot here is that despite various weaknesses of perceptual models of the emotions, we can still draw valuable conclusions based on the *dissimilarities* between our perceptual experiences and the distinctively moral subset of our emotional experiences. While the fact that emotional experiences in general respond to reasons makes them importantly dis-analogous to perceptual experiences (thus rendering them poor candidates for providing direct evidence for the truth of their appraisals), this difference actually lends *support* for a model that takes a subset of these emotional experiences – those that correspond to moral appraisals – to provide indirect evidence. The very fact that emotional experiences of the negative reactive attitudes respond to reasons, in addition to the fact that the truth of their corresponding appraisals is still an open question even when we have full knowledge of the relevant nonevaluative facts, suggests that these emotional experiences themselves constitute indirect evidence that the appraisal is correct.

While resentment itself is not a reason for believing that an agent is its appropriate target, the experience of this emotion is a reason to think that there are such reasons around. In fact, the experience of resentment may even turn out to be the *best* indirect evidence we have that there are reasons for thinking that an agent is the appropriate target of the negative reactive attitudes. Even if we do not have direct access to those reasons, our experience of resentment provides (barring obvious defeaters) at least some reason for thinking that this appraisal is true. And so, insofar as we experience the negative reactive attitudes we have at least some reason for thinking that agents can be deserving of blame in the basic sense.

4.4 Conclusion

The goal of this chapter has been to argue that we have good reason for thinking that even reactive blame can plausibly meet both the value-based (NAV) and desert-based (NAD) desiderata for normatively adequate blame, and thus that the problem of blame can be resolved. As discussed in Section 4.1, a strong case can be made for the claim that even reactive blame meets NAV. This kind of blame, warts and all, is uniquely suited to allow us to properly value the objects of value themselves, and to sustain our membership in moral communities along with the moral norms that constitute them. Finally, if the fittingness account of basic desert of blame is plausible, then both the parity of reasons argument discussed in Section 4.2 and the argument that our moral emotions constitute indirect justificatory evidence for their corresponding appraisals discussed in Section 4.3 support the claim that NAD can be met.

At this juncture, some bookkeeping is called for. I have granted that a normatively adequate account of reactive blame must provide some reason to think not only that reactive blame is valuable, but further that agents are deserving of blame in the basic sense. I have gone on to argue that both of these desiderata can be met. Skeptics about the permissibility of blame are welcome to challenge any number of components of this view. But how might such challenges go? Here shifting focus to the broader discussion of *moral responsibility* will be instructive.

By now, skeptical challenges to success theories about moral responsibility are familiar – the claim that the kind of agency that these success theorists defend is *not enough*, such theories do not deliver *genuine* freedom, and what they call "basic desert" is really some watered-down version of the real deal. Here I anticipate the same kinds of objections to the account I offer. While the fittingness account might be an interesting proposal, it is still not an account of what we are "really after" in debates about moral responsibility and the permissibility of blame.

But here is the rub. Once skeptics lodge this charge, it is not at all clear how to assess it. At the level of disagreements about basic desert and what counts as *true* or *genuine* responsibility,[30] we reach a kind of impasse. My goal in the remainder of this book will be to provide a methodological scaffold for adjudicating these questions. My hope is to clean up the methodological mess that arises from attempts to respond not only to skeptics, but also to full blown *eliminativists* about moral responsibility and blame. While I cannot hope to defuse such positions decisively, I will argue that we can at least go much further in articulating the methodological burdens for such views. With a clearer picture in hand, I argue that in fact a strong case can be made for *preserving* reactive blame. Not only is reactive blame permissible, but prescriptively we *ought* to go on blaming even in this unpleasant way.

[30] See Galen Strawson (1994).

Prescriptive Preservationism and Eliminativism

CHAPTER 5

The Methodological Burdens for Eliminativism

Taking stock, thus far I have argued for the permissibility of blame in a way that is intended to meet skeptics on their own terms. Unlike standard success theories about moral responsibility, I have tried to pay particular attention to the role that basic desert plays in this debate, and show systematically that there is a plausible way to analyze basic desert of reactive blame that provides the groundwork to then argue that: (1) reactive blame is sufficiently valuable to meet NAV, (2) we have good reason to think that agents are deserving of reactive blame in the basic sense and that reactive blame meets NAD, and so (3) contra skeptics, even reactive blame is permissible.

At this juncture, a shift in focus is called for. While the goal of Part I was to defuse skeptical arguments about the *permissibility* of blame, my arguments have thus far been silent on the *prescriptive* varieties of skepticism. As discussed in the Introduction, these two branches of skepticism can and sometimes do come apart, and the arguments in Part I are unlikely to do much to persuade a full-blown *eliminativist* about reactive blame – one who thinks that, regardless of the case for permissibility, we *still* ought to eliminate this kind of blame from our conceptual and practical lives to the fullest extent that we are able.[1]

The remainder of this project will focus on attempting to defuse this second kind of challenge to reactive blame. Doing so will require a significant shift away from many of the issues central to Part I (such as the nature of our negative reactive attitudes, basic desert, and the right kind of reasons to blame) and toward a new set of particularly thorny issues (those concerning methodology and reference foremost among them). Any attempt to counter full-blown eliminativism will also require us to broaden our focus from reactive blame itself to the closely related concepts of free

---

[1] Here again my targets include, for example, Pereboom (2001, 2013), Caruso (2012, 2015, 2020), Strawson (1994), and Waller (1990, 2011, 2015, 2020).

will and moral responsibility. Arguments for eliminativism have thus far
proceeded exclusively in this broader domain, where conclusions about the
nonexistence of certain kinds of free will and correspondingly *genuine*
(basic desert-entailing) moral responsibility are taken to entail that we
ought to give up reactive blame along with them. As such, in what follows
I will shift from talk of reactive blame to talk of free will and moral
responsibility, keeping in mind that the kind of free will at issue is the
kind relevant to moral responsibility, and that the kind of moral responsibility at issue is the kind that entails basic desert of reactive blame.[2]

I begin in this chapter by addressing a significant gap in the literature –
thus far little attention has explicitly been paid to the *methodological
burdens* for eliminativist views about free will, moral responsibility, and
blame. While such views are pervasive across a wide swath of philosophical
areas of interest – metaphysics, philosophy of mind, philosophy of science,
and moral philosophy to name a few[3] – there is little consensus on what
these views must establish in order to persuasively argue that we ought to
abandon some familiar feature of our ontology, conceptual schema, or
practical and moral lives. While these burdens may differ across different
domains,[4] there are at least two methodological burdens that clearly
emerge for eliminativism about moral responsibility (and, correspondingly,
reactive blame) in particular. My goal in this chapter is to elucidate both of
them, and to begin to assess eliminativists' prospects for meeting them.
The picture that will emerge by the end of this chapter is that a successful

[2] Where possible, I will try to make the link between these arguments and concepts explicit, but to do
so throughout would be, stylistically, deeply unpleasant for the reader to wade through. For ease of
exposition in what follows, I will assume that any conclusions about basic desert entailing moral
responsibility apply equally to reactive blame that is deserved in the basic sense. Whether such
conclusions extend to *other* kinds of blame is an interesting and complex question, as are questions
about kinds of freedom and control that are not relevant to moral responsibility, and types of
responsibility (perhaps, for example, the kind that tracks only attributability or answerability) that
are not relevant to basic desert of reactive blame in particular. However, I will not take up any of
these questions here. Despite expanding the focus of discussion to include free will and moral
responsibility in the second part of the project, my goal is still to restrict its parameters only to the
kinds of freedom and responsibility relevant to reactive blame.
[3] For example, Unger (1979) and van Inwagen (1990) on composite objects (though van Inwagen
allows for the existence of composite living organisms), Churchland (1981, 1986) and Stitch (1983)
on common sense folk-psychological concepts like belief, Feyerabend (1962) and Laudan (1984) on
scientific realism, Griffiths (1997) on emotion, Machery (2009) on concepts, Mackie (1977) and
Blackburn (1985) on moral properties, and Appiah (1995), Andreasen (2000), and Mallon (2006)
on the existence of race.
[4] For instance, the burdens for eliminativism might shift in interesting ways as we move from varieties
of eliminativism concerning *normative* concepts like moral responsibility to other purely *descriptive*
concepts like composite objects.

case for eliminativism cannot sidestep questions about reference and essence. And so I turn to tackling those questions head-on in Chapter 6.

I begin in Section 5.1 with some terminological stage setting. While I have already discussed the distinction between skepticism and full-blown prescriptive eliminativism in the Introduction, a more careful look at this distinction is called for. In Section 5.2, I motivate and assess the first methodological burden for eliminativists about moral responsibility – the fact that they must *fix the skeptical spotlight*. In Sections 5.3 and 5.4, I focus on the second of these burdens – the fact that eliminativists must meet *the motivational challenge*. Eliminativists have thus far pursued two main strategies for meeting this burden. First, they have offered arguments that we *should not* retain our responsibility-related attitudes and practices via appeal to the gains and losses of retaining versus eliminating them. Using the prescriptive elements of Derk Pereboom's hard incompatibilism as an instructive example in Section 5.3, I argue that this strategy is problematic. Either it is unpersuasive, or it collapses into the second strategy. This second strategy – the focus of Section 5.4 – is to assess arguments that we *cannot* retain our responsibility-related attitudes and practices via appeal to some error regarding a necessary feature of moral responsibility or its essence. Using Galen Strawson's impossibilism as an instructive example, I argue that this potential path to eliminativism ultimately bottoms out in controversial claims about reference and essence. Such questions merit their own separate treatment, and so I turn to them in Chapter 6.

Here it is worth noting that I do not take the arguments in this chapter and in Chapter 6 to decisively refute eliminativism about moral responsibility and reactive blame. Rather, I take them to more clearly articulate burdens thus far overlooked which eliminativists must address if they hope to successfully motivate their view. Here my goal is to shift the overall *dialectic burden* in favor of some variety of preservationism by showing that eliminativists' prospects for meeting these burdens ultimately look grim. However, even if my arguments in Chapters 6 and 7 are successful, I still anticipate worries about what some have called "the dark side" of free will, responsibility, and reactive blame to linger.[5] And so, in Chapter 7, I conclude by explicitly addressing these worries, and offering a final *argument from empathy*, which highlights the comparative dark side of *eliminativism* that emerges when we adopt a more victim-centered approach to these issues.

---

[5] I credit Nadelhoffer and Tocchetta (2013) for this particularly ominous sounding way of characterizing worries about the negative practical consequences of retaining our current beliefs and practices in regard to free will, moral responsibility, and reactive blame.

5.1 Terminological Stage Setting

It often turns out that some feature of the world differs significantly from what we think about it. Whales are not fish; solid objects are actually composed of tiny subatomic particles with relatively large swaths of open space between them; witches of the kind persecuted for centuries do not exist; and there is no such thing as phlogiston. Perhaps, too, some of the concepts that give rise to many of our most vexing philosophical questions are not as we think they are. This point will perhaps seem obvious. Philosophy is, after all, largely in the business of refining our concepts and bringing to the surface various errors and inconsistencies that afflict them. Less obvious is what we should do in light of such realizations. Most radical among our alternatives is some variety of eliminativism: given the error or inconsistency identified, the thing in question should be abandoned. It does not exist, the term we have been using fails to refer, or our concept of it is fatally flawed in some way, and so we should eliminate it from our conceptual, linguistic, and normative practices, at least insofar as we are able.

Such a move has been suggested regarding a wide array of philosophically significant concepts including beliefs and other mental states, ordinary objects like tables and chairs, race, and even our moral claims. As discussed at the outset of this book, this kind of skeptical position has also garnered interest and support in discussions of free will and moral responsibility. The error identified by the proponents of these skeptical positions has varied and includes appeal to the implausibility of ultimate sourcehood, the incompatibility of moral responsibility and the pervasiveness of luck, and even the claim that moral responsibility is incoherent, requiring the power to be *causa sui*.[6] Here, though, I am interested in a feature that many of these positions have in common – the move from identification of a *descriptively* significant error to some version of *prescriptive* eliminativism.

What I will here refer to as *descriptive skepticism* and *prescriptive eliminativism* calls for at least some clarification. By descriptive skepticism, I mean any and all views that identify a significant error regarding our standing concept or ordinary language attributions of "moral responsibility." This characterization allows for the possibility of both conceptually

---

[6] For arguments for the implausibility of ultimate sourcehood, see Pereboom (2001, 2014). For arguments regarding the incompatibility of moral responsibility and the pervasiveness of luck, see Levy (2011) and Haji (2016). For arguments regarding logical incoherence and the power to be *causa sui*, see Galen Strawson (1994).

motivated forms of skepticism, and ontologically motivated versions.[7] The former often involves identification of some significant error in our folk concept of moral responsibility.[8] Conceptually motivated skeptics claim that our concept is fragmented, naturalistically or normatively implausible, or downright incoherent or inconsistent.[9] I take most of the skeptical views about moral responsibility currently on offer to be conceptually motivated, but explicitly ontologically motivated versions of skepticism are also possible. Rather than pointing to some error in our concept, one might argue that the term "moral responsibility" fails to refer and do so in a way that is largely silent on our widespread conceptual commitments. This path to skepticism is more common in regards to empirically verifiable kind terms,[10] and I will focus on it exclusively in Chapter 6.[11] In this chapter, I will set it aside and focus exclusively on *conceptually motivated* views. Regardless of the path to skepticism, what both conceptually and ontologically motivated varieties have in common is that they identify some fatal error in either our folk concept of moral responsibility, or our discourse involving the term "moral responsibility." Precisely the nature

---

[7] Thanks to Ley Cray for helpful and insightful discussion of this distinction in conversation.

[8] There is considerable disagreement about what our folk concept of moral responsibility amounts to. Here I wish to avoid making a commitment to any particular view of concept individuation and the distinctions between concepts, conceptions, and mere beliefs. One's stance on these issues will be particularly relevant to assessing versions of descriptive skepticism – in order to show that our concept is fatally flawed, the skeptic will of course have to say something about what this concept amounts to in the first place. I leave this as a task for the skeptic, and here take the following stipulative, working definition of the "folk concept" to be sufficient for my current purposes: our folk concept is a set of widely shared semantic commitments about moral responsibility, in particular those commitments that allow us to avoid talking past one another on the topic. For further discussion of these points, see McCormick (2013, 2017a).

[9] For arguments that our folk concept of moral responsibility might be fragmented, see Feltz and Cokely (2008). For arguments that it is naturalistically and normatively implausible, see Vargas (2013). And for arguments that our folk concept of moral responsibility might actually be inconsistent, see Weigel (2013).

[10] Consider here the classic example of our elimination of phlogiston from scientific theory and discourse.

[11] For example, see Nichols' (2015). While Nichols does not endorse an explicitly skeptical or eliminativist view, arguing instead that we should be *discretionists* about free will and moral responsibility, facts about reference success primarily motivate the distinctions that he draws between these positions. One might also offer an ontologically motivated skeptical position via appeal to claims about the metaphysical nature of the universe. If, say, the falsity of determinism is necessary in order for the term "moral responsibility" to refer to any form of control or agency in the actual world, and it turns out determinism is true, this could also lay the groundwork for an ontologically motivated variety of skepticism. Thanks to Michael McKenna for suggesting the possibility of this kind of view. However, given the unlikelihood of our ever truly *discovering* or *verifying* that determinism is in fact true, this kind of skeptical view would of course be quite difficult to motivate, and so I do not discuss it in depth in what follows.

of the error may be a point of disagreement, but where skeptics converge is on the claim that there is one.

By prescriptive eliminativism, I mean to pick out views that draw a substantive conclusion about what we should do in light of the purported error identified by some variety of skepticism. Namely, the error in question is sufficient to block a "business as usual" stance regarding our blaming practices. I discuss the forms that such preservationist prescriptive alternatives to eliminativism might take in further detail in Section 5.3, taking Manuel Vargas' (2005, 2009, 2011, 2013) *revisionism* as the most thoroughly developed and defended example currently on offer. In contrast, the defining feature of eliminativism is that we should reject such attempts to sustain our responsibility-related practices in light of the purported error(s) identified by some form of descriptive skepticism. Eliminativists claim instead that we should abandon these practices, at least to the extent that we are able, rather than attempting to revise, to justify, or otherwise sustain them.

So, prescriptive eliminativist views presuppose some variety of descriptive skepticism.[12] But this dependence does not run in both directions. *Mere* descriptive skepticism, without an additional eliminativist prescriptive conclusion, is a coherent position. In Section 5.2, I look closer at why this is so regarding descriptive skepticism about the kind of moral responsibility that entails basic desert of reactive blame in particular. While I take the arguments in Part I to have established a plausible account of the permissibility of reactive blame capable of defusing descriptive skepticism, the goal here is to show that even if some variety of skepticism *were* true, the move to full-blown eliminativism still is not warranted without a great deal of further work.

5.2   Eliminativism and the Skeptical Spotlight

Descriptive skepticism about moral responsibility fails to entail, on its own, prescriptive eliminativism. It is possible to carve out a coherent position such that our concept of responsibility suffers some significant error, while at the same time denying that we should eliminate

---

[12] At least as I have defined the positions here. It is of course conceptually possible that a prescriptive eliminativist might argue that we should abandon our practices *despite* the fact that there is no purported conceptual error (perhaps, for example, this prescriptive position is motivated entirely by pragmatic considerations). While to my knowledge no one has as yet endorsed or defended this kind of position, it is helpful to mark it in conceptual space. Thanks to Neal Tognazzini for suggesting this point.

responsibility and blame from our discourse, attitudes, and practices insofar as we are able. The diagnostic portion of Manuel Vargas' revisionist program, for example, can be categorized as a form of mere descriptive skepticism.[13] On this reading, Vargas offers a conceptually motivated brand of descriptive skepticism in particular – our folk concept of moral responsibility is significantly libertarian, and these libertarian strands render the concept naturalistically and normatively implausible.[14] Despite this problematic feature, Vargas (2013: 88) argues that we need not be moved to eliminativism. Instead, we might either perform a kind of conceptual surgery (connotational revision), or a kind of conceptual transplant (denotational revision).[15] Regarding the former, connotational revision, we might excise the problematic libertarian features from our concept in a way that still preserves the reference of "moral responsibility" and the work of this concept to sustain our responsibility-related discourse, attitudes, and blaming practices. Regarding the latter – denotational revision – we might abandon our standing concept of moral responsibility but reanchor reference with a distinct but similar nearby concept capable of doing the same work as the original to sustain our responsibility-related discourse, attitudes, and blaming practices. According to Vargas, either strategy represents a live preservationist prescriptive alternative to eliminativism despite the significantly problematic libertarian features of our folk concept identified.[16] If Vargas is right, then even if we embrace a descriptively skeptical position about moral responsibility, we have at least two live preservationist alternatives to prescriptive eliminativism. The move from mere skepticism to full-blown eliminativism requires at least some further work.

5.2.1 The Logical Gap between Error and Elimination

At this point, it will be helpful to move from general talk of skepticism and eliminativism to a more concrete instance of the former. Here I will use Ishtiyaque Haji's luck-based view as an instructive example. Haji motivates a kind of dual skepticism about obligation and blameworthiness by

---

[13] For a comprehensive look at Vargas' revisionism, see Vargas (2005, 2009, 2011, 2013).
[14] See Vargas (2013: 60–70; 2005: 52).
[15] See also Nichols (2015) for an alternative characterization of this distinction in terms of causal-historical and descriptive views of reference.
[16] For arguments that revisionists would do well to abandon connotational revision in favor of denotational revision, see McCormick (2017a: 116–117). Here I will grant Vargas' claim that both versions of revisionism are tenable.

identifying a conflict between the pervasiveness of luck and three independently plausible commitments: that motivation requires ability, a version of ought implies can is correct, and blameworthiness requires impermissibility. While Haji concludes that impermissibility and blameworthiness are threatened most by this conflict, here I will argue that this kind of skeptical conclusion requires a further *comparative* defense of the commitments that generate it. Given that Haji himself takes each of these commitments to be independently plausible, why think that it is specifically the connection between blameworthiness and impermissibility that cannot be salvaged?[17]

Haji's (2016) skeptical argument proceeds as follows:

1. Regardless of the truth of determinism or indeterminism, luck is pervasive; the way that we are, our actions, and the circumstances in which our actions occur are often out of our control.
2. If luck is pervasive, then we frequently lack alternatives.
3. Obligation requires alternatives.
4. So, the range of obligation in our world is, at best, significantly less than we take it to be.
5. But, there is a deontic requirement for moral responsibility.
6. There are two plausible ways of understanding this deontic requirement: (a) *blameworthiness requires impermissibility*, or (b) *blameworthiness requires nonculpable belief in impermissibility*.
7. If the deontic requirement is understood in terms of (a), then luck's restriction of the range of our obligations also restricts the range of our responsibility.
8. If the deontic requirement is understood in terms of (b), then blameworthiness could be sustained only by our being mistaken about the

---

[17] Here it may be helpful to identify a related problem for arguments like Haji's – a problem of intricacy. It is perhaps obvious that the more background commitments one depends on to build her argument, the more avenues there are for potential objectors to target. It will therefore be natural for those who wish to resist arguments like Haji's to immediately press back on what he claims are independently plausible principles. In particular, they are likely to target the chosen formulation of these principles. Though perhaps independently plausible at a certain level of generality, how precisely we should interpret them is an ongoing and controversial question (thanks to Michael McKenna for making this point). This is in part what I mean to capture in thinking about what I call the *shifting skeptical spotlight* below. But there may also be a related problem for arguments like Haji's – the very fact that each of the background commitments Haji appeals to require such a complex, intricate, and somewhat technical defense might itself give us pause in assessing the claim that such principles are indeed even *independently* plausible (thanks to Manuel Vargas for suggesting this point).

primary moral statuses (obligatory, permissible, impermissible, etc.) of our actions.

9. And so, at best blameworthiness "hangs on a thread."

Haji's argument here is a kind of *dual* skepticism, in that he claims that luck threatens obligation and, via this threat to obligation and some additional principles, so too does it threaten blameworthiness and moral responsibility. For my purposes, the key premises of the argument are (2), (3), and (5), which are each supported by what Haji takes to be relatively uncontroversial principles. Regarding (2), we have *Motivation/Ability*:

> *Motivation/Ability:* If S believes that it is morally impermissible as of t1 for S to perform A at t2, and S lacks any desire to perform A at t2, and in the relevant temporal interval (between t1 and t2), S cannot acquire a desire to do A at t2, then as of t1 S cannot do A at t2. (Haji, 2016: 132)

Haji assumes that the desires we have and can acquire at a time are often a matter of luck (regardless of the truth of determinism or indeterminism). If one cannot intentionally perform an action that one has no desire (and cannot acquire a desire) to perform, and whether or not we have (or can acquire) such a desire is often itself a matter of luck, then the pervasiveness of luck significantly restricts our alternatives.

In support of premise (3), Haji appeals to *Kant's Law*:

> *Kant's Law:* If S morally ought, as of time, t1, to do A at t2, then at t1 S can do A at t2; and if S morally ought, at t1, not to do A at t2, then at t1 S can refrain from doing A at t2. (Haji, 2016: 20)

If *Kant's Law* is correct, then obligation requires alternatives. In conjunction with *Motivation/Ability* and the pervasiveness of luck, *Kant's Law* then delivers the intermediate conclusion that obligation "hangs on a thread." In other words, if we assume that some version of *Kant's Law* is correct and obligation requires alternatives, and luck rules out alternatives, then luck also undermines the range of our obligations. At best, the scope of our obligations in the actual world is significantly less than we take it to be.

But if blameworthiness requires impermissibility, then this restriction on the range of our obligation also restricts the range of our responsibility. And Haji argues that there is such a deontic requirement on blameworthiness. The initial formulation of this requirement is the following:

> *Blameworthiness/Impermissibility:* (Necessarily) one is blameworthy for doing something only if it is impermissible for one to do this thing. (Haji, 2016: 50)

Haji considers, but ultimately rejects an objective interpretation (premise 6 (a) in the argument above) of *Blameworthiness/Impermissibility* and instead defends a complex subjectivist interpretation:

> *Complex Subjective (Blameworthiness/Impermissibility):* Necessarily, one is morally blameworthy for doing something only if it is either nonculpably believed that it is impermissible for one to do it, or it is nonculpably believed that it is morally deontically inferior to something else one could have done instead. (Haji, 2016: 158)

But even if this subjective interpretation of *Blameworthiness/ Impermissibility* (premise 6(b) in the argument above) is correct, a significant restriction on the scope of our obligation would significantly restrict the scope of our blameworthiness. If, as Haji argues, the scope of our obligation is significantly restricted, then we are often *mistaken* when we (even non-culpably) believe many of our actions are impermissible. And so while this kind of belief would leave open the possibility of meeting the deontic condition on blameworthiness, it would still leave blameworthiness precariously dependent on a kind of widespread "deontic irrationality" (Haji, 2016: 9). Thus for Haji blameworthiness, like obligation, is seriously threatened by the pervasiveness of luck.

One of the many merits of Haji's argument is that it explicitly identifies the problematic feature of moral responsibility, motivating a concrete variety of skepticism – the commitment to some version of *Blameworthiness/Impermissibility*. Further, Haji's argument is also explicit about why this feature is problematic. It is in direct tension with the pervasiveness of luck and at least two other independently plausible commitments: *Motivation/Ability* and *Kant's Law*. However, Haji notably says very little about the prescriptive upshot of this argument. In fact, he leaves us only with the following remarks:

> I conclude on this note. Not being grandiose but limited, the skepticism concerning the scope of obligation and blameworthiness I have argued for shows that our world is messy . . . How we would negotiate our way through this moral mess – how, for example, we would go about treating people who have violated the law, or react to people who have done what it is seemingly impermissible for them to do, or what agenda we would set for the moral education of our children – invites careful thought. (Haji, 2016: 339)

Haji himself seems aware of the gap between the skeptical position he argues for and further prescriptive conclusions. While the final questions he poses suggest the possibility of prescriptive eliminativism, he does not explicitly endorse such a move. And the details of the argument for skepticism sketched previously allow us to see clearly why doing so requires further work. As things stand, Haji has identified an inconsistent set of conceptual commitments. A specific feature of our concept of responsibility – some version of *Blameworthiness/Impermissibility* – is in direct tension with the conjunction of two additional independently plausible commitments: *Motivation/Ability* and *Kant's Law*. If we are to maintain our commitment to these two principles, and *Blameworthiness/Impermissibility* is a constitutive feature of our folk concept of moral responsibility, then indeed we have a problem. Haji has successfully identified a significant error in our folk concept and thus motivated a descriptively skeptical position. Moral responsibility *cannot* be what we thought it was, at least if we hold fixed other important background commitments such as our commitment to *Motivation/Ability* and *Kant's Law.*[18]

But should we hold fixed these other background commitments? Motivating the move from skepticism to full-blown eliminativism requires, as a first step, an affirmative answer to this question. The fact that a set of our standing – even widespread and independently plausible – commitments are inconsistent tells us little about how we should *resolve* the relevant inconsistency. Perhaps in this case the best way to do so is instead to abandon *Motivation/Ability* or *Kant's Law.*[19] Upon further consideration, we might have better reason to give up one of these two commitments than we do *Blameworthiness/Impermissibility*. If so, then we have no clear reason to think that this commitment, and along with it moral responsibility, ought to be abandoned.

5.2.2   *Fixing the Skeptical Spotlight*

This possibility highlights an interesting feature of skeptical arguments more generally: They are vulnerable to what I will call *the shifting skeptical spotlight*. One shifts the spotlight when they argue that we should resolve an inconsistency identified by skeptics by rejecting a different plank of the

---

[18] Insofar as we also accept Haji's own interpretation of these commitments.
[19] The fact that Haji (2016: 45–128) himself devotes significant attention to defending *Kant's Law* from numerous objections suggests that it might be a good candidate. One might also argue that *Motivation/Ability* is not nearly as independently plausible as Haji suggests. For example, in regards to actions with a moral valence, it looks as though this principle presupposes a Humean picture of moral motivation, and perhaps even some variety of reasons internalism (see Williams, 1981). These are both substantive, controversial commitments (see, for example, Anscombe's (1963) argument that the former is incoherent).

inconsistency identified. This is of course akin to G. E. Moore's (1962) famous response to skepticism about knowledge. When faced with an apparent inconsistency between a plausible definition of knowledge and the belief that I know anything at all, skeptics claim that I should resolve the inconsistency by giving up the latter. But, as Moore points out, this is not the only possibility. When we examine the inconsistent set more closely (and see that the belief that I have two hands entails the belief that I know anything at all) perhaps we should conclude that we have better reason to shift the skeptical spotlight to a different member of the set. If one must choose between giving up a plausible definition of knowledge and giving up the belief that one has two hands, Moore makes the persuasive case that perhaps we should take a closer look at the definition of knowledge. It is open to us to shift the skeptical spotlight to what we previously took to be an independently plausible definition of knowledge, and away from the seemingly commonsensical belief we now see that it stands in tension with.

In Haji's case, we might grant the plausibility of his overall skeptical argument but resist a further prescriptive move to eliminativism about blameworthiness and moral responsibility. Rather than abandoning a deontic requirement on blameworthiness, perhaps we have better reason to shift the skeptical spotlight to one (or both) of the independent commitments it is at odds with: *Motivation/Ability* or *Kant's Law*.

This discussion serves to highlight one important feature of eliminitivists' burden: given the identification of some significantly problematic feature of our concept of moral responsibility, eliminativists must show further that *this feature*, and not one or more of the commitments it is in tension with, is the one that we should abandon in order to resolve the tension identified. In other words, eliminativists must *fix the skeptical spotlight*.

5.2.3   Is Fixing the Spotlight a Fair Burden?

Is this a reasonable burden to hold eliminativists accountable to? Haji, of course, might argue that he has already met it by defending *Motivation/Ability* and *Kant's Law* at length independently.[20] Surely we do not expect eliminativists to *prove* that the other principles that give rise to the inconsistency motivating a skeptical position are true. Such a burden would indeed be far too heavy. It is thus important to emphasize that this

---

[20] Haji (2016: 45–128) defends *Kant's Law* extensively, and also *Motivation/Ability* (2016: 129–154).

is not what fixing the skeptical spotlight requires. Instead, a more charitable interpretation is that fixing the spotlight requires a *comparative* defense of these commitments, one that is Moorean in spirit. Fixing the skeptical spotlight requires only that skeptics provide *some* further motivation for resolving the inconsistency in the way that they recommend. The burden for skeptics on the path to eliminativism is to show that, once we have clearly identified the fact that one of these commitments must go, our reasons weigh heavily in favor of abandoning the problematic feature of the thing to be eliminated, rather than one or more of the other commitments that it is in tension with. In regards to Haji's skeptical position, we need further argument that, in light of the tension between *Motivation/Ability*, *Kant's Law*, and *Blameworthiness/Impermissibility*, it is *Blameworthiness/Impermissibility* that should go, regardless of the independent plausibility of each of these three principles.

Here eliminativists might pursue a further line of objection. They might grant that fixing the skeptical spotlight is theoretically desirable, but deny that meeting this burden is in fact necessary.[21] Why can't eliminativists simply help themselves to a presumed fixing of the spotlight and proceed conditionally on the path to eliminativism from there?

It seems clear that whether or not eliminativists can get by with a promissory note regarding the skeptical spotlight will depend heavily on what the ultimate practical implications of the eliminativist view on offer turn out to be. The higher the "stakes" are for an eliminativist view of moral responsibility (in other words, the more drastic the view is in regard to the ways it rationally entails we must revise our responsibility and blaming practices, and the potential costs that go along with such sweeping changes), the heavier the burden on eliminativists to proceed on firmer ground and fix the spotlight before doing so. If the brand of eliminativism on offer turns out to be particularly "low stakes" in terms of its practical implications, then perhaps a promissory note regarding the spotlight will be sufficient.

However, I take it to be a characteristic feature of any *robust* eliminativist view that it will have at least some significant practical implications. If not, then it is not at all clear what motivates tackling the methodological hurdles of framing the view as eliminativist in the first place. Varieties of eliminativism are, at least in paradigm cases, not ho-hum affairs. Furthermore, any brand of eliminativism that targets our *reactive blaming* practices as among those in need of elimination will not be of the low

---

[21] Thanks to Manuel Vargas for suggesting this possible further line of objection.

stakes variety. And so, while there may be room for some uncharacteristically low stakes versions of eliminativism to initially sidestep the skeptical spotlight with a promissory note, there is good reason to think that it is a genuine burden that *most* varieties of eliminativism must attend to.[22] This will certainly be so for any variety of eliminativism attempting to motivate the conclusion that we ought to abandon reactive blame, and any responsibility-related practices and systems of criminal punishment that presuppose that it is permissible and can be deserved in the basic sense. And, at the very least, those varieties of eliminativism that do attempt to circumvent fixing the skeptical spotlight are saddled with the related burden of explaining why they are licensed to do so. They ought to make explicit the low practical stakes of the view on offer, and explain why eliminativism in this case is still a worthwhile pursuit, given its high methodological price tag.

I take fixing the skeptical spotlight to be a first step on the path from skepticism to full-blown eliminativism. But while this step is necessary, it is not sufficient to fully motivate eliminativism. Even if skeptics can show that the purportedly problematic feature of our concept of responsibility (for example, *Blameworthiness/Impermissibility*) is the commitment that should go, they must further motivate the claim that some variety of preservationism (like Vargas' revisionism) cannot or should not be pursued instead of full-blown elimination.

5.3   The Motivational Challenge

Let us assume that skeptics are able to fix the skeptical spotlight.[23] Some feature of our concept of moral responsibility (perhaps *Blameworthiness/ Impermissibility*) is incoherent, implausible, or gives rise to an inconsistency with other independently plausible background commitments, and skeptics can persuasively argue that the relevant feature of our concept of

---

[22] Here it is worth noting that Pereboom's early characterizations of hard incompatibilism (2001) seem to cast the view as a "high stakes" variety of eliminativism. However, more recent characterizations (2014), and explicit attempts to carve out space for plausible *nonreactive* varieties of blame (2013, 2020) suggest that he may now wish to lower the stakes. Questions about the stakes for hard incompatibilism will ultimately determine the burdens that the prescriptively eliminativist component of the view is saddled with, but here I assume a "high stakes" interpretation, given that Pereboom is at the very least committed to abandoning *reactive blame* and any of the responsibility-related practices and systems of criminal punishment that depend on it.

[23] In fact, for the remainder of this chapter and the next, I will grant the assumption that each specific eliminativist account considered is able to successfully fix the skeptical spotlight, and argue that even so the prospects for fully motivating eliminativism look grim.

moral responsibility is the most vulnerable. In order to move from skepticism to eliminativism, there is a further challenge: eliminativists must meet what I will hereafter call *the motivational challenge*. They must motivate eliminativism over preservationist prescriptive alternatives able to accommodate the same error, such as revisionism. In light of the error identified by the skeptical argument they endorse, full-blown prescriptive eliminativists must argue either that we *cannot*, or that we *should not* retain our responsibility-related attitudes and practices. In this section, I will assess each of these possible strategies for meeting the motivational challenge in turn. While the first is either unpersuasive or collapses into the second, the second depends on controversial assumptions about reference and essence that will be the focus of discussion in Chapter 6.

5.3.1 A General Eliminativist Argument

First, Derk Pereboom has argued extensively that we would not suffer significant losses if we were to give up the responsibility-related attitudes and practices that presuppose basic desert of praise and blame, and in fact we might be better off if we did so. According to Pereboom, many of the relevant attitudes that we value (forgiveness, gratitude, and feelings of achievement and self-worth among them) can either be rationally retained even if no one is ever deserving of praise and blame in the basic sense, or they can be replaced with satisfactory analogues. Furthermore, those attitudes (foremost among them the varieties of moral anger that characterize reactive blame) and practices (especially retributivist systems of criminal punishment) that we would be rationally forced to give up are, on the whole, features of human life that do more harm than good. And, those practices that we do value (for example, moral education) can be rationally retained even if no one is ever deserving of praise and blame in the basic sense.[24]

These claims can be used to construct a *General Eliminativist Argument* (GEA) that we should not retain our responsibility and blaming attitudes and practices:

1. If no one is ever deserving of praise and blame in the basic sense, and the attitudes and practices that depend on basic desert of praise and blame do not make us better off, then we should not retain them.

---

[24] For Pereboom's full argument for the claim that we would be no worse off without the attitudes and practices that rationally depend on basic desert of praise and blame, see Pereboom (2001, 2009b, 2011, 2014).

2. No one is ever genuinely deserving of praise and blame in the basic sense.

3. The attitudes and practices that depend on basic desert of praise and blame do not make us better off.

4. So, we should not retain these attitudes and practices.

Though Pereboom himself does not make it explicit, something much like GEA seems to be what motivates the prescriptive element of his hard incompatibilism.[25] Premise (2) is motivated by a series of familiar arguments against a variety of success theories about moral responsibility, including the disappearing agent objection to libertarian incompatibilism, Pereboom's own Four Case Manipulation Argument (FCMA) against compatibilism, and his wild coincidences objection to agent-causal libertarianism (Pereboom, 2001, 2014). If these arguments are successful, and these positions represent an exhaustive picture of the only plausible success theories of moral responsibility, then no one is ever deserving of moral praise and blame in the basic sense. Premise (3) is motivated by Pereboom's own assessment of the gains and losses of abandoning the responsibility-related attitudes and practices that rationally presuppose basic desert of praise and blame, and I will not rehearse these arguments here. Finally, premise (1) appears to be an uncontroversial platitude. If in fact no one is ever deserving of praise and blame in the basic sense, and furthermore the attitudes and practices that depend on basic desert of blame have no consequentialist, contractualist, or pragmatic justification either, then it is difficult to see why we would have any reason to retain them. Especially if, as Pereboom argues, doing so makes us worse off by subjecting agents to harmful, undeserved reactive blame and punishment.

On the face of things, GEA looks like a plausible argument. However, appeal to an argument of this form will not allow eliminativists to meet the motivational challenge. Upon closer inspection, arguments like GEA offered in service of meeting the motivational challenge are not likely to be persuasive. Eliminativists must show that, in light of the descriptive error they cite in fixing the skeptical spotlight, our blaming attitudes and practices cannot or should not be retained. GEA represents one possible

---

[25] In light of the discussion about stakes at the end of Section 5.2, it is important here to flag the fact that the stakes of Pereboom's own prescriptive view are somewhat unclear. In what follows, I will first assume for the sake of argument a "high stakes" reading of the practical implications of hard incompatibilism, but return to questions about how the way these practical implications turn out might influence the way we assess the adequacy of attempts to meet the motivational challenge shortly.

argument that we *should not* retain them via appeal to the claim that doing so would not make us better off, and in fact might make us worse off. But this claim will only be plausible to those who have *already rejected* the arguments from eliminativists' preservationist competitors.

To see why, consider again revisionism as a possible preservationist alternative to eliminativism. When faced with GEA, revisionists can and should point out that the plausibility of (3) depends on antecedent assumptions regarding what, if anything, might play the role of sustaining and justifying our blaming attitudes and practices. In Pereboom's case, it is because these attitudes and practices give rise to widespread unfairness and undeserved harm that we are no worse off (and perhaps even better off) without them. But his arguments in favor of this claim depend crucially on the following two assumptions:[26]

> **(AP1):** Being the ultimate source of one's action is the only kind of *responsible agency* capable of sustaining and justifying basic desert of praise and reactive blame.

> **(AP2):** Basic desert is the only kind of *fittingness relation* capable of sustaining and justifying reactive blaming practices that are permissible.

Is a preservationist of any stripe – or even a relatively neutral party without prior eliminativist leanings – likely to accept these assumptions?

Preservationists certainly will not. Returning to revisionism as an instructive example, a rejection of either (AP1) or (AP2) is precisely what motivates the claim that some form of revision is possible despite the problematic feature of our concept of moral responsibility identified by revisionists' initial descriptive project.[27] On this view, even if our standing concept is fatally flawed, we might still be able to sustain and justify even

---

[26] Pereboom makes (AP1) explicit in his arguments against compatibilism, event-causal libertarianism, and agent-causal libertarianism. In regards to (AP2), it is worth noting that Pereboom (2013, 2020) defends an explicitly forward-looking, nonbasic, and nonreactive account of blame, which he argues that even responsibility skeptics like hard incompatibilists can accept. For this reason, I have restricted the scope of these two assumptions to apply only to our *reactive* blaming practices, which are precisely those Pereboom argues we should abandon, and which raise the stakes for the hard incompatibilist variety of eliminativism.

[27] Might the explanatory work proceed in the other direction – namely the apparent possibility of revision is what motivates revisionists' willingness to reject (AP1) or (AP2)? Perhaps, though as a piece of anecdata my own initial skepticism about the plausibility of (AP1) and (AP2) has largely motivated a willingness to embrace the potential for plausible revision. Regardless of which direction the motivational work is done, though, the relevant point here is that preservationists will ultimately be committed to rejecting one or both of these assumptions in order to make room for their prescriptive project to get off the ground in the first place.

our *reactive* blaming practices with a significantly revised or replacement concept.

To see how, consider again both the connotational and denotational varieties of revisionism. For connotational revisionists, it is possible to revise our concept in such a way that still leaves us with a view of responsible agency capable of sustaining and justifying basic desert of praise and blame. And so, the connotational revisionist will reject (AP1) out of hand, and with it premise (3) of GEA. For the denotational revisionist, the standing concept is in fact too flawed to meet the task. But the denotational revisionist will still claim either that the kind of agency picked out by the flawed concept is not the only one capable of doing this work (and thus reject AP1), or that basic desert is not the only fittingness relation capable of sustaining reactive blaming practices that are permissible (and thus reject (AP2)). If this is correct then an argument like GEA will have no motivational force for revisionists, or for those who take revisionism as a live option. Premise (3) will not be persuasive to anyone who is at least open to preservation without further argument in support of (AP1) and (AP2).

This discussion suggests that what eliminativists who appeal to the gains and losses of abandoning our reactive blaming practices need is some *further* argument in support of something like (AP1) and (AP2). Generalizing from hard incompatibilism to eliminativism more broadly, what eliminativists need in order to meet the motivational challenge by way of appeal to some assessment of gains and losses is support for each of the following assumptions:

> **The Necessity Assumption (AP-Necessity):** the error that the skeptical spotlight is fixed on is a *necessary or constitutive* conceptual feature of the kind of moral responsibility that entails basic desert of reactive blame, or part of the *essence* of basic desert entailing moral responsibility.

> **The Basic Desert Assumption (AP-Desert):** basic desert is the only kind of fittingness relation capable of sustaining and justifying blaming practices that are permissible.

Appeals to gains and losses will do little to motivate the conclusion that we ought to abandon our blaming practices unless one is also convinced that the error identified by a given variety of skepticism is in fact *necessary* for creatures like us to ever be deserving of reactive blame in the basic sense, and also that there this no relation other than basic desert that could possibly account for the permissibility of reactive blame.

5.3.2   *Solving the Problem of Blame (Again)*

Here it will come as no surprise that I reject AP-Necessity as it applies to Pereboom's view. Pereboom fixes the skeptical spotlight on ultimate sourcehood, arguing that this kind of control is at best naturalistically implausible given our best scientific views. But, as argued in Part I, once we narrow our focus to precisely the kind of harmful, reactive blame that skeptics like Pereboom are worried about a positive picture of basic desert understood in terms of fittingness emerges, and there is no reason to think that the right kind of reasons to blame will depend on anything like ultimate sourcehood. In fact, it would come as a great surprise if this metaphysically esoteric kind of agency turned out to play a constitutive role in the propositional content of our evaluative beliefs about others' quality of will and failure to meet the expectations constitutive of our interpersonal relationships.[28]

What of AP-Desert? Here I am inclined to accept this assumption. I take it to be relatively uncontroversial that basic desert is, at the very least, the *best* fittingness relation to appeal to in order to resolve the problem of blame. This is precisely why I have chosen to pursue the line of argument that I have in Part I. But AP-Desert makes a stronger claim that basic desert is the *only* fittingness relation that can do this work. While I am not aware of any positive arguments for accepting this claim, the role that something like AP-Desert seems to play in the dialectic between eliminativists and preservationists about moral responsibility at least suggests that we ought to take this assumption seriously. In a debate rife with disagreement, something like AP-Desert does seem to be a rare point of agreement. Perhaps, then, even if there are no plausible arguments that can be offered in its favor we ought to take AP-Desert to be just the sort of bedrock intuition that cannot be analyzed further. Like basic desert itself, it is a sort of elephant in the room, but one that we cannot say much more about. If this is the case, what are the implications for the arguments I have offered thus far?

If we assume that AP-Desert is a bedrock, widely accepted intuition that does not admit to further challenge, then I take my arguments in favor of the fittingness account to show that one can accept it and still offer persuasive arguments for thinking that reactive blame is in fact deserved in the basic sense. But, an eliminativist like Pereboom might still push back against the fittingness account itself, and reject this relation of fit as

---

[28] I discuss this point further in Chapter 6.

robust enough to deliver the kind of basic desert of blame relevant to *genuine* moral responsibility.

Addressing concerns about "genuine" responsibility requires diving into thorny issues about reference and essence. What counts as *genuine* responsibility will depend on what, if any, features are essential to our concept of moral responsibility, and what determines the extension of the terms "free will" and "moral responsibility." These issues will be discussed further in Chapter 6, and so for the moment I will set them aside.

However, here it is worth noting an alternative strategy for avoiding this kind of worry altogether. Even if a persuasive case can be made for thinking that the reactive account I have defended somehow falls short of "true" or "genuine" responsibility, it might still be a plausible variety of *denotational revisionism* worth taking seriously. Perhaps at the end of the day what the fittingness account offers is a way to *revise* our concept of *either* basic desert or of basic desert-entailing moral responsibility, in light of a shift in focus to reactive blame and (as I will discuss further in Chapters 6 and 7) a more victim-centered approach to thinking about these issues. Given the arguments in Part I, it is not clear *what more we might reasonably want* when it comes to the justification of our reactive blaming practices. On this account, we have good reason to think that our actual attributions of reactive blame are sometimes appropriate and have just the same evidentiary status as a variety of other epistemically privileged and relevantly similar affective attitudes. Insofar as we have good reason to think that the evaluative propositional content of the latter is an accurate representation of the way that the world is, so too do we have good reason to think that the propositional evaluative content of resentment, indignation, and guilt is as well.

While the negative reactive attitudes can indeed be harmful, the combination of their value and the kind of appropriateness captured by the fittingness account is sufficient to motivate the claim that they are permissible. Eliminativists who attempt to object further that these considerations are not sufficient to motivate permissibility are stuck either in the position of offering a direct argument for some version of AP-Necessity, or landing themselves in a vicious circle by again appealing to AP-Desert. However, opting for the former ultimately collapses the gains and losses approach to eliminativism discussed in this section into the second possible strategy for meeting the motivational challenge – offering an argument that we *cannot* retain our responsibility-related attitudes and practices without the erroneous feature that the skeptical spotlight has been fixed on. I turn now to a brief discussion of this kind of strategy, but will address it more fully in Chapter 6. What I ultimately take the discussion of gains and losses to show is that a persuasive case for eliminativism requires some argument for AP-Necessity – any case for thinking that the gains of eliminating free will and moral responsibility outweigh the losses will not be persuasive without further support for this assumption.

5.3.3 *Responsibility Realism and the Practical Implications of Eliminativism*

Before turning to direct eliminativist arguments that we *cannot* retain our responsibility-related attitudes and practices (and thus in turn arguments in support of AP-Necessity), it will be helpful to discuss two potential objections to the arguments offered in this section. The first objection concerns the nature of moral responsibility facts, and the second a return to questions about the practical implications of the variety of eliminativism on offer.

First, one might argue that whether or not revisionists can and should reject (AP1) and (AP2) in the way I originally formulate them above itself depends on a broadly realist assumption about the nature of moral responsibility facts. What is really going on at the heart of this discussion is that preservationists see rejecting (AP1) and (AP2) as live options only because they assume that there could be some broadly realist facts about agency and fittingness capable of grounding basic desert of praise and blame and the overall fairness of our blaming attitudes and practices, facts that are distinct from those eliminativists claim *should* do this grounding work, given our normative framework as it currently stands. But, eliminativists might argue further that there are no such facts, reject this broadly realist assumption, and argue that there is reason to think that the facts that ground (AP1) and (AP2) cannot be disconnected from our normative framework in this way. Perhaps instead the truth of these claims is more heavily grounded in the framework itself.

Here it is well beyond the scope of my current purposes to adjudicate this potential disagreement. I wish only to identify it as a potential place eliminativists might plausibly push back on the claim that arguments like GEA are incapable of meeting the motivational challenge, and as a larger issue that might bear on the plausibility of AP-Necessity and AP-Desert for relatively neutral parties. However, it is worth noting that the account of reactive blame defended in earlier chapters avoids any such realist assumptions. Rather, as a descriptive account of blame this view is in fact heavily grounded in our normative framework as it currently stands, with the added benefit of being psychologically plausible. And so, if the fittingness account of reactive blame is at all plausible, then again we have at least one prospect for rejecting these two eliminativist assumptions that does not depend on any realist assumptions of its own.

Second, the adequacy of GEA for meeting the motivational challenge might also depend in important ways on the practical implications of the variety of eliminativism on offer. In particular, the previous discussion proceeds under the assumption that Pereboom's hard incompatibilism is sufficiently high stakes – it recommends at least some significant revision to our responsibility-related attitudes and practices, at least those that pertain to harmful reactive blame. But Pereboom (2013, 2020) himself has recently defended a largely Scanlonian view of blame, one that, if correct, might still be preserved even by hard incompatibilists. In light of this, one might argue that the practical implications of Pereboom's particular brand of eliminativism are relatively low stakes, and as such there are alternative routes to meeting the motivational challenge that appeal to gains and losses but need not have the form of GEA. On an especially low stakes reading of Pereboom, for example, perhaps all that is needed is appeal to the fact that giving up the attitudes and practices that depend on basic desert of praise and blame itself costs us very little. And so why not err on the side of caution with low stakes eliminativists and give them up?

In response, it is worth echoing my remarks on the practical implications of varieties of eliminativism in Section 5.2. It seems to me that low stakes varieties of eliminativism are, to an important extent, nonstandard varieties of eliminativism. Here I am concerned primarily with the potential for more robust or paradigmatic varieties of eliminativism to meet the motivational challenge, in particular those that target the kind of free will and moral responsibility relevant to basic desert of *reactive blame*. How we should classify Pereboom's own view, and whether there are alternative strategies for meeting the motivational challenge available to low stakes eliminativists are both important questions that merit their own separate treatment. However, given the discussion in previous chapters, it will perhaps be obvious that I reject this kind of low stakes eliminativism as a possible answer to the problem of blame. At best, it represents a potential strategy for *avoiding* the problem of blame altogether. Because I take the problem of blame to arise only in the context of high stakes, harmful, reactive blame, I will set explicitly low stakes eliminativism aside. At best, this kind of view fails to address the problem of blame head-on.

5.4 Necessity Arguments

If the aforementioned arguments are correct, then any persuasive path to eliminativism will depend on some direct argument in favor of eliminativists' preferred version of AP-Necessity. Either this argument is needed to render something like GEA's appeal to the gains and losses persuasive, or it can be used to argue directly that we *cannot* retain our responsibility-related attitudes and practices in light of the error identified by fixing the skeptical spotlight.

Eliminativist arguments of this sort claim that we should not retain our responsibility-related attitudes and practices because we *cannot* do so. How might such arguments proceed? Here I will take Galen Strawson's (1994) Basic Argument for *impossibilism* as an instructive example.[29] What arguments like Strawson's reveal is that this kind of argument – whether it is intended as a direct argument in favor of elimination or an indirect one by way of offering support for AP-Necessity – will depend on substantive assumptions about reference and essence. Here in this final section, I wish only to highlight this dependence, and will turn to the task of assessing the prospects for the success of this kind of argument in Chapter 6.

Galen Strawson' *impossibilism* is motivated by what he calls The Basic Argument, which can be stated as follows:

1. Nothing can be *causa sui*.
2. In order to be truly morally responsible for one's actions, one would have to be *causa sui*, at least in crucial mental respects.
3. Therefore nothing can be truly morally responsible.

(Strawson, 1994: 5)

Premise (2) is a claim about a necessary or constitutive feature of our concept of moral responsibility. According to Strawson, *true* moral responsibility requires being a self-caused cause, at least in crucial mental respects. However, acting as a self-caused cause requires control over these crucial mental aspects "all the way back," a notion that has notoriously faced charges of incoherence or logical impossibility. If it is, and premise (2) is

---

[29] However, it is important to note that Strawson himself is somewhat cagey on the prescriptive implications of impossibilism. Elsewhere (1993) he argues that concerns about the objective attitude might be sufficient to motivate us away from full-blown elimination. This conflict between Strawson's descriptive and prescriptive conclusions is difficult to interpret, and I do not wish to attempt to do so here. However, regardless of Strawson's own position on the issue, many others have taken his impossibilism to motivate some variety of eliminativism, and so I will treat the view as such in what follows.

true, then it follows that being truly morally responsible is logically impossible. No one can ever be truly responsible for what they do.

Strawson takes the kind of moral responsibility at issue, *true* moral responsibility, to be just the one presupposed by any blaming attitudes and practices intended to deliver differential treatment of one another that is fair. As he himself puts the point, it is the only kind of responsibility which would allow us to *make sense* of our notions of heaven and hell, the religious presupposition that it could be just to punish individuals for what they do with eternal torment and reward them with eternal salvation (Strawson, 1994: 9–11). Given this understanding of the kind of responsibility at issue, if (2) is correct then we have good reason to think that any blaming attitudes and practices intended to deliver fair differential treatment *cannot* be sustained and justified. A necessary or constitutive feature of our concept of moral responsibility – and furthermore *any* revised or replacement version capable of doing the required work of the concept – is logically impossible to instantiate, and so the blaming attitudes and practices that presuppose it cannot be fair.[30]

Strawson's Basic Argument serves to highlight one possible way eliminativists might offer support for AP-Necessity, and in doing so meet the motivational challenge. However, this strategy gives rise to notoriously difficult questions about reference and the nature of our concepts. Strawson and other eliminativists often lean heavily on locutions regarding *true* or *genuine* responsibility, but what justifies the restriction of our target concept to whatever it is they have in mind? Here Strawson's own argument suggests that some set of practical and normative considerations are relevant – true responsibility, the kind Strawson has in mind and for which being causa sui is purportedly necessary, is the only kind of responsibility that might make sense of holding agents responsible in "the heaven and hell sense." But why think that *this* is what we're after? This kind of responsibility certainly seems to be a far cry from what we have in mind when we hold one another to the kinds of expectations constitutive of our interpersonal relationships. When I reactively blame my partner for saying something hurtful, I certainly do not *think* that I am presuming them responsible for the features of their character that gave rise to the insult "all the way back." The kind of God-like, eternal damnation-

---

[30] Here it will be helpful to note that I do not take this last line of argument to be Strawson's own. Strawson (1993), after all, has himself suggested that despite the skeptical conclusion of impossibilism, it may not be in our best interest prescriptively to abandon our responsibility-related attitudes and practices. Rather, here I wish to point out only that something like premise (2) is precisely what prescriptive eliminativists *need* in order to meet the motivational challenge directly.

justifying perspective from which Strawson's "true" responsibility would be of interest is drastically removed from our everyday blaming practices.

This is, of course, precisely the *elder* Strawson's point that our responsibility-related attitudes and practices as we find them are tethered to the moral ground we actually stand on in ways that metaphysically ambitious kinds of freedom and control (like being *causa sui* and ultimate sourcehood) seem to have little to do with. And so, at this juncture, we find ourselves at a familiar impasse. In order to fully assess the prospects for eliminativists to meet the motivational challenge, we need some way of adjudicating questions about *what we are talking about* when it comes to debates about free will and responsibility in the first place. I address this task head-on in Chapter 6.

5.5 Conclusion

Here I hope to have identified the two primary burdens for eliminativism often obscured by running the view together with mere descriptive skepticism. Full-blown eliminativism requires not only identifying some significant error for our concept of moral responsibility, but showing further that the error cannot be resolved by jettisoning some other feature of our concept, and that even if this is so the overall concept cannot be adequately revised (or replaced) rather than abandoned. What this discussion reveals is that adjudicating between eliminativism and preservationism requires diving into thorny issues about what the target concept of disagreement really is. I turn now to discussion of how to resolve these questions.

CHAPTER 6

Free Will, Responsibility, and Reference

How do the terms "free will," and "moral responsibility" refer? Like questions about basic desert, this question seems to lie at the center of debates about whether our responsibility-related attitudes and practices ought to be preserved or eliminated. In this chapter, I tackle questions about reference head-on, and argue that even recent elimination-friendly work on how "free will" refers suggests that the prospects for offering support for AP-Necessity and meeting the motivational challenge discussed in Chapter 5 look grim.[1]

While assumptions about reference are rarely made explicit in debates about free will and moral responsibility, there are several noteworthy exceptions. In Section 6.1, I begin by canvassing some of the early work, highlighting the role that assumptions about reference might play in debates about free will and moral responsibility, focusing in particular on the work of Mark Heller (1996) and Susan Hurley (2000). Heller and Hurley both offer insights about the way different *reference conventions* might inform how we adjudicate between eliminativist and preservationist views about free will and moral responsibility. And Hurley in particular offers a powerful argument against the plausibility of one prominent path to elimination, namely positing a necessary feature of free will that is *impossible* to instantiate. Here I focus on Hurley's arguments to this end, and conclude that they provide ample reason to think that paths to

---

[1] In this chapter, I will frame these views as accounts of how the term "free will" refers, as this is the language that much of the literature has assumed thus far. Here I assume, as others do, that in the contemporary discussion the kind of free will at issue is whatever kind of freedom is needed to ground basic desert-entailing responsibility, and in turn any plausible account of permissible reactive blame. I take this assumption to be an innocuous one and those interested in different kinds of freedom will be changing the subject in regard to what it is *high stakes* eliminativists and preservationists are arguing *about*. Whatever it is, it is the kind of freedom or control that *would* or *could* allow for basic desert of moral responsibility and reactive blame for creatures like us.

elimination like Galen Strawson's are best abandoned by hopeful eliminativists.

In Section 6.2, I turn to noteworthy recent work by Shaun Nichols (2015) to systematically account for the way our reference conventions shape the debate between eliminativists and preservationists about free will. I focus on Nichols' arguments for a *discretionary view* of free will, which takes "free will" to be an ambiguous kind term. Nichols concludes that despite his own diagnosis of a significant error in our folk thinking about free will and moral responsibility, preservationists might ultimately speak truly when they say, "Free will exists," and so too can eliminativists when they say, "Free will does not exist." This is because on Nichols' view, preservationists and eliminativists are each appropriately deploying different reference-fixing conventions for the term "free will," one that allows the term to successfully refer and another that does not.

However, Gregg Caruso (2015) has recently argued that even granting the bulk of Nichols' claims we should still be moved to accept eliminativism over preservation, and in Section 6.2.2, I discuss Caruso's discretionary case for eliminativism. In Section 6.3, I argue that Caruso's attempt to motivate eliminativism by way of Nichols' discretionary view fails. Caruso's argument is both subject to a dilemma regarding his ability to hold fixed a causal-historical account of reference, and further there is a far more plausible candidate for the target of our initial baptism of "free will" than the one he identifies. I conclude that the path to elimination offered by Caruso also fails to meet the motivational challenge.

In Section 6.4, I take stock of the prospects for eliminativists to meet the motivational challenge. While I do not take the arguments in this chapter to be decisive, I do take them to shift the dialectical burden quite powerfully toward preservation. Even when we grant some significant error or the plausibility of some variety of descriptive skepticism, it is far more difficult to motivate full-blown elimination than eliminativists themselves assume. However, I do offer some proposals for what I take to be the most plausible remaining possible paths to elimination, and some eliminativist-friendly insights about the way that appeals to reference might help to motivate elimination in the future. At the end of the next and final chapter, though, I offer a positive case for preservationism based on some features of the discussion of reference here. If this *argument from empathy* is plausible, then so much the worse for eliminativism.

6.1 Early Reference-Based Arguments against Elimination

Both Mark Heller (1996) and Susan Hurley (2000) can be credited with initiating much early discussion about free will and reference. Here my discussion of Heller will be brief, as his own conclusion concerns the prospects for traditional compatibilism, and its extension to debates between prescriptive preservationists and eliminativists is therefore largely suggestive. Much of the discussion in this section will focus on Hurley, and her insights about how the distinction between descriptive and causal-historical theories of reference might shape the plausibility of one kind of eliminativist view about free will in particular – a view like Galen Strawson's that posits a necessary feature of free will, or *essence* that is impossible to instantiate. Ultimately, I take Hurley's arguments to provide a strong case against the prospects for this particular kind of eliminativism to meet the motivational challenge, though they do not count equally against other varieties such as Pereboom's.

6.1.1 "Free Will" as a Kind Term

To my knowledge, Mark Heller (1996) is the first to suggest that influential twentieth-century insights about reference might fruitfully be extended to traditional debates about free will. Heller's key insight is that we might think of "free will" as a *kind term*, and that doing so raises the possibility of distinguishing between the extension of this kind term and the concept associated with it. As Putnam (1962) and Kripke (1980) famously note, the two might come apart in interesting ways. Putnam (1962, 1975) suggests that we might come to *discover* facts about kinds that are absent from – or even at odds with – our concepts of them. The essential properties of a kind might not fit our concept, but this does not entail that the associated kind term fails to refer.

   Here Heller cites Putnam's famous robot cat example. If we came to discover that the cuddly companions that we have been calling cats turned out to be automata controlled by Martians, this does not entail that we should conclude that there are no cats. Of course, if our *concept* fixed reference, then we would have to conclude that the extension of "cat" turns out to be empty. But Putnam famously argues that there is another possibility. Perhaps instead the extension is determined by *paradigm cases*. Cats are just anything that is of the same *kind* as whatever the paradigm cases turn out to be. One such paradigm is staring at me now as I type this. If it turns out that this thing I have been calling a cat (his proper name is

"Butters") has been a robot controlled by Martians all along, then insofar as the other paradigms (for example, the other fluffy thing I have been calling a cat named Coco, and my friends' cats Thom, Ethel, and Esther) turn out to be of the same kind, then Putnam's recommendation is that we ought to revise our concept of cats. For Putnam, the essential nature of a genuine kind is an empirical matter, something to be discovered, and like many discoveries the results might be (and often are) surprising.

Heller's own suggestion is that we might extend this line of reasoning to free will. It is at least prima facie plausible that free will is a genuine kind. If so, and Putnam's insight on how kind terms refer is also correct, then Heller suggests that the standard method of subjecting views of free will to "death by counterexample" is misguided (Heller, 1996: 334). The standard method presupposes that conceptual analysis is the appropriate methodology for theorizing about free will, and that it is ultimately our concept of free will that fixes its reference and thus determines its extension. But once we consider free will as a kind, this method is no longer obviously appropriate. Instead, we ought to take *paradigms of free action* as our starting point, and work to discover what the essential nature of those paradigms is.[2]

While Heller takes these insights to suggest a possible line of defense for compatibilism, many have taken Heller's proposal to lay the groundwork for other *meta*-methodological work on free will.[3] In particular, the suggestion that existence claims about free will might depend in interesting ways on the operative theory of reference (and, in particular, whether extension is determined by a concept or description doing the relevant reference-fixing work, or some paradigm or initial baptism) has become central to debates between free will eliminativists and preservationists. I turn now to Hurley's arguments for thinking that one variety of eliminativism in particular is unlikely to gain a footing *regardless* of which reference-fixing convention is operative.

6.1.2   The Impossibility of Impossibilism

Susan Hurley (2000) takes a more expansive approach to thinking about the role of reference and essence in assessing the plausibility of eliminativist

---

[2] Heller's own proposal is that these insights might be used to defend purportedly counterintuitive varieties of compatibilism in particular. For further discussion of Heller's specific argument, and objections to it, see Daw and Alter (2001).

[3] See, for example, Oisin Deery's (2021a, 2021b) work systematically unpacking the way that taking free will to be a *natural* kind (understood in terms of homeostatic property clusters) suggests a new and fruitful way to approach existence claims about free will.

views about moral responsibility. While Hurley's discussion here is rich, I will restrict my focus to her argument that eliminativist views appealing to an *impossible* essence fail to motivate eliminativism regardless of one's preferred reference-fixing convention. I take Hurley's argument to offer powerful reason to think varieties of eliminativism like Galen Strawson's impossibilism cannot meet the motivational challenge discussed in Chapter 5.

Hurley lays the groundwork for her argument with a set of initial observations about how different accounts of reference and essence tend to accommodate revision versus elimination:

> The general issue is: when does a theory change, revise, or resolve our beliefs about some entity or property, and when does it eliminate that entity or property? That general issue is closely linked to another, the issue of what determines the necessary, or essential properties of some entity or kind. Do the contexts in which a term has been applied and its causal history determine what is essential to its referent, or does some theoretical role assigned to it? The answer might be different for terms of different kinds. When essence is context-driven, we can be very wrong in our theoretical descriptions of a given entity or kind. We can discover surprising things about what is essential to that stuff we've been talking about. On the other hand, when essence is theory-driven, we can be very wrong in our applications of a term. We can discover to our surprise that nothing occupies the theoretical role essential to the entity or kind in question, that there is no such thing as what we took ourselves to be talking about. Entities or properties with context-driven essences are more hospitable to revision than to elimination. Eliminativism tends to assume theory-driven essences. What isn't clear in general is what counts as horse and what as cart. Are issues about eliminativism responsible to issues about essence, or vice versa? (Hurley, 2000: 230–231)

Like Heller, Hurley points out that reference-fixing conventions that treat an entity or property like a genuine kind (in Hurley's terms, *context-driven* approaches to essence) tend to be more hospitable to significant revision of our beliefs about that thing, while reference-fixing conventions that give priority to our concept of an entity or kind as determined by its theoretical role (in Hurley's terms, *theory-driven* approaches to essence) tend to be more hospitable to eliminating the entity or property. However, certain attempts to motivate elimination seem particularly ill suited even on a theory-driven approach. On Hurley's view, this is precisely the case for attempts to motivate eliminativism that appeal to an essence (a necessary feature of our concept or the theoretical role) that is impossible to instantiate.

Hurley argues that it is difficult to see how a call for elimination based on appeal to an impossible essence could be motivated on any account of essence. First, if one is operating within a context-driven view then essences have explanatory depth and must do the relevant explanatory work in relation to our contexts of use (Hurley, 2000: 236). So, when it comes to responsibility, on a context-driven view the essence of responsibility must go some way toward explaining our actual attributions of moral responsibility, and why in some cases we hold people responsible and in others we do not. But if the essence of moral responsibility is impossible to instantiate, then it simply cannot do the explanatory work required. A necessary condition for responsibility that we do not and cannot ever satisfy cannot explain these attributions. How, for example, could the property of being *causa sui* serve to explain our earliest paradigmatic attributions of responsibility, when this property is both logically and conceptually impossible? Perhaps a metaphysically impossible essence might still be capable of doing this explanatory work (I return to this point in the discussion of possible versus impossible essences below), but the prospects for a property that we cannot even coherently *conceive* of seems clearly out. This condition is not a plausible candidate for the essence of responsibility on a context-driven account where actual contexts of use determine the extension of "responsibility." Any attempt to motivate eliminativism on the assumption of a context-driven approach that posits a conceptually impossible essence for responsibility is doomed to failure, given that it is not at all clear how such an essence might explain our earliest attributions of moral responsibility and how their corresponding practices managed to get off the ground in the first place.

Here one might initially object that this argument should not trouble eliminativists who appeal to some necessary but impossible feature of responsibility, because context-driven accounts rule out elimination *anyway*. And so, eliminativists of all stripes will have already abandoned a context-driven approach and assumed a theory-driven one. Hurley points out, however, that the issue here is not that context-driven approaches render eliminativism a nonstarter. There is at least one possible way in which a context-driven account might still recommend elimination, namely if the kind in question turns out to be grue-like, with no causal or functional unity (Hurley, 2000: 237). And Heller makes the same point in regard to "free will," noting that even on a paradigm-based, causal-historical approach "free will" might still fail to refer if "the acts we take to be free form no kind at all" (Heller, 1996: 336). A context-driven approach is especially hospitable to preservation and revision, "but it does not

guarantee that there actually are free acts" (Heller, 1996: 336). The upshot
here is that this first horn of Hurley's argument against elimination via
appeal to an impossible essence does not simply fall out from facts about
context-driven approaches. While context-driven approaches are less
elimination-friendly than their theory-driven counterparts, they are not
so hostile as to rule out even the *possibility* of motivating eliminativism.
Only those varieties of eliminativism which assume responsibility has some
essential feature that is impossible to instantiate are vulnerable to Hurley's
argument. Other varieties of eliminativism might still succeed on a
context-driven approach if they can demonstrate that even our paradigmatic attributions of responsibility in actual contexts of use fail to cohere as
a plausible, genuine kind.

How does elimination by way of appeal to an impossible essence fare on
a theory-driven approach? Hurley notes that theory-driven accounts of
essence also require explanatory depth, though in relation to the theory
itself rather than the contexts of application.

> Explanatory depth within a theory-driven account would relate to the
> theory itself. It would have a coherentist character. A subset of the proper-
> ties the theoretical role assigns to the kind *F* may do better than any other
> subset at preserving the internal coherence and point of the theory. Such
> explanatory depth has a theory-internal normative and justificatory dimen-
> sion. (Hurley, 2000: 239)

But it is clear that an impossible essence cannot do this explanatory
work, either. If the point of a theory of moral responsibility is to provide an
account of when attributions of praise and blame are warranted, then a
property that is logically impossible for us to possess or conceptually
impossible for us to coherently conceive of clearly will not do the best
job of preserving the internal coherence of that theory. And it seems that
the property of being *causa sui* is again of precisely this type. So, regardless
of one's chosen reference-fixing convention, it looks as though attempts to
motivate eliminativism by way of appeal to an impossible essence are
bound to fail.

Again, the point here is not that elimination could *never* be motivated
on a theory-driven account. In fact, as noted previously, theory-driven
accounts tend to be relatively elimination-friendly. It could turn out that
we discover that the property (or properties) that best explain our responsibility system is never actually instantiated. Take, for example,
Pereboom's proposal for the relevant property – ultimate sourcehood.
Being the ultimate source of one's action need not require being *causa
sui*. If this is not obviously the case for Pereboom's own characterization of

ultimate sourcehood[4] consider, for example, Robert Kane's characterization.[5] On Kane's view, we need not be responsible for our character and motives "all the way back" in order to be the ultimate sources of our actions, only insofar as they trace back to the kind of self-forming actions that build our ownership of these features *gradually* over time. On a view like Kane's, it might turn out that we discover that even this kind of ultimate sourcehood is not something that creatures like us are capable of in the actual world. In this were then case, then a theory-driven approach might recommend elimination over revision when it comes to responsibility, especially if we think ultimate sourcehood is the *only* thing capable of doing the relevant explanatory work in our responsibility system. The upshot here is that the problem Hurley identifies is not that theory-driven approaches rule out elimination in general, only that those that appeal to impossible essences like being *causa sui* look to be nonstarters given that it is unclear how they might possibly do the explanatory work needed to fix reference in the first place.

So, if Hurley is right neither context- nor theory-driven approaches have the potential to motivate elimination over revision when they appeal to an impossible essence. Eliminativists who claim either that a necessary feature of the kind of thing we are talking about in our actual contexts of use (on a context-driven approach) or a property assigned by the theoretical role of a kind needed to preserve the internal coherence of the theory itself (on a theory-driven approach) is either logically or conceptually impossible will be hard pressed to show how such a thing could ever do the explanatory work needed to fix reference and get our talk of responsibility off the ground in the first place.

I take this line of argument to provide persuasive reason for thinking that versions of eliminativism that appeal to impossible essences cannot meet the motivational challenge discussed in Chapter 5. Impossibilists cannot hope to show that we ought to eliminate rather than *revise*, when they cannot even establish that they are talking about *the same thing* that preservationists and ordinary folk are when they use the term "responsibility." Far from generating radical conclusions about *true* or *genuine* responsibility (to borrow Strawson's own preferred locutions), it seems that such views are in fact guilty of changing the subject. While the kind of impossible responsibility they are talking about might be theoretically interesting, it is not likely to match up with ordinary usage regardless of

---

[4] If it is, so much the worse for Pereboom's own prospects for motivating eliminativism.
[5] See Kane (1985, 1996, 2007, 2011).

one's preferred account of how the extension of "responsibility" is fixed. So much the worse for this kind of eliminativism.[6]

6.1.3   Assessing Impossible Worlds?

The main thrust of Hurley's argument is that impossible essences cannot do the explanatory work needed to fix reference on any plausible approach to reference and essence (Hurley, 2000: 242). However, before moving on, it is important to make clear that the relevant kind of impossibility needed to motivate this argument is restricted to logical or conceptual impossibility.[7] A property that is, say, merely nomologically impossible to instantiate might still be considered a *possible* essence, capable of the doing the relevant explanatory work. Hurley illustrates this point with the following example: let us say that we are interested in wizards, and think that it is essential to being a wizard that one has magical powers. The fact that it is impossible (let us say) in a world like ours for beings to have magical powers does not mean that it is logically or conceptually impossible for beings to have such powers. We can imagine possible worlds in which they do. If, in such worlds, having magical powers does the relevant explanatory work regarding who counts as a wizard or to a theory of wizard kind, then having magical powers is a possible essence for wizards.

But we cannot assess the relevant counterfactuals for a logically and conceptually impossible essence like being *causa sui*. There are *no* possible worlds where we might assess whether something being the cause of itself does the relevant explanatory work for a theory of responsibility or paradigmatic attributions of responsibility. For Hurley, this is why there is no room for a logically or conceptually impossible essence to do the relevant explanatory work on either a context- or theory-driven approach. There is simply no way for us to be *so* mistaken about the actual world for such an essence to fix reference. While we might discover all sorts of erroneous

---

[6] Hurley acknowledges, however, that the distinction between context- and theory-driven accounts is not exhaustive. In addition to a straightforwardly context- or theory-driven view, one might also take a meaning-driven approach to essence, or something akin to a reflective equilibrium approach that requires trade-offs between context- and theory-driven considerations (Hurley, 2000: 234). Hurley sets aside the tenability of a meaning-driven approach in light of worries regarding disagreement and skepticism about the analytic/synthetic distinction (Hurley, 2000: 233). And it is unclear how adopting a reflective equilibrium approach might avoid inheriting the same problems for impossible essences that plague both context- and theory-driven approaches. Therefore, in lieu of some alternative approach to essence, attempts to motivate elimination by appeal to impossible essences look deeply problematic on any plausible picture.

[7] Metaphysical impossibility might also turn out to be sufficient.

beliefs about responsibility on either approach, there is a sense in which this particular mistake is off the table for us. Making such an error would be like Johan Becher hypothesizing that phlogiston is both a substance and not a substance. While Becher could (and certainly did) make plenty of errors in regard to positing the existence of this now-eliminated kind, it is not at all clear how he possibly could have made *that* one.

But here one might take issue with an assumption that Hurley seems to be making about impossible worlds, namely that reasoning about such worlds is not theoretically useful because all claims about them are trivially true. Some, like Daniel Nolan (1997), have argued to the contrary that we can make sense of the idea that claims about impossible worlds are not just trivially true. In fact, Nolan argues that they can be quite useful when reasoning about possibility. If this is correct then why think that we cannot reason fruitfully about what would be the case in logically impossible worlds in which beings are *causa sui*?

While a detailed response to this objection is well beyond my current purposes, I think it is helpful to briefly outline a potential response on behalf of Hurley – even those who take impossible worlds to be theoretically useful do not go so far as to claim that *all* impossible worlds are theoretically useful. In particular, while we may be capable of principled reasoning about comparatively "close" impossible worlds, this does not mean that we are capable of such reasoning when it comes to those that are especially distant. Perhaps there is some fact of the matter about what would be the case in worlds where *I* was born in the eighteenth century rather than the twentieth century.[8] But intuitions about what would be the case in a world like this are far clearer than intuitions about what would be the case in a world in which all the logic books are false.[9]

The point here is that Hurley can grant that in some cases appeal to impossible worlds can be theoretically useful, but it seems reasonable and relatively uncontroversial that their usefulness declines as one moves from "nearby" to very distant impossible worlds. And *logically* impossible worlds – like those in which there are entities acting as self-caused causes – are a long way off indeed. Thus, any appeal to facts of the matter about what would be the case in such worlds should be, at best, viewed with a healthy amount of skepticism. In particular, there seems little reason to think that our judgments about whether or not particular properties do the

---

[8] Of course, you would only take this world to be metaphysically impossible if you accept Kripke's (1980) view of the necessity of origins.
[9] If we accept something like Lewis (1979) similarity conditions between possible worlds.

relevant explanatory work in such worlds are at all reliable or informative.[10] And this is even more obvious for *conceptually* impossible worlds that include features that we do not even have imaginative access to.

This concludes discussion of Hurley's arguments against certain subsets of eliminativism like Strawson's impossibilism. I take these arguments to generalize for any variety of eliminativism that attempts to meet the motivational challenge by way of a direct necessity argument that appeals to a logically or conceptually impossible essential feature of responsibility. I turn now to the prospects for other varieties of eliminativism.

6.2   An Elimination-Friendly Approach to Reference

Like Heller and Hurley, Shaun Nichols (2013, 2015) also makes explicit the distinction between eliminativist and preservationist views of free will and moral responsibility, and the role that our reference-fixing conventions play in motivating each of these positions. As the only view currently on offer that makes a positive case for the possibility of eliminativists' claims that free will does not exist given an explicit and plausible account of the appropriate reference-fixing conventions for "free will," if a case can be made for thinking that even Nichols' approach ultimately recommends preservation over elimination then we will be well positioned to conclude that eliminativists' prospects for meeting the motivational challenge are grim. In this section, I discuss the contours of Nichols' unique account of how "free will" refers, which he calls the *discretionary view*. While Nichols himself endorses a kind of pluralism about existence claims about free will – in some contexts reference succeeds, but in others it does not, and so *both* eliminativists and preservationists can speak truly without contradiction – Gregg Caruso (2015) has recently attempted to make use of Nichols' discretionary view to motivate full-blown eliminativism rather than pluralism. In this section and the next, I will also argue that by Caruso's own lights, this line of argument actually motivates *preservation*, not elimination.

I begin in Section 6.2.1 by discussing the main features of Nichols' discretionary view. In Section 6.2.2, I turn to Caruso's argument that the discretionary view motivates full-blown elimination. In Section 6.3, I turn to my own arguments for the conclusion that, by both Nichols' and Caruso's own lights the discretionary view in fact motivates preservation

---

[10] For further discussion of these issues, see Williamson (2007).

over elimination, despite its initial appearance as the most elimination-friendly account of how "free will" refers currently on offer.

6.2.1 Nichols' Discretionary View

Nichols (2015) first tackles a variety of descriptive questions about our folk concepts of agency, determinism, and moral responsibility in the service of providing a folk psychological diagnosis of the problem of free will. He argues that this problem stems from fundamental conflicting intuitions about the nature of agency: that starting from childhood, we are compulsive seekers of causal explanation, though at the same time find it deeply counterintuitive to think of our own decisions as determined. Further, the belief that our decisions are indeterministic is unjustified because it rests on the faulty assumption that if our decisions were determined, we would know that they were. All this, Nichols argues, suggests a debunking argument that might supplement traditional arguments against libertarianism.

But, should any of this lead us to believe that free will does not exist? Here Nichols offers a novel approach to assessing the disagreement between eliminativists and preservationists, and proposes that we can adopt a *discretionary view* about who is correct. According to this view, the term "free will" is an ambiguous natural kind term. For Nichols, this means that the referent of its tokens is fixed by different reference conventions in different circumstances. So, when eliminativists say, "Free will does not exist," and preservationists say, "Free will does exist, it's just not what we thought it was," it is possible that both speak truly. Something about the circumstances in which these two utterances occur could make different reference conventions operative for each.

In order to more fully explain how this could be so, it will be helpful to begin with a few remarks about what the discretionary view is *not*. First, while it is a view about the way that a term ("free will") refers, it is not easily situated within standard discussions of meaning and reference. It is easy – though of course not entirely uncontroversial – to find examples of terms that have a different extension in different circumstances. Take, for example, straightforwardly context-sensitive terms such as "left," "near," and perhaps even "knows." Nichols makes a further and far more controversial claim about "free will." Not only is it possible that the extension of "free will" differs in different circumstances, but furthermore this is precisely because the operating reference *convention* that picks out the extension for a given token itself differs in different circumstances.

Second, the claim that "free will" is an *ambiguous* kind term has some potential to be misleading. What Nichols has in mind here is not that "free will" is ambiguous in the standard sense, namely that the term has multiple meanings. Rather, on the discretionary view the meaning of "free will" remains fixed.[11] It is only the operative reference convention that is ambiguous.[12]

According to Nichols, the appropriate reference convention for a token of the term "free will" depends in some way on practical interests:

> Although the actual historical role of practical interests is unclear, it is very plausible that practical interests can have important effects on ontological claims ... it does seem likely that practical considerations can impact which [reference] conventions we adopt. In addition, if Pinillos, Mallon, and I are right about the availability of different reference conventions, then there need be no mistake in adopting one convention or the other [Nichols et al., 2016]. As a result, we might appeal to practical interests in deciding which convention to adopt and impose. (Nichols, 2015: 69)

Importantly, on the discretionary view, there could be sufficient differences in the practical interests relevant to the circumstances of eliminativists' utterance, "Free will does not exist," and the practical interests relevant to the circumstances of preservationists' utterance, "Free will exists, it's just not what we thought it was," such that different reference conventions for the term "free will" are operative for each. For example, a conservative descriptive reference convention (in Hurley's terms, a theory-driven approach) may be operative for eliminativists. When eliminativists say, "Free will does not exist," the extension of "free will" is picked out by a description of a kind of agency that has no application (perhaps, again, ultimate sourcehood). Thus, like "phlogiston," for eliminativists the extension of "free will" is empty, and what they say is true. In contrast, a more liberal causal-historical reference convention (in Hurley's terms, a context-driven approach) may be operative for preservationists. When preservationists say, "Free will exists," the extension of "free will" is picked out by the intentions of a speaker in an initial baptism along with the similar

---

[11] Perhaps as "the kind of control needed for creatures like us to be deserving of moral praise and blame in the basic sense," since this seems to be the rare point of agreement among all parties engaged in this debate.

[12] Of course, this entails that the extension of the term picked out by these conventions is also ambiguous, and so if one takes meaning and reference to be one and the same then the discretionary view can be understood as the view that the meaning of the term "free will" is ambiguous. Here I wish only to flag that the kind of ambiguity at issue here is distinct from what those who take meaning and reference to be distinct are usually appealing to.

intentions of subsequent speakers who make paradigmatic attributions of "free will." When this causal-historical reference convention is operative, it is charitable to assume that the speaker intends to pick out an existing form of agency, even if she has some mistaken beliefs about it. For preservationists, then, the extension of "free will" is not empty and what she says is also true.

The upshot here is that on Nichols' discretionary view there is an important contextual difference between eliminativists' utterances and preservationists' utterances such that a different reference convention is available for each. So, while eliminativists and preservationists are both genuinely talking about the same thing – free will – they have very different practical interests in regard to it. While the referential ambiguity of free will allows for the fact that both a conservative descriptive reference convention and a liberal causal-historical reference convention are available, which convention it is *appropriate* for each of these parties to adopt will in some way depend on their reasons for being interested in free will in the first place.[13] If this is the case, then there need not be a genuine disagreement between eliminativists and preservationists, both speak truly. And the appearance of disagreement can be explained via appeal to a discretionary view of free will.

Nichols ultimately seems to embrace this possibility, and suggests that both eliminativists and preservationists *do* in fact speak truly. He demonstrates the way that this *pluralist* position might go using Galen Strawson's eliminativist impossibilism and Manuel Vargas's preservationist revisionism as instructive examples:

> Now we can finally get to the issue concerning eliminativism and preservationism about free will. We have been assuming that the folk conception of free will contains significant error. If the foregoing story about the diversity of reference conventions is right, how should we interpret Galen Strawson when he says "Free will doesn't exist"? Descriptively, of course. He is keying on the false description associated with "free will," and pointing out that nothing meets that description. To interpret Strawson's use of "free will" causal-historically would be manifestly uncharitable. What reference-convention is in place when Manuel Vargas says "Free will isn't what we thought"? Presumably *not* restrictive descriptivism, or what he says is, by his own lights, false. *This allows us to say that Vargas is right and Strawson is also right.* It is just that the term "free will" operates with a different reference convention in the different contexts. (Nichols, 2013: 212; emphasis my own)

---

[13] I will say more about what these different interests might plausibly be shortly.

Here Nichols acknowledges that this pluralism "deflates somewhat the importance of the metaphysical dispute between eliminativists and preservationists," a feature which has unsurprisingly drawn criticism from both eliminativists and preservationists alike.[14] In Section 6.3, I offer my own criticism, but first turn to an eliminativist criticism recently offered by Gregg Caruso (2015).

6.2.2   An Eliminativist Account of Initial Baptism

Gregg Caruso (2015) has pushed back on Nichols' pluralist conclusion that the discretionary view entails a deflationary position about the disagreement between eliminativists and preservationists. According to Caruso, even if we grant Nichols' discretionary approach to reference along with several other substantive assumptions, we still ought to conclude that the discretionary view recommends elimination over preservation when it comes to free will.

Caruso's argument proceeds by first granting a number of Nichols' own assumptions:

> I am willing to grant for the sake of argument that (1) the concept of "free will" is enmeshed in significant error, (2) the free will debate depends on substantive assumptions about reference, (3) not all theoretical terms embedded in false theories should be eliminated, and (4) reference is systemically ambiguous. (Caruso, 2015: 2827)

As discussed earlier, Nichols himself takes these claims to support a pluralistic, deflationary conclusion about the disagreement between preservationists and eliminativists. Caruso argues, to the contrary, that even if we hold fixed these features of Nichols view there is actually good reason to think *only* eliminativists speak truly. Caruso agrees with Nichols' conclusion that the conservative descriptive reference-fixing convention is appropriate to eliminativists' use of the term "free will," and that when this convention is operative eliminativists speak truly when they claim that free will does not exist. Where Caruso pushes back is in regard to the claim that a liberal causal-historical convention can render preservationists' claim that free will does exist true as well. Rather, Caruso argues that even when this liberal reference-fixing convention is operative, we have good reason to think that "free will" *also* fails to refer. And so, regardless of the appropriate

---

[14] See, for example, Kane (2017), Vargas (2017) and McCormick (2017b). For Nichols' responses to these arguments, see Nichols (2017).

reference-fixing convention, eliminativists speak truly when they claim that free will does not exist, but preservationists' claim that free will does exist is false.

As noted in the discussion of Hurley's argument in Section 6.1, causal-historical (in her terms, context-driven) reference-fixing conventions tend to encourage quantification over actual features of the world, but they do not *guarantee* successful reference. Whether or not a term does successfully refer when a causal-historical convention is operative will depend on three things: (1) the causal chain between initial baptism and the present speaker; (2) facts about the initial baptism itself; and (3) whether or not the paradigms in our contexts of use are sufficiently similar to take them as involving a genuine kind. In regard to (1) the question is whether or not the intentions of the speaker in the initial baptism plausibly connect up with current usage via a nondeviant causal chain.[15] In regard to (3), we might get a failure of reference even when a casual-historical convention is operative if it turns out our paradigm uses (in this case attributions of free will and moral responsibility) are similar only to such a grue-like extent that we have good reason to think that they fail to pick out a genuine kind. Here (2) and (3) are distinct, though closely related. While failure for our current paradigms to pick out a genuine kind would entail reference failure even on a causal-historical convention, so too would failure to pick out a genuine kind in the initial baptism of the term. And it is the latter path to reference failure that Caruso is interested in, arguing that the most plausible account of the initial baptism of "free will" fails to pick out a genuine kind.

On Caruso's view, "free will" fails to refer even if a causal-historical convention is operative in much the same way that "phlogiston" would have failed to refer if we imagine such a convention had been operative for Johan Becher. Had Becher posited the existence of phlogiston by demonstratively pointing to a pile of rust, and then to some smoke rising from a fire, his attempt to pick out a unified feature of the world would have failed. In simpler terms, such an attempt to successfully fix reference would have been a swing and a miss, given that it turns out there is nothing that unifies the phenomenon Becher would be attempting to get at via ostension. At best, Becher would be attempting to baptize something like, "that

---

[15] For example, a gradual shift in speakers' intension over time allows for continued successful reference, even while tolerating significant revision. But, a sudden and drastic shift (for example, a new assertion that we ought to be talking about *this new stuff* rather than *that old stuff*) might in turn shift reference to the extent that we have changed the subject.

stuff released when wood burns or metal rusts." But, of course there is no such substance. Becher would have been "swinging" at an arbitrary disjunction of two different reactions involving oxygen, and simply struck out at picking out some unified feature of the actual world.[16]

Caruso begins by noting (I think correctly) that there is an initial difficulty in imagining how the initial baptism for "free will" might go, given important differences between free will and other concepts that seem clearly subject to a causal-historical convention like *observable* kinds. While the initial baptism for these things (for example, water and whales) were likely demonstrative, it is not at all clear what the demonstrative target might be in the case of free will.[17] Here Caruso helpfully notes a common point of obscurity for those who assume a causal-historical reference-fixing convention for "free will," and he goes on to suggest several candidate targets:

> It is possible, for example, that the initial baptism was to whatever power or ability is required to justify ascriptions of desert-based moral responsibility, or to that feature of choice and action that justifies our reactive attitudes, or to a set of compatibilist-friendly capacities (e.g. reasons responsiveness). While I cannot adequately address all these possibilities here (although I will say something about them below), my proposal is that we should look elsewhere, i.e. to the *phenomenology of free agency*. (Caruso, 2015: 2828)

There are several reasons for thinking that the initial baptism for "free will" plausibly appealed significantly to our first-person experience of agency. First, our first-person experience is "more primitive and basic" (Caruso, 2015: 2828). Here Caruso appeals to our intuitions about possible worlds in which we *lack* any first-person experience of free agency. Even if the other reference-fixing candidates mentioned above (for example, compatibilist friendly capacities) were present in such a world, Caruso suggests that without the first person experience of free agency it is prima facie plausible to think that term "free will" and the corresponding concept of FREE WILL would never have been introduced.

Caruso argues further that the phenomenology he appeals to cannot be reduced to a distinction between the voluntary and involuntary. Citing the example of automatisms as a clear instance of the first person experience of *lacking* free agency, he points out that such actions still appear to be

---

[16] Here I am tempted to say that not even this path to elimination works if we *genuinely* adopt a causal-historical account of reference, and do not implicitly sneak in theory-driven considerations. I discuss these considerations further below, and if I am right all the worse for Caruso.
[17] For further discussion of this kind of concern, see McKenna (2009).

voluntary in that they are "clearly caused by the agent, are driven by goals and intentions, and involve sophisticated actions and movements (unlike the herky-jerky movements of many involuntary actions)" (Caruso, 2015: 2829). According to Caruso, it would be implausible to think that we would ever introduce the concept of FREE WILL in a possible world in which we experienced all of our actions as automatisms, even while clearly retaining the voluntary/involuntary distinction.

Second, Caruso cites the prominent role that appeals to the phenomenology of free agency have played historically in arguments for libertarianism, especially those that cite our *feeling of freedom* as providing some degree of evidence for the existence of libertarian free will. While Caruso himself doubts the plausibility of such arguments, here he cites only what he takes to be their undeniable intuitive appeal, both among philosophers and the folk more generally.[18]

Finally, Caruso argues that in contrast to the phenomenology of free agency the other plausible candidates for causal-historical reference fixing (such as reasons-responsiveness) are historically anachronistic (Caruso, 2015: 2830). While a minimal condition of agency like reasons-responsiveness might be an obvious essential component for any plausible contemporary account of free will, it seems far too narrowly focused to capture "in *totality* our pre-theoretical self-conception as agents" (Caruso, 2015: 2830). Any plausible candidate for fixing the reference of "free will" with an initial baptism must accommodate the fact that our use of this term and some corresponding concept stretches back millennia. As such it ought to be compatible with our prescientific, pretheoretical views of ourselves as agents.[19] While the phenomenology of free agency looks to be an especially plausible candidate on this dimension, Caruso suggests that other more theoretically sophisticated compatibilist-friendly candidates are not.

Caruso concludes that the phenomenology of free agency is the best candidate for the demonstrative target of any plausible reference-fixing initial baptism of "free will." This widely shared, basic, intuitive, and historically central first person experience looks like just the sort of thing our ancestors might have been trying to get at in introducing the term

---

[18] Here Caruso emphasizes that appeals to the phenomenology of free agency have played a prominent role in many agent-causal libertarian views in particular, for example Campbell (1957), O'Connor (1995), Taylor (1992).

[19] Caruso (2015: 2830) discusses the need for the relevant reference-fixing feature to be compatible with dualism, in particular.

"free will" in the first place. It is *that* feeling – the feeling that your action is *up to you* in a specific way.

However, if Caruso is correct then by Nichols' own lights the discretionary view would not yield pluralism. Even when a causal-historical reference-fixing convention is operative, if the initial baptism of "free will" targets the phenomenology of free agency then we find ourselves with one of the rare instances that leads to reference failure even when the liberal convention is operative. Much like the hypothetical example of Becher above, our ancestors would have been swinging and missing at ostensively picking out some actual, unified kind of thing in the world.

As discussed above and noted by Caruso, Nichols himself has gone to great lengths to argue that our first person phenomenology of agency is *libertarian* and *incompatibilist*, and also that this phenomenological experience is *in error*.[20] If the phenomenology of agency is libertarian, but this illusory first person experience is the demonstrative target intended to fix the reference of "free will," then even on a causal-historical reference-fixing convention the term "free will" will fail to refer. And so, Caruso argues, even by Nichols' own lights we should be moved by the discretionary view to embrace eliminativism over preservationism. When eliminativists say that free will does not exist a conservative descriptive reference-fixing convention may very well be operative, the term "free will" fails to refer, and so their non-existence claim is true. But, if Caruso is right about the initial baptism of "free will," then when preservationists say that free will does exist (it is just different than we thought) a liberal casual-historical reference convention may very well be operative, but the term "free will" still fails to refer. And so preservationists' existence claim is false. So, if Caruso is right, we have good reason to think that eliminativists are getting things right while preservationists are getting things wrong, and we should be moved to embrace elimination over preservation.

Here I think Caruso suggests a powerful potential line of argument in favor of elimination, one of the few which addresses issues having to do with the way that "free will" refers head-on. If Caruso is right, then this argument might offer hope for eliminativists' prospects for meeting the motivational challenge. However, in the next section, I present two objections to Caruso's argument. First, I suggest that there is in fact a *better* candidate for the target of our initial baptism of "free will," namely *the phenomenology of resentment*. Further, even if a case can ultimately be made for thinking that the phenomenology of agency is the best candidate

[20] For further argument in support of this claim, see also Deery et al. (2013).

for the target of our initial baptism, Caruso's argument would still fail to motivate elimination over preservation. This is due to a misunderstanding about our hypothetical initial baptism of "free will" that appears to be central to Caruso's argument. The problem here is that Caruso seems to sneak in an implicit theory-driven approach to reference-fixing, and in doing so overlooks the significant degree of flexibility for causal-historical reference-fixing conventions.

6.3 Against a Discretionary Case for Eliminativism

Caruso's proposal that our first person experience of libertarian agency could be the target for the initial baptism of "free will" seems initially plausible. Here I will grant Caruso's claims that this experience is basic, widespread, historically pervasive, and intuitive. However, in this section, I will argue that it cannot be the best candidate for the target of an initial baptism of "free will" for two reasons. The first involves a dilemma regarding whether or not Caruso is in fact able to motivate his argument while holding fixed a causal-historical reference-fixing convention. The second appeals to the fact that there is a far better candidate for the target of our initial baptism of "free will," and this candidate suggests that Nichols' original claim that preservationists speak truly when they say that free will exists is correct.

6.3.1 Caruso's Dilemma

Caruso's argument is subject to a dilemma regarding whether or not he in fact holds fixed an operative causal-historical reference-fixing convention throughout. On one hand, his argument for taking the phenomenology of libertarian agency as a plausible target of our initial baptism for "free will" seems to depend on implicit appeal to *theory-driven* considerations. On the other, when we take care to ensure that these descriptive considerations do not infect a causal-historical reference-fixing convention, it is not at all clear why accepting the phenomenology of agency as the best candidate for our initial baptism of "free will" would entail reference failure. In fact, even if we accept Caruso's account of initial baptism two clear paths to preservation will remain.

I begin with the first horn of the dilemma. In order to make his proposal for initial baptism plausible it seems that Caruso must appeal implicitly to *theory-driven* considerations. The very distinction between causal-historical and descriptive reference-fixing conventions hangs on the fact that the kind of thing ostensively identified in an initial baptism is *not* wedded to any particular corresponding *concept* or theoretical role. Therefore, in claiming that the target of our initial baptism is the phenomenology of specifically *libertarian* agency, Caruso implicitly sneaks theory and other considerations relevant only to a descriptive reference-fixing convention into his account.

As Caruso notes, for paradigmatic examples of things for which a causal-historical reference-fixing convention is operative – namely observable kinds like water, or cats – the way that baptism occurs is relatively straightforward. We observe that certain features of the world seem to share *some* kind of similarity sufficient to motivate our picking out *that* kind of thing as "x." So, to return to Putnam and Heller's example, we observe a kind of thing in the world that seems similar to other things in the world, and this similarity is sufficient to motivate our choosing a term to pick out the relevant kind of thing – "cat."

But "free will" is not an observable kind, at least not on the face of things. Perhaps this is why Caruso seems to assume that if a causal-historical reference-fixing convention is operative for "free will" then its initial baptism will require appeal to *some* conceptual content in order to do the relevant reference-fixing work. However, this is a mistake. In such circumstances it seems that the right conclusion to draw is in fact that a causal-historical reference convention is not really *appropriate* in the first place. This conclusion would, of course, only serve to strengthen Caruso's argument. If it turns out that a causal-historical convention is not even appropriate for "free will," then Nichols' pluralism would fall to eliminativism by default. But this conclusion is not a charitable one, given the strong case that Heller, Nichols himself, and others have made for thinking that a causal-historical convention *is* appropriate, at least in some contexts.[21] And so, on this horn of the dilemma Caruso's argument is subject to the charge of employing an uncharitable interpretation of causal-historical reference-fixing conventions. Perhaps a case can be made for thinking that this liberal convention is not even appropriate for "free will," but that is not the argument that Caruso offers. If that is the approach he wishes to take, then Caruso owes us an argument explaining why Nichols, Heller, and others are mistaken to think that it is, and where each of their arguments goes wrong.

So much for the first horn of the dilemma for Caruso's argument. What of the second? Here the problem is that once we hold fixed a charitable

[21] See also Deery (2021b).

interpretation of how an operative causal-historical reference-fixing convention for "free will" might work Caruso's argument no longer motivates the claim that "free will" fails to refer, even if we grant his claim that the best candidate for the target of initial baptism is the phenomenology of free agency. Once the *libertarian* restriction on this initial baptism is dropped, there is no reason to think that the target phenomenology entails reference failure.

First, given Hurley's arguments earlier, we have good reason to think that, whatever the kind of agency our first person experience picks out, if a causal-historical reference-fixing convention is operative, then it is at least *more likely* than not that it is a kind of agency we actually instantiate. If not, then it is difficult to see how it might be capable of doing the required explanatory work to unify our paradigmatic attributions of free will over time after the initial baptism. As discussed in Section 6.1, it is not impossible that this initial baptism is best characterized as a "swing and miss," aiming at what we *thought* was some feature of the world that it turns out we were wrong to think was a genuine kind. But even if this were so, it would be puzzling to find out that it had taken us *so long* to discover this given, as Caruso himself notes, the basic, widespread, historically pervasive, and intuitive nature of whatever kind of agency this phenomenology picks out.

But, as Hurley notes, context-driven approaches like a causal-historical reference-fixing convention do not *rule out* this possibility. And so, let us assume for the sake of argument that Caruso is right about the claim that the relevant kind of agency (as Nichols himself also supports) is libertarian. Even so, it is not at all clear why we should conclude that "free will" fails to refer. To see why, consider how things might go when we grant this assumption and actually hold fixed a causal-historical reference-fixing convention. On this picture the initial baptism would proceed via some manner of ostensive introspection. We introduce the term "free will" to talk about *the kind of control or agency* we exercise when we experience a first personal sense of freedom. If Caruso is right, then the similarity that unifies our experiences of this kind of agency as relevantly similar to motivate the claim that they are of the same kind and in need of a term to denote them is their libertarian features. This is one way that initial baptism specifically targeting *libertarian* free agency might get off the ground on a genuinely causal-historical account, without sneaking in any conceptual or theory-driven considerations. And if we take this as a plausible account of the initial baptism of "free will" then it would support at least one of the claims that Caruso is after – that when we introduce the term "free will" it is a "swing and miss" scenario. We aim at some feature of the world that turns out not to be a genuine kind.

However, here the second horn of the dilemma arises most clearly for Caruso. Even if we grant this claim, it *still* does not entail eliminativism. True, on this picture (keeping in mind that it emerges only after granting a rather long list of assumptions) our initial baptism of "free will" fails to secure reference. But that fact alone does not entail that our *current use* of the term fails to refer. Here Caruso is overlooking one possible path to preservationism discussed in Chapter 5 – *denotational revision*.[22] It is open to preservationists to allow that our initial baptism of "free will" failed to successfully fix the extension of "free will" to denote some genuine kind in the actual world. They can grant that this initial baptism involved a swing and a miss. However, preservationists can still argue that this shows merely that we *should change the subject* when it comes to free will. There is some very closely related kind of agency that *is* instantiated capable of doing all the same work that we were trying to get at in our first attempt at initial baptism.[23] Rather than adjusting our swing, we can adjust the placement of the ball.

A causal-historical reference-fixing convention is particularly hospitable to this kind of referential *shift* over time. If we come to find out that the kind of thing we were aiming at with our initial baptism turns out not to be a genuine kind instantiated in the actual world but that there is a nearby kind sufficiently similar, then it is open to preservationists to argue that a kind of *rebaptism* is in order. Importantly, this kind of move would acknowledge that eliminativists are getting something right – our initial baptism of "free will" failed to secure reference. But they are also getting something wrong – this failure does not entail *current* reference failure and elimination, because we may have plausibly *replaced* the empty extension with a second baptism that does successfully fix reference to a genuine kind.

This path to preservationism – some variety of denotational revision – represents a path to preservation that can also take on board many of the concerns of eliminativists. In fact, eliminativists like Caruso might here object that it *is* a variety of eliminativism. On a certain reading this is true; denotational revision does grant that our initial attempt at baptism for

---

[22] Elsewhere (McCormick, 2017a), I have suggested it may be helpful to think about this variety of revisionism as *replacementism*.

[23] For an even fuller account of the kind of explanatory work, or "work of the concept" required to *anchor* reference and avoid an unacceptable kind of subject changing, see Vargas (2013) and McCormick (2013).

"free will" got things so wrong that it failed entirely. But (and perhaps I have sufficiently beaten a dead horse in terms of the baseball analogy at this point) why think that our success at fixing the reference of a term is a one-strike-only-affair? Surely it is not the case that every time we try to pick out a feature of the world with a new term and get things wrong, that term is suddenly off limits in perpetuity. Human language and concepts simply do not follow such rules, they are far messier. And so it should come as no great surprise if, for a feature of our lives that stretches so far back as free will, we will have gotten things pretty terribly wrong *at least* once. But that in itself does not entail the impossibility of current (or future) success. While eliminativists like Caruso seem to assume that successfully fixing reference is a one-strike-and-you're-out affair, this strikes me as a particularly implausible way to think about how reference might evolve over time, especially if a causal-historical convention is operative.

This of course is not a definitive argument against Caruso. It does, however, significantly defuse the force of his discretionary argument for eliminativism. On one hand, it looks as though the motivation for this argument depends on an uncharitable characterization of causal-historical reference-fixing conventions that sneaks theory-driven considerations in implicitly. On the other, it is not at all clear that if we hold fixed a genuine causal-historical reference-fixing convention for "free will" and grant Caruso's account of initial baptism, then this pair of assumptions entails elimination. While Caruso's argument might motivate the *possibility* of a discretionary eliminativist conclusion, it cannot fully meet the motivational challenge without further argument that *denotational revisionist preservationism* should or must be abandoned in favor of full-blown elimination. And considerations having to do with reference alone will fail to adjudicate this dispute.[24]

However, it is not at all clear that we ought to grant Caruso's proposed account of the initial baptism of "free will." In fact, I turn now to arguments for thinking that there is a far better candidate target than the phenomenology of libertarian agency. If these arguments are successful, then, in combination with the dilemma discussed in this section, I take them to provide ample reason to reject Caruso's argument as a successful path to eliminativism.

---

[24] One thing that might help adjudicate it is a return to considerations having to do with gains and losses. I revisit these considerations in Chapter 7.

6.3.2   A Better Account of Baptism

In listing possible candidates for initial baptism, Caruso himself mentions "that feature of choice and action that justifies our reactive attitudes" (Caruso, 2015: 2828). Here I offer a related but distinct proposal – that the target of our initial baptism of "free will" is most plausibly *the kind of thing that triggers the negative reactive attitudes.* If the view defended in Part I is correct, then there is a sufficiently unified kind for this baptism to successfully fix reference, namely the kind of action or quality of will that violates a non-extraneous expectation. However, I do not wish to argue here that this is the only plausible candidate. Rather, this feature of the overall view I have been offering is largely modular, and I take this to be a merit of the view. Given a causal-historical reference-fixing convention for "free will" we would do well to retain some flexibility in regard to new discoveries about the kind of thing we are talking about. And, for my current purposes any account of the target of our initial baptism that is a better candidate than the phenomenology of free agency will be sufficient to defuse Caruso's attempt to motivate eliminativism via a discretionary view of reference. So, here I will restrict my focus to assessing my proposal comparatively against Caruso, and argue that by his own lights the kind of thing that triggers the negative reactive attitudes is a better candidate for the target of our initial baptism of "free will." And if this is in fact the best account of how reference is fixed, then the discussion both here and in Part I constitutes a systematic attempt to show that we have good reason to think "free will" successfully refers. So, once we have paid closer attention to the various ways "free will" might refer, we see that none of these approaches offers a persuasive path to motivating eliminativism.

Like Caruso, I take some kind of first person experience to play a significant role in fixing the target of our initial baptism of "free will," but that is where the similarities end. Contrary to Caruso I do not think that any first person experience is *itself* a plausible target. On Caruso's view the demonstrative target of our initial baptism seems to be our apparent experience of a particular kind of agency itself – libertarian agency. However, as discussed in the previous section, on this view the *content* of the experience seems to be doing a great deal of reference-fixing work. Without the further restriction to our first person experience of *libertarian* agency (which again smuggles in theory-driven considerations and seems to shift the operative reference-fixing convention to a descriptive one) the phrase "the phenomenology of free agency" does little to narrow our focus to some feature of the world we might plausibly pick out ostensively. If we are careful to hold fixed a causal-historical reference-fixing convention and avoid smuggling in any descriptive content, then it immediately becomes clear that *the phenomenology of free agency* is a puzzling candidate for the target of initial baptism. As Caruso himself notes, there is a wide array of candidate experiences we might be attempting to get at by ostensively picking out *that* kind of first person experience. If what we are doing is trying to pick out what we think is a genuine kind of thing in the world, then appealing to *that* kind of thing is likely to give rise to confusion and further questions about *which* kind of free agency we are trying to talk about. Thus, as discussed above, the phenomenology of free libertarian agency actually looks like a fairly poor candidate for the target of our initial baptism, at least if we are attempting to reconstruct how a genuine causal-historical reference-fixing convention might have initially gotten off the ground, and not smuggling descriptive content based on our current knowledge back into the reconstruction.

So, what might a better candidate for initial baptism look like? As noted above, I think that Caruso is on the right track to suggest that some feature of our first person experience must play a role in doing this reference-fixing work. Given that free will is not an *observable* kind, there must be some other observable feature of the world that allows us to *get at* the kind of thing that we are introducing the term "free will" to talk about. And here our phenomenology looks to be the best candidate. But, again, the phenomenology of some kind of agency is a puzzling place to look, given the wide array of different kinds of experience one might be after. A more *unified* and *widely shared* experience would be better suited to help ostensively identify the kind of thing in question. And luckily there is an obvious candidate – *our experience of the negative reactive attitudes*. Here the claim is not that the attitudes themselves are the kind of thing targeted by our initial baptism. Rather, our first person experience of resentment, indignation, and guilt are what allow us to focus ostensively on *the kind of thing that they respond to*, the kind of thing that we want to talk about when we introduce the term "free will."

To use Caruso's own intuitive test for plausibility, imagine a world in which agents experience the phenomenology of free agency, but do not experience any corresponding negative reactive attitudes. Such a world might resemble, as Michael McKenna (2012) has suggested, the planet Vulcan in the Star Trek universe. In such a world it does seem plausible that agents might introduce the term "free will" in order to ostensively capture some experience of free agency. But, in such a world "free will" would *refer to something different* than it does for us, assuming preservationists are right. At the very least, it would refer to something different than whatever it is preservationists are *trying to preserve* in debates about free will, moral responsibility, and reactive blame – the kind of freedom or agency needed for agents to be deserving of blame in the basic sense. While Vulcan agents might sensibly talk about "free will" in the possible world we imagine, and in such a world Caruso's diagnosis that the term fails to refer due to the illusory nature of the phenomenological experience they use to ostensively fix reference (at least if it turns out there is good reason to think they too lack such libertarian agency) would be correct, this does not tell us much about the possible referent of *our* term "free will."

Whatever free will turns out to be, by Caruso's own lights it must be the kind of thing at issue in and historically relevant to the long-standing discussion of free will over millennia. While I grant that the first person experience of some kind of libertarian agency might be a plausible candidate here, this will only be so holding fixed its correlation with other *emotional first person experiences*, namely our experience of the negative reactive attitudes. As discussed in Part I, it is precisely the experience of the varieties of moral anger associated with certain kinds of agency that focus and *hold our attention*. Thus a plausible candidate for fixing the target of our initial baptism must have at least something to do with our experience of these attention grabbers themselves. Without them, we have no clear reason to introduce "free will" as a term needed to capture some feature of the world relevant to our responsibility-related practices of praising and blaming in the basic sense.

So, the phenomenology of the negative reactive attitudes looks to be a more plausible candidate for fixing the reference of "free will" by targeting the kind of thing that triggers them (whatever that turns out to be!). Our first person experience of the negative reactive attitudes is more widespread and historically pervasive than even our experience of the kind of libertarian agency that Caruso suggests. While the experience of the kind of agency Caruso cites *might* be plausibly found wherever in human history we find practices of moralized praising and blaming, the experience of resentment is *most* plausibly found in all of these contexts, often (if not always) as a constitutive feature of the practices themselves. Our experience of the negative reactive attitudes is also at least as intuitively powerful as the phenomenology of free agency. Whereas the latter does seem to play a prominent role in a wide range of *libertarian* arguments for the existence of free will, appeals to the experience of resentment as the kind of thing that can be *rendered appropriate* features prominently in almost *every* descriptive success theory or preservationist account of free will. Finally, as discussed by McGeer (2013), moral anger is a *basic emotion*. As such it is difficult to see how Caruso might argue that the phenomenology of free agency is somehow *more* widespread and primitive.

To sum up, my proposal is that the phenomenology of the negative reactive attitudes is a better reference-fixing candidate for the initial baptism of "free will" than the phenomenology of free agency. Our experience of these attitudes is a pervasive and seemingly unavoidable feature of any context in which the introduction of the term "free will" might occur, at least if we restrict our focus to *the kind of thing* relevant to debates about moral responsibility and praise and reactive blame. As such, by Caruso's own lights I think that we ought to take seriously the proposal that on a causal-historical reference-fixing convention the target of our initial baptism for "free will" is fixed ostensively by our experience of the negative reactive attitudes. Our experience of these attitudes is what allows us to target the kind of thing that appropriately triggers them as the feature of the world that we aim to pick out with the term "free will." Finally, this proposal does not guarantee successful reference – we might come to find out that there is no genuine kind that could render the negative reactive attitudes appropriate. But, if the arguments in Part I are correct then we have good reason to think that there is and that "free will" refers successfully, at least if a casual-historical reference-fixing convention is operative.

I conclude that Caruso's attempt to motivate eliminativism by appealing to Nichols' discretionary view fails. In order to motivate the conclusion that "free will" fails to refer on either reference-fixing convention, Caruso must smuggle in descriptive reference-fixing content. On a genuine causal-historical account, there is no good reason to think that "free will" fails to refer. Even if we grant Caruso's claim that the phenomenology of free agency is the best candidate for the target of our initial baptism, he fails to consider the possibility of successful reference via referential shift or downright replacement. However, there is a deeper worry for Caruso's attempt to motivate eliminativism, namely that the phenomenology of free agency is not a plausible candidate for the target of our initial baptism of "free will." Not only does this proposal constitute a puzzling candidate for initial baptism in and of itself, but there is by Caruso's own lights a far more plausible candidate in the phenomenological neighborhood – the kind of thing (on my preferred view, the violation of a non-extraneous expectation) that is the object of the negative reactive attitudes.

6.4 A Discretionary Case for Preservationism

If indeed there is a strong case for thinking that "free will" refers success-fully when its extension is fixed by a causal-historical convention, where does this leave the disagreement between preservationists and eliminati-vists? Even if direct necessity arguments (like Strawson's arguments for impossibilism) fail to meet the motivational challenge, and explicit elim-inativist appeals to reference failure (like Caruso's) are also unpersuasive, does this leave us with any positive case for preservationism? Or, is accepting something like Nichols' pluralist conclusion and acknowledging that in some contexts the claim, "Free will does not exist," is true an appealing compromise for those who wish to retain our responsibility-related and reactive blaming practices?

It seems to me, first, that even some variety of pluralism would be a victory for preservationists about free will and reactive blame. Prescriptive preservationists (in contrast to descriptive success theories) are already proceeding under the assumption that there is (or may be) something problematic about our folk concept of free will. On this point, prescriptive preservationists and eliminativists can agree. Where they disagree is in regard to *what we ought to do* in light of this. While eliminativists – at least the high stakes varieties – take both the theoretical and practical implica-tions of the error in question to be drastic, preservationists think that we can justify leaving things well enough alone. And so, to the extent that there are *any* contexts in which the claim, "Free will exists" turns out to be true, even if it turns out to be quite different than we thought it was, preservationists will have won the day.

However, I think that an even stronger case for preservationism emerges from the various insights about the essence and reference of free will discussed in this chapter. What Heller, Hurley, and Nichols' arguments all reveal is how crucial it is for eliminativists to make a case for some kind of *necessity claim* regarding either some *essential feature* of free will that it turns out we have good reason to believe is nowhere instantiated in the actual world, or for the claim that the reference-fixing convention(s) operative for "free will" entail reference failure. I take the arguments in this chapter to show that, at least thus far, eliminativists have not offered sufficient support for either claim. But preservationists can and should say more. Following this rich and growing literature attending explicitly to questions about the essence and reference of free will suggests a further *positive argument* in favor of preservation.

I will end this chapter by sketching the contours of this argument. Like Caruso, I will build on the scaffold that Nichols' discretionary account sets up for understanding the *possible* ways that "free will" refers. While Caruso accepts Nichols' claim that *both* a conservative descriptive and liberal causal-historical reference convention can be appropriate in fixing the reference of "free will" in certain contexts (and goes on to argue that *both* conventions lead to reference failure) here I will argue that we have reason to think that a conservative descriptive reference-fixing convention is not appropriate for "free will" at all.

First, I find it plausible to think (like Pereboom, Vargas, and so many others) that our concept or folk theory of free will is a mess. It is likely fragmented (rather than univocal), and we have good reason to think that ordinary folk deploy different criteria for free will in different contexts.[25] Rather than sort through this mess, I think that preservationist do well to sidestep it entirely (after all, there are more than enough messes regarding free will to sort through). Instead, a more fruitful strategy has emerged, one that evolves from Heller's initial suggestion that compatibilists might benefit from more closely attending to the implications of thinking about free will as kind with an extension fixed by paradigm cases, and the deeper analysis of the ways that "free will" might refer elucidated by Nichols' discretionary view. My proposal is that preservationists can assume something akin to Nichols' discretionary view as a plausible account of the *possible* reference-fixing conventions for "free will." However, when we attend more closely to a deeply problematic implication of the pluralist conclusion that Nichols himself reaches, a case for outright preservation emerges.

6.4.1   The Problem with Practical Interests

In discussing the role that practical interests might play in fixing the propriety of different reference conventions Nichols appeals to historical examples, focusing in particular on the term "witch," and contrasting it with the term "magician" (Nichols, 2015: 67–70). In certain historical contexts, a more restrictive reference convention (the extension of "witches" is picked out descriptively by something like, "does black

---

[25] For example, for arguments that empirical evidence suggests that the folk concept is fragmented, see Feltz and Cokely (2008). And for arguments that empirical evidence suggests that we ought to take seriously some form of *variantism* about moral responsibility – that different people apply different criteria for moral responsibility in different eliciting conditions – see Knobe and Doris (2010).

magic/has a pact with Satan") is appropriate because it pushes us to be eliminativists in a domain where failing to be eliminativists is likely to have seriously negative practical consequences. For example, a liberal reference convention that is more permissive when it comes to the truth of existence claims about witches will result in the execution and torture of those to whom the term refers. With respect to "magician," on the other hand, there are no such practical considerations pushing us in the direction of a restrictive reference convention. Here our practical interests are less weighty, and so a more liberal convention is appropriate.

But how should we understand the claim that a certain reference convention is appropriate? Consider again what Nichols says about witches. When we consider the claim that practical considerations regarding avoiding harming and torturing those to whom the term "witch" might refer make a restrictive reference convention appropriate, how are we to understand this claim? Here is one option:

(1)   We *can* use this reference convention.

This option implies that the relevant convention is available, or that it is permissible to use it. There is nothing inconsistent, irrational, or normatively problematic about doing so. However, when considering this option in regard to the term "witch" in the historical context at issue, (1) is obviously too weak. It seems that the whole point of appealing to practical interests as considerations that appropriately shift the reference convention of an ambiguous kind term in a particular context is that there is a reason to think that they *should* operate in the relevant context. So perhaps instead we should consider a stronger claim:

(2)   We *ought* to use this reference convention.

Based on the example above (witches) it seems charitable to interpret this as an all things considered ought. If we are more permissive in allowing for the existence of witches, then we will be more permissive in allowing torture and execution in the particular context we are considering. And so we ought not, all things considered, use a reference convention that allows for a proliferation of witches. If this is correct, we now have a more detailed picture of which practical interests the reference conventions of ambiguous kind terms depend on: *all of them*. Given that the consequences of using a more liberal convention for "witch" are on the whole negative we should, all things considered, adopt the more restrictive convention. Little would be gained by allowing for a proliferation of witches, and a great deal of harm can be avoided by adopting the elimination-friendly restrictive convention. The latter convention is thus appropriate in the sense that we ought to adopt it.

Unfortunately, given what Nichols says about "free will," it seems he actually rejects this picture, or at least that he should if he hopes to maintain that eliminativists and preservationists can both speak truly. It is not at all clear how it could be appropriate for an eliminativist and preservationist to be using different reference conventions if what the appropriateness of these conventions depends on is our all things considered practical interests. True, an eliminativist and a preservationist might each, individually, have very different practical interests. For example, an eliminativist might plausibly care more about avoiding unfairness and harm to the *targets* of blame than a preservationist. Likewise a preservationist might plausibly care more about preserving social cooperation, or the advantageous features of our responsibility-related practices for the broader moral community and for *victims* than an eliminativist. But, there is some fact of the matter about how these interests shake out, all things considered. We may of course be unsure of how the balance is tipped, but on this view either a restrictive reference convention will turn out to be all things considered appropriate or a more liberal convention will be.[26] If the appropriate reference convention for an utterance that includes "free will" depends on our all things considered practical interests then our current practical interests must fix the appropriate convention one way or the other. Preservationists and eliminativists might very well be motivated by different goals, and have different reasons motivating their interest in free will, but there will be some fact of the matter about which reasons turn out to be the weightiest, all things considered. But then eliminativists and preservationists cannot both speak truly after all – at least not if they are *contemporaries* or members of the same moral community, making their utterances in the same context relative to their all-things-considered practical interests.

Is there an alternative interpretation we can appeal to, capable of preserving the claim that contemporaneous eliminativists and preservationists might both speak truly? In order to get this result the appropriate reference convention for "free will" would have to depend more narrowly on the context of the speakers' utterance. And given that we are considering practical interests as the only kinds of contextual considerations

---

[26] I attempt to address this in Chapter 7, by assessing what seem to be the *worst* features – or highest *costs* – of both preservationism and eliminativism about free will, responsibility, and reactive blame.

relevant to determining the appropriate reference convention,[27] it seems that we would have to circumscribe the relevant practical interests to, at best, the all things considered interests of the individual speaker. In this case the fact that an eliminativist cares most about avoiding unfairness and harm yields the result that *for her* a more restrictive, descriptive reference convention is genuinely appropriate. And so her utterance, "Free will does not exist" is true. On the other hand, the fact that a preservationist cares most about the benefits of social cooperation and the utility of our responsibility practices yields the result that *for her* a more liberal, causal-historical reference convention is genuinely appropriate. And so her utterance, "Free will exists" is also true. Further, these two utterances could be made by contemporaries, in the same place, time, and circumstance – even in the same *conversation* – without inconsistency. This picture of how the reference of "free will" operates also looks like a promising way of explaining why we often have the pervasive sense that eliminativists and preservationists are talking past one another. If the view just sketched is correct then there is a sense in which they are, and they do so because of the drastic differences in their individual views about which free will and responsibility-related practical considerations they think that we should care about most.

Unfortunately, this picture of how the reference of "free will" operates is not one we should accept. First, it makes "free will" more akin to a straightforwardly context-sensitive term. But Nichols is not attempting to argue that "free will" is context-sensitive in the way that terms like "left" or "near" are, just that it is *ambiguous* in regard to the reference conventions that are appropriate for a given tokening. Furthermore, circumscribing the practical interests that these reference conventions depend on to the practical interests of individual speakers hangs reference directly on the narrow context of the speaker at the time of the utterance. On this view, we would get the result that the truth of utterances that include tokens of "free will" depend on a variety of subjective, individual considerations. At best, this straightforwardly context-sensitive interpretation yields a far more constructivist view of free will than Nichols himself seems comfortable with. At worst, it makes "free will" not merely ambiguous, but *wildly* so.[28]

---

[27] Here I am restricting the scope of the relevant contextual considerations to practical interests because this is the only proposal Nichols himself suggests. There may be other considerations a proponent of a discretionary view of free will might appeal to, but exploring such alternatives constitutes its own potentially fruitful project and is beyond my current scope.

[28] Another way of putting the worry is that this version of the discretionary view runs the risk of running afoul of a version of the Humpty Dumpty Problem (see Donnellan (1966, 1998), and McKay (1968)), allowing for the possibility that "free will" refers in radically counterintuitive ways.

Furthermore, there are serious normative considerations that count against this interpretation of the discretionary view. In order to make this worry clear and avoid appeal to any controversial assumptions regarding free will, consider again the consequences of adopting a similar view of the term "witch" in a particular historical context, say sixteenth-century Salem. If "witch" were context-sensitive in precisely the way described above, this would have deeply problematic consequences. When the witch-persecutor says, "Witches exist," she speaks truly. According to *her* practical interests, a more liberal causal-historical reference convention is appropriate. After all, what she cares most about is preventing potential worshipers of Satan from destroying the moral fiber of her community. And a more liberal reference convention is better suited to promoting these interests. But, when the family and friends of the accused say, "Witches don't exist," they too speak truly. According to *their* practical interests, a more restrictive descriptive reference convention is appropriate. After all, what they care most about is the well-being and survival of the loved one who stands accused. Of course she does not actually have a pact with Satan, and so the more restrictive, descriptive convention is better suited to promoting their interests. But surely only one of these utterances is true. If our practical interests are to be at all relevant to determining the appropriate reference convention for a term like "witch," then they must yield a result that provides some indication of what should be done in the circumstances we are considering. Who is right, and should we hang the accused or not?

Unfortunately, if the interpretation of the discretionary view we are currently considering is correct then there is no right answer to this question. And, we get similar results if we apply this view to "free will." Tokens of the term "free will" are uttered in circumstances bound up in the same kinds of weighty practical interests as the term "witch" in the historical context we have been considering, especially when we are trying to decide whether or not someone is the appropriate target of reactive blame. For example, in at least some circumstances the all things considered practical interests of the victim will make a more liberal reference convention appropriate. For them, what matters most might be holding the person who has wronged them responsible and bringing them to justice. But, in at least some circumstances the individual who has acted wrongly will have all things considered practical interests that shift the reference convention in the opposite direction. For them, what matters most is that they not be treated harshly or unfairly, and that we take seriously potential excusing conditions. So here a more restrictive, descriptive reference convention is appropriate.

But then what should we *do*, practically speaking? Is the target of blame actually blameworthy, or not? Should we reactively blame them, or even punish them? A discretionary view of "free will" that takes the appropriate reference convention of an utterance to depend on narrowly circumscribed practical interests is no help to us here.

I take this to be a persuasive reductio of this version of the discretionary view, and furthermore any version that entails pluralism about whether eliminativists or preservationists speak truly. This is not an argument against a discretionary view of kind terms in general, only those for which this practical problem is salient. Whales (as members of a kind) do not care about what reference convention is at play for a given utterance of "whale." But accused witches and potentially blameworthy agents certainly do. I turn now to a version of the discretionary view that preserves the insight that both a descriptive and causal-historical reference-fixing convention are possible *candidates* for determining the extension of "free will" in a given context, but that abandons the corresponding pluralism of embracing them both. Instead, I think that what these considerations about practical interests shows is that we ought, all things considered, to embrace the causal-historical convention and preservationism along with it.

6.4.2 A Positive Case for Preservation

Where does this leave the discretionary view? Here I will defend one option for preserving the spirit of the discretionary view by way of abandoning its pluralism and giving up the claim that *contemporaneous* eliminativists and preservationists can both speak truly. This need not undermine the more basic claim that "free will" is an ambiguous kind term, and that the reference conventions for this term depend in some way on our practical interests. If we take the relevant practical interests to be *all things considered* practical considerations – perhaps those shared by members of the same moral community – then the view on offer would avoid the normative worry raised above. Like the original discretionary view, on this view it is ambiguous which reference convention fixes the extension of tokens of the term "free will." Unlike the original discretionary view, on this view what makes a particular reference convention appropriate is the all things considered practical interests of the shared moral community of which the speaker is a member. On this view, we must give up the claim that contemporaneous eliminativists and preservationists might both speak truly, at least when they are members of the same moral community.

One might initially think that this undermines any useful insights that the discretionary view buys us in the first place. But this conclusion would be wrong. What this revised version preserves is the insight that *practical interests matter* when it comes to how the term "free will" refers. We should take the practical interests of our shared moral community seriously in matters related to free will. There is, of course, serious work to be done in determining how our all things considered practical interests shake out here. Which concerns are in fact weightiest? Is it concerns about, for example, fairness and the avoidance of harm for blame's targets, or concerns about preserving social cooperation and protecting and defending victims? Either eliminativists or preservationists are *right* here, and we need to know which one in order to resolve fundamental and ongoing disagreement about what kind of agency we are *aiming* at when we talk about free will.[29]

Here I will conclude with two quick remarks on shallowness and direction of fit. What I find most appealing about Nichols' insight that practical interests might shape what "free will" refers to is that it provides a new way to give such considerations pride of place in theorizing about free will and moral responsibility, one that sidesteps traditional worries about consequential shallowness. To say that the way "free will" refers depends on our all things considered practical interests is not to say that the *justification* for our free will practices is purely consequentialist. How these practices are to be justified would still be an open question. We might still be moved to eliminativism, for example, even if it turns out that we should adopt a liberal reference convention, because we conclude that our responsibility practices cannot themselves be justified. In saying that our all things considered practical interests help determine what it is we are trying to talk about, we can (at least for the moment) remain silent on the justification of the larger practices that free will and responsibility are central to. Furthermore, this kind of view captures the appealing idea that what we care about should play a central role in determining what it is we are trying to talk about when we use these terms. Unless one is inclined toward a particularly spooky form of realism about moral responsibility, one that takes the kind of agency picked out by "free will" to be one of the ways that nature is carved at its joints independent of creatures like us with interests like ours, then this will be a merit of the view.

---

[29] In Chapter 7, I hope to make a further case for preservationists on just this front.

6.5   The Prospects for Eliminativism

So, it seems all paths lead back to the assessment of our all things considered practical interests when it comes to ultimately adjudicating between preservationism and eliminativism about the kind of free will relevant to moral responsibility and basic desert of reactive blame. First order appeals to gains and losses (like Pereboom's discussed in Chapter 5) are unlikely to be persuasive unless paired with arguments for a further necessity claim. And, Hurley's arguments demonstrate that the success of these arguments are unlikely if they appeal to essential features of free will that are impossible for creatures like us to instantiate. But, even if we explore the prospects for non-impossibilist brands of eliminativism and assume elimination-friendly views of reference like the discretionary view, at best eliminativism still seems under-motivated, and at worst (for eliminativists) we might actually have reason to opt for preservationism. I have not yet said much by way of argument in favor of this last claim. Its plausibility will depend on at least *some* initial assessment of our all things considered practical interests when it comes to free will, moral responsibility, and reactive blame. This will require a return to gains and losses in the next and final chapter, though with a different motivation and through a different lens – namely taking the "dark side" of free will into serious consideration, and showing that our all things considered interests *still* motivate preservation over elimination.

At this point, it will be helpful to take stock. The goal of this chapter has been to defuse potential arguments that various kinds of eliminativism can successfully meet the motivational challenge by more carefully examining background assumptions about the way "free will" and "moral responsibility" refer. I first considered and rejected one possible path to elimination – necessity arguments appealing to an essential feature of moral responsibility that is logically or conceptually impossible – based on what I take to be a powerful argument from Susan Hurley. I then turned to an account of the way that "free will" refers that is especially friendly to eliminativism, Shaun Nichols' discretionary view, and a further argument from Gregg Caruso that the discretionary view actually motivates full-blown eliminativism. In Section 6.3, I argued that Caruso's proposal fails, even by his own lights and on this particularly elimination-friendly view of reference. Finally, the kind of pluralism that Nichols' himself endorses as the outcome of the discretionary view faces a significant practical challenge. As such, I argue that a more plausible version of the discretionary view must take our all things considered practical interests to be what determines whether a descriptive or causal-historical reference-fixing convention is operative for "free will" for a given speaker. This shift to consideration of the all things considered practical interests of, say, the moral community of which the speaker is a member suggests: (1) that only one reference convention will be appropriate in a given context, (2) that preservationists and eliminativists cannot both speak truly (at least if they are members of the same moral community), and (3) that we ought to abandon Nichols' pluralist conclusion. While fully assessing the all things considered practical interests of those engaged in debates about the existence of free will and responsibility is not a project I will be able to take up fully, in the next and final chapter, I will argue that we have genuine reason to favor preservationism.

Of course, my arguments here in Part II do not offer an exhaustive treatment of every possible path to eliminativism. However, at this point I hope to have shown that the burden for motivating eliminativism is far heavier than eliminativists themselves acknowledge. As discussed in Chapter 5, eliminativists often seem to assume that by meeting *one* burden – fixing the skeptical spotlight – the jump to elimination will be relatively simple. They need only show that the gains of embracing eliminativism outweigh the costs of retaining attitudes and practices grounded in a false assumption that we are sometimes deserving of praise and blame in the basic sense. Or, they need only claim that the problematic feature identified by fixing the skeptical spotlight is necessary or essential to our concept of free will. But, as discussed in Chapter 5, appeals to gains and losses will do little to persuasively and independently motivate eliminativism. They must be paired with at least some further argument for a version of AP-Necessity that would render it plausible that "free will" and "moral responsibility" fail to refer.

However, what the arguments in this chapter have shown is that this path to elimination is not particularly fruitful, either. When we do attend more carefully to the possible ways that "free will" and "moral responsibility" might refer, what we find is that one direct path to elimination (the impossibilist path) is especially ill suited to do the relevant motivational work. But, even when we consider views of reference that are especially *hospitable* to eliminativism (like Nichols' discretionary view) attempts to motivate full-blown eliminativism (like Caruso's) also seem to fail.

So where does this leave the prospects for eliminativism? While several paths to elimination remain open, we can now isolate what successfully motivating this kind of view would require. First, a successful eliminativist view about free will and moral responsibility must fix the skeptical spotlight. They must not only identify a significant error, but also argue comparatively that there is no better way to resolve the inconsistency that it gives rise to than by giving up this apparently problematic feature itself. Second, eliminativists must meet the motivational challenge by motiving elimination over preservation. Here matters are trickier, but at least two common paths to meeting this challenge will prove unsuccessful: (1) appeals to gains and losses without any corresponding support for AP-Necessity, or (2) direct arguments for elimination via appeal to the necessity of a conceptually or logically impossible essence. Further, any attempt to meet the motivational challenge ought to make explicit any background assumptions about the way "free will" and "moral responsibility" refer.

Returning to reference, it should now be clear that the prospects for eliminativism will be best on a conservative, descriptive reference-fixing convention. Eliminativists might therefore do well to simply acknowledge this fact and tackle the project of offering explicit arguments for why this kind of reference-fixing convention is operative (or at least appropriate) for "free will" and "moral responsibility." For example, pairing Derk Pereboom's hard incompatiblism with an explicitly descriptive reference-fixing convention might be the best path to defending AP-Necessity, and arguing that failure to instantiate ultimate sourcehood would entail reference failure for "free will" and "moral responsibility."

On the other hand, eliminativists will do well to avoid causal-historical reference-fixing conventions. While such conventions might fail to secure reference, the objections to Caruso's argument above serve to highlight how ill-suited this kind of background assumption is for *motivating* eliminativism. However – and on a more positive note for eliminativists – any argument that can be made for thinking that a proposed preservationist account is subject to concerns about reference failure *even if a causal-historical reference-fixing convention is operative* might itself provide indirect support for eliminativist attempts to meet the motivational challenge. This is because meeting the motivational challenge ultimately depends on which view – elimination or preservation – we have better reason to endorse. Therefore, arguments against preservationism via appeal to reference failure on even their own preferred convention will count equally in favor of eliminativism.

Finally, eliminativists might retreat to some version of pluralism, perhaps the kind generated by Nichols' discretionary view. However, I take this to be the weakest option available to eliminativists, due to a further concern with how Nichols' pluralism might play out in practice discussed above.

6.6 Conclusion

After wading through these waters, my own conclusion is that attending more carefully to how issues of reference and necessity play an implicit but significant role in the debate between eliminativists and preservationist suggests a strong prima facie case for preservation over elimination. While I do not take my arguments here and in Chapter 5 to be definitive, when combined with the arguments offered in Part I, they do substantially shift the dialectical burden to eliminativists. Eliminativists must show that we ought to abandon our responsibility-related attitudes and practices, perhaps foremost among them those involving reactive blame. This strikes me as a difficult task for three reasons: (1) there are powerful arguments for a naturalistically plausible and normatively adequate descriptive account of reactive blame capable of resolving the problem of blame; (2) most paths to elimination currently on offer fail to meet the motivdational challenge; and (3) there is a positive preservationist alternative also in the offing. In the final chapter, I turn to making a further case for (3), and argue that we have good reason to think that our all things considered practical interests count in favor of preservation over elimination, especially when we focus on "the dark side" of each of these positions.

CHAPTER 7

Facing the Dark Side

In Chapter 6, I offered a case for thinking that (contrary to Caruso's eliminativist conclusion and Nichols' pluralist one) a discretionary view of the way "free will" refers can be used to motivate preservation over elimination. If this is correct, then there is a positive case for preservationism about free will, moral responsibility, and blame, even assuming a view of reference that is especially friendly to elimination. While I take the extensive arguments in Part I to undermine most skeptical descriptive worries about the permissibility of reactive blame, and the arguments in Chapters 5 and 6 to undermine the persuasiveness of arguments for prescriptive eliminativism, here I still anticipate lingering pragmatic worries about "the dark side" of free will and reactive blame.[1]

While highlighting the *value* of blame is a necessary step in any successful defense of reactive blame (as discussed in Part I), defenders ought not attempt to downplay its harms. On this front, skeptics and eliminativists are correct – reactive blame has costs. As such, defenders of reactive blame do best to acknowledge this fact and address the dark side of blame head-on. Doing so is the goal of this final chapter. Here I canvass some recent work by eliminativists who identify what they take to be some of the *worst* features of belief in free will and our reactive blaming practices, focusing on two concerns in particular. The first is the worry that empirical evidence suggests a correlation and potential causal connection between our free will beliefs and a constellation of morally troubling political beliefs. The second is a worry that I take to be a primary motivation for both descriptive skepticism and prescriptive eliminativism – the fact that without a high degree of *confidence* that we are sometimes deserving of reactive blame in the basic sense we are left at best *hoping* that our

---

[1] I credit Nadelhoffer and Tocchetto (2013) for this impactful way of describing the relevant worries.

blame-related attitudes and practices are justified.[2] Without such confidence, we ought to embrace skepticism and elimination in order to uphold one of our most basic moral reasons – the prohibition on harming the innocent undeservedly.

While I grant the force of each of these concerns, I argue that neither can be used to successfully motivate elimination over preservation. In regard to the relation between our free will beliefs and morally troubling conservative political beliefs, I argue that we have good reason to think that the observed correlations are not suggestive of a deeper causal relationship. In regard to harming the innocent, I argue that when it comes to sustaining a prohibition on harming the innocent undeservedly, eliminativists in fact find themselves on even shakier ground than preservationists.

In the final section of this chapter, I offer some concluding remarks, and suggest that part of the *problem* with the problem of blame and corresponding debates between eliminativists and preservationists harkens back to Nichols' insights about how our interests play a substantive role in fixing the target of the discussion. Here I shift to a more personal tone and make explicit the interests that I myself value most deeply in approaching questions about free will, responsibility, and blame – the importance of *protecting and defending victims*. I suspect that, in contrast, many approaches that end in eliminativism tend to place concerns about harming the potential targets of blame more centrally. This is, in many ways, an admirable approach. Eliminativists' concerns about who we harm and how seriously we harm them when we blame, given that we can recognize the significant extent to which we are not the ultimate sources of our actions, are also important moral considerations not to be overlooked.

However, I do not think that we ought to prioritize such concerns over our concern for the victims of harm. When we take into consideration *actual victims* and the additional harms they might endure were we to embrace eliminativism fully, a brute pragmatic *argument from empathy* emerges in favor of preservationism. I take the rational requirements of eliminativism on how we ought to treat victims – especially those who have suffered further *failures* to hold those who have harmed them responsible in the broader moral community – to be deeply troubling when made

---

[2] In fact, this worry seems to resonate beyond skeptical and eliminativist camps. Manuel Vargas (2013) appeals to precisely this concern about his own diagnostic account of moral responsibility, in that the libertarian strands of our folk concept would leave us hanging the justification of our responsibility system at best on the mere hope (and a slim one at that) that we have such libertarian agency.

explicit. In other words, there is an often overlooked dark side for *eliminativism* as well.

7.1 Belief in Free Will, Just-World Beliefs, and Right-Wing Authoritarianism

To begin, one of the most serious proposed costs of retaining reactive blame is grounded in empirical work that attempts to explore correlations between belief in free will and a family of deeply problematic moral, political, and religious beliefs. Recently, Thomas Nadelhoffer and Daniela Goya Tocchetto (2013) have surveyed and attempted to replicate empirical work initially suggestive of these correlations, and the bulk of this data has also been heavily emphasized by skeptics such as Caruso (2020) and Bruce Waller (2020).

Nadelhoffer and Tocchetto utilize two previously established psychometric instruments for measuring people's beliefs and attitudes about free will and related concepts, The Free Will and Determinism Scale (FAD-Plus) and The Free Will Inventory (FWI).[3] FAD-Plus is a twenty-seven-item scale that consists of four primary subscales:

> (a) Free Will – which measures intuitions about responsibility, free will, and "ultimate" control, (e.g., "People have complete free will"); (b) Scientific Determinism – which measures intuitions about the biological and environmental causes of human behavior (e.g., "As with other animals, human behavior always follows the laws of nature"); (c) Fatalistic Determinism – which measures intuitions about the inevitability of the future (e.g., "Whether people like it or not, mysterious forces seem to move their lives"); and (d) Unpredictability – which measures intuitions about the potential impossibility of predicting human behavior (e.g., "Chance events seem to be the major cause of human history"). (Nadelhoffer and Tocchetto, 2013: 125)

FWI is a twenty-nine item tool for measuring both the strength of people's beliefs about free will, determinism, and dualism, and the relationship between these beliefs and related beliefs about punishment and responsibility, with each item scored on a seven-point Likert scale ranging from 1 (strongly disagree) to 7 (strongly agree). Nadelhoffer et al. (2014) split the FWI into two parts, the first involving three subscales:

---

[3] See Del Paulhus and Carey (2011) for the development of FAD-Plus, and Nadelhoffer et al. (2014) for the development of FWI. For earlier psychometric instruments developed for these purposes, see Viney et al. (1984), Stroessner and Green (1990), Paulhus (1991), and Rakos et al. (2008).

(a) Free Will – which measures intuitions about free will and the power to do otherwise (e.g., "People always have the ability to do otherwise"); (b) Determinism – which measures people's intuitions when it comes to whether the universe is purely deterministic (e.g., "Every event that has ever occurred, including human decisions and actions, was completely determined by prior events"); and (c) Dualism/Non-Reductionism – which measure intuitions about both the existence of an immaterial soul and the irreducibility of the mind and the body (e.g., "The fact that we have souls that are distinct from our material bodies is what makes humans unique"). (Nadelhoffer and Tocchetto, 2013: 128)

Part 2 of FWI is then a series of fourteen statements designed to probe people's more fine-grained intuitions about free will and how they relate to other beliefs about responsibility, determinism, dualism, punishment, and scientific explanation (Nadelhoffer and Tocchetto, 2013: 128).

Nadelhoffer and Tocchetto (2013) survey the empirical literature employing FAD-Plus and FWI and also present the results of a pair of studies they employ using FWI in the hopes of shedding light on the "illusionism" debate (assuming some variety of skepticism, would we be better off retaining the illusion of free will or abandoning it and embracing eliminativism?). While they conclude that their own findings "raised more questions than they answered," and that "as things presently stand, we simply don't have enough data to know what the impact would be if people came to believe that they don't have free will," there seems to be growing consensus regarding the apparent correlation between belief in free will and a pair of troubling political beliefs – Right-Wing Authoritarianism (RWA) and Just-World Beliefs (JWB).[4]

RWA is typically defined as "submission to established and legitimate authorities, sanctioned general aggressiveness toward various persons, and adherence to the generally endorsed social conventions" (Nadelhoffer and Tocchetto, 2013: 131). The scale used to measure these beliefs and attitudes is the following:

The Right-Wing Authoritarianism Scale:
- "The established authorities generally turn out to be right about things, while the radicals and protestors are usually just 'loud mouths' showing off their ignorance."

[4] For the development of empirical tools for assessing these beliefs, see Altemeyer (1996, 1981) (for development of the RWA Scale), and Lerner (1980) and Lerner and Simmons (1966) (for development of the JWB Scale and the origin of the just-world conception, respectively).

- "Our country desperately needs a mighty leader who will do what has to be done to destroy the radical new ways and sinfulness that are ruining us."
- "It is always better to trust the judgment of the proper authorities in government and religion than to listen to the noisy rabble-rousers in our society who are trying to create doubt in people's minds."[5]

In turn, JWB capture the tendency to blame the victims of misfortunes for their own fate. Based on earlier empirical findings (Lerner and Simmons, 1966), Lerner (1965) formulated the Just-World Hypothesis that people might "need to believe that they live in a world where people generally get what they deserve" (Nadelhoffer and Tocchetto, 2013: 132). In order to measure the degree to which people believe this, Lerner (1980) developed the following scale:

The Just-World Belief Scale:
- "By and large, people deserve what they get."
- "Although evil men may hold political power for a while, in the general course of history good wins out."
- "People who meet with misfortune have often brought it on themselves."

Nadelhoffer and Tocchetto's primary concern regarding the potential dark side of free will is that utilizing FAD-Plus and FWI in conjunction with RWA and JWB has thus far yielded empirical evidence for a correlation between beliefs about free will and the latter pair of morally troubling worldviews.[6] While their own pair of studies yield puzzling results on a number of fronts, Nadelhoffer and Tocchetto confirmed their predictions that free will beliefs would correlate with RWA and JWB.[7]

In light of these correlations, Caruso (2020) argues that belief in free will can encourage us toward disproportionately harsh punishment, to overlook the underlying systemic causes of criminal behavior, and to ultimately excuse and perpetuate deeply problematic social and economic inequalities. With a clearer picture of the dark side of the belief in free will in hand, he goes on to defend a public health-quarantine model of criminal

---

[5] See Altemeyer (1966).

[6] See, for example, Paulhus and Carey (2011) who found that scores on the FAD-Plus subscale were positively correlated with JWB ($r = .28$, $p < .005$), and raw scores on the free will subscale correlated with RWA ($r = .30$, $p < .001$), though controlling for religiosity eliminated the latter association.

[7] In particular, they did not find predicted correlations between free will beliefs and religiosity, political conservatism, retributivism, social dominance orientation, or economic system justification, and predictions that specifically libertarian beliefs would correlate with dualism and negatively correlate with determinism fared only marginally better (Nadelhoffer and Tocchetto, 2013: 135–139).

justice. This model places heavy emphasis on how inequities such as poverty, preexisting medical conditions, mental illness, educational inequalities, and environmental health can causally contribute to criminal behavior. Further, identifying these inequities suggests a variety of potential opportunities for crime prevention. So, insofar as we find the conservative political beliefs and their corresponding practical implications troubling, we ought to be moved to abandon our free will beliefs and instead toward embracing these alternatives (Caruso, 2020: 62).

Waller emphasizes the correlation between free will beliefs and the following related set of politically conservative beliefs: belief that individuals justly deserve punishment and reward, belief in rugged individualism, and belief in a just world (Waller, 2020: 79). He further contrasts the broadly Neoliberal worldview associated with this set of beliefs with social democratic alternatives. While the former is heavily grounded in retributivism and individualism, social democratic alternatives are instead oriented toward a more egalitarian perspective. These alternatives acknowledge that the world is not just and that offenders are often themselves the victims of systematic injustices; it also promotes a greater willingness to assume collective responsibility for criminal offenses. Waller suggests that we ought to follow the model of our social democratic counterparts and free ourselves from the problematic retributive systems that we are enmeshed in. Like Caruso, he suggests that we would do better to shift our attention toward diagnosing the variety of systemic injustices that constitute the underlying causes of criminal behavior, while abandoning the false assumption that offenders are capable of the kind of self-creation that could render them free and responsible in the first place (Waller, 2020).

Nadelhoffer and Tocchetto, Caruso, and Waller all cast a bright light on what threatens to be a significant cost for preservationism. If it turns out that belief in free will (and correspondingly belief that reactive blame is sometimes deserved in the basic sense) not only correlates with, but actually plays some *causal* role in generating this suite of conservative political ideologies, then many will find the cost of belief in free will too high to bear *regardless* of the theoretical virtues of any preservationist arguments. However, it is not at all clear that the case for a *causal* relation between free will beliefs and these disturbing political beliefs is anywhere near as strong as eliminativists like Caruso and Waller seem to assume.

Even if the correlation between free will beliefs and JWB and RWA holds, it is still far from obvious that belief in free will plays any role in *generating* the latter beliefs, or even that free will beliefs are a necessary condition for adopting them. If, for example, we have reason to think that the vast majority of non-skeptics – especially ordinary folk who comprise much of the data that Nadelhoffer and Tocchetto, Caruso, and Waller all cite – believe that we *do* have free will, then mere correlation will not tell us much at all. In fact, if the majority of the folk believe that we do have free will, then we would *expect* to see a high correlation between these two kinds of beliefs. But this prediction would not be due to any special causal relation between our free will beliefs, JWB, and RWA. Rather, we would expect to see the relevant correlations simply because of the widespread nature of free will beliefs themselves. If the majority of the folk believe that we have free will – as, in fact, it seems they do if Nichols and others are correct[8] – then we should expect to find *trivial* correlations between our free will beliefs and almost any other set of beliefs we might consider.

However, these considerations do not themselves *rule out* the possibility of an underlying causal relation. I take the initial force of this worry about the relation between free will beliefs, JWB, and RWA to be tracking the fact that the presence of a deeper causal connection also feels intuitive. Even as a preservationist, I myself can feel the force of the idea that it would *make sense* for at least some of the beliefs that constitute the constellation of JWB and RWA to depend in some way on the assumptions that we have free will, and are sometimes deserving of praise and blame in the basic sense. However, even this intuition will be more or less plausible depending on which particular features of JWB and RWA we focus on. And while there may admittedly be an intuitive connection between some of these features that calls out for further explanation and empirical scrutiny, such explanations seem unlikely for precisely those features that seem most problematic. Here I will set RWA aside, as Nadelhoffer and Tocchetto note that even the mere correlation identified between RWA and free will beliefs is slightly weaker than that between our free will beliefs and JWB. Further, it is concerns about JWB that skeptics like Caruso and Waller emphasize most heavily.

When it comes to moral concerns about the constellation of conservative beliefs at issue, one feature of the JWB Scale is likely to stand out as the most troubling:

"People who meet with misfortune have brought it upon themselves."

There is a noteworthy contrast between this item and the other two. While the other two items – that people in general deserve what they get,

---

[8] For example, see also Nichols and Knobe (2007).

and that good wins out in the long run – have at least some clear positive implications (both psychologically and pragmatically) because they include the notion that *good* things happen to *good* people, it is this third item that has an especially objectionable air to it. As Nadelhoffer and Tocchetto, Caruso, and Waller all note, the beliefs tracked by this item characterize the morally troubling phenomenon of *victim blaming*.

But, when we focus on this item in particular, even the apparent intuitive connection between free will beliefs and this especially troubling aspect of JWB dissipates. That is because there is an obvious and far better alternative explanation for the source of victim blaming than our free will beliefs. To see why, focus on the context in which both Caruso and Waller emphasize the morally disturbing nature of victim blaming:

> The case of rape victims is the most obvious and extensively studied example of this phenomenon. Rape is a brutal, demeaning, and trauma-producing crime; in a just world, no innocent person would be subjected to such a horrific fate. Thus there is a powerful tendency to see rape victims as really not quite so innocent: they dress provocatively; they were "loose" women; they did something to put themselves in that situation (they were careless about where they walked, or they drank too much); they "led him on" or were "asking for it" (thus in some parts of the world, rape victims are subject to death by stoning). Harsh cross-examination of those who claim to be rape victims are notoriously common; those harsh cross-examinations are common because they are often effective; and they are often effective because juries – eager to preserve their belief in a just world – are already inclined to see the victim of this terrible ordeal as other than innocent. (Waller, 2013: 73)

Here Waller offers a powerful list of the ways in which victim blaming can and often does re-traumatize its targets, especially in rape cases. But, I must admit that I find it puzzling that Waller (and Caruso) so easily make a leap to attributing some causal relation between this phenomenon and our free will beliefs. Given their focus on rape and the other examples appealed to in order to motivate the troubling nature of the phenomenon – blaming those in poverty for their own circumstances and labeling those on welfare as lazy in particular – it is odd that they do not acknowledge that another set of troubling beliefs is an obvious candidate for causally generating the victim blaming phenomenon. That is the fact that the paradigm victims blamed in these examples are members of *marginalized groups*.

If we were to accept Caruso and Waller's proposal that free will beliefs play some causal role in generating the victim blaming subset of our JWB, then we would expect to see this phenomenon born out *equally* across a wide range of groups. But, of course, we do not. When the victim is a person of privilege – take, for example, a well-off white male robbery victim – we do *not* find the same robust phenomenon of victim blaming. Why not? Surely Caruso and Waller would not claim that there is some kind of widespread background belief that well-off, white male victims are *less free*. Rather, the most obvious explanation seems to be the correct one here. Victim blaming clearly correlates more strongly with a different set of beliefs than our free will beliefs – namely background beliefs that are biased, sexist, racist, and classist.[9]

I therefore suggest this set of familiar background biases as a better explanation of the possible causes of the victim blaming subset of our JWB than our free will beliefs. But this subset is precisely what motivates the troubling nature of the broader JWB category. I therefore take the force of the worry about the relation between free will beliefs, JWB, and RWA to be – at least in its current state – insufficiently empirically motivated to tip the scales in favor of eliminativism all on its own. While there may be an intuitive link between these two kinds of beliefs, and genuine evidence of a causal connection might be significant blow to preservationism, the arguments and the evidence just are not there.[10]

7.2   Harming the Innocent

The next feature of the dark side of free will and reactive blame that seems most central to eliminativists' concerns is the motivation for the problem of blame itself – harm. Interestingly, this concern is rarely made explicit. For an exception, consider the following remarks from Pereboom:

> The reason we should take skepticism about free will seriously is that it engages a basic moral reason in a way that sets it apart from skepticism about induction and also from skepticism about the external world. The basic moral reason is the reason we have to oppose intentionally harming others. If we

---

[9] For an excellent analysis of how sexual assault victims often suffer a credibility deficit while perpetrators are often accorded a credibility excess, see Yap (2017).

[10] But what if the evidence does get stronger, would this *then* be a significant blow to preservationism? As I will discuss in Section 7.3, I think that the weightiest reasons in favor of preservationism arise out of adopting a *victim-centered* approach. And so, if it turns out that preserving our belief in free will and our reactive blaming practices directly causes or increases the phenomenon of victim blaming, then it is *possible* that the relevant evidence could count against preservationism. However, even in this case, I do not think that the relevant evidence would provide any definitive motivation for eliminativism. At worst (for preservationists), it might motivate a more careful analysis of precisely how the harms of victim blaming stack up comparatively against the value of protecting and defending victims. It would come as no great surprise that reactive blame turns out to be a kind of *double-edged sword*, but that fact in itself need not entail that we should stop wielding it altogether.

lived in accord with external-world or inductive skepticism, many intuitive applications of this reason would be undercut. But free will skepticism denies only the potential overrider to this basic moral reason that basic desert justifications for harming would provide. (Pereboom, 2014: 154)

Skeptics are motivated by their concern that we have "a basic moral reason" to avoid the harms of reactive blame and its corresponding practices, absent what looks to be one of the only plausible reasons that might outweigh it – the fact that this harm is deserved. This, of course, will be familiar from the discussion of the problem of blame in Part I. While the goal of Part I was to show that reactive blame *is* sometimes deserved in the basic sense, here I wish to consider only how lingering concerns that it is *not* deserved might be used to try to directly motivate prescriptive eliminativism.

It will be helpful to first consider precisely what concerns about under-served intentional harm amount to, and the nature of the basic moral reason Pereboom cites. I propose that the simplest way of characterizing the relevant reason at issue is a standing reason to oppose *harming the innocent*. At the heart of things, what skeptics and eliminativists are perhaps most concerned about is the widespread harm of the innocent that undeserved reactive blame would entail. However, when we consider this concern in its most basic form, it takes on some puzzling features as a potential motivation for eliminativism. That is because one prominent objection to eliminativism is that this prescriptive view *itself* cannot adequately explain how such a prohibition on harming the innocent might possibly be grounded. Saul Smilansky (2011, 2016, 2017, 2020) and John Lemos (2016, 2018) have persuasively developed this line of argument against eliminativist views of free will. Both take Pereboom as a representative target and raise concerns about whether hard incompatibilism (and the corresponding quarantine model of punishment Pereboom endorses) can truly sustain the sort of deontological constraints against using persons "merely as means" needed to uphold the prohibition against harming the innocent (Smilansky, 2020: 30).

Lemos (2018), for example, is particularly interested in whether or not Pereboom's quarantine model can preserve *respect* for the innocent, and ultimately argues that it cannot. Pereboom offers his quarantine model as an alternative to problematic retributive and consequentialist models, in large part because quarantine would reduce undeserved harm to criminals. But, as Lemos points out, even those criminals subject to minimally harmful punishment on the quarantine model are actually innocent, by Pereboom's own lights, because they do not deserve blame in the basic sense. Lemos argues further that the quarantine model lacks the resources to explain why we should not enact policies and procedures that would lead to the detention of *more* innocent people who have committed no crimes but are likely to. Such procedures would reduce even more undeserved harm to victims at the cost of only minimally harmful detention of innocent potential criminals. If this is correct, then Pereboom's hard incompatibilism seems to require abandoning the inherent wrongness of punishing the innocent, or at least inherits familiar consequentialist difficulties for explaining it.[11]

Likewise, Smilansky argues that by definition free will "denialists" are committed to the fact that "morally, in the deep sense, *everyone* is innocent" because no one is deserving of blame in the basic sense, and so "no one can be justly punished" (Smilansky, 2020: 33; emphasis my own). Therefore, any unequal treatment by way of *any* variety of eliminativist punishment will be unjust, even if morally justified. While the most straightforward path to justification would of course be consequentialist in spirit, eliminativists must find some alternative means to sustain genuinely deontological constraints against treating potential criminals as mere means, or familiar worries for pure consequentialist deterrence theories regarding harm to the innocent rear their ugly head. Smilansky sums up the objection here nicely:

> Once the sanctity of moral innocence is violated (because some are to be punished although everyone is morally innocent), the overwhelming concern with who is to be punished, rather than with how many unjust harms of the innocent (including victims of crime) are to occur, seems to lose much of its moral weight. Once the difference between offenders and nonoffenders is not held to be reflective of moral guilt and innocence, focusing on it loses much of its moral motivation. It can no longer serve as a formidable basis for deontological constraint, as it can when we are concerned with agency-related fault and desert as giving permission for using as a means, or the absence of such permission. (Smilansky, 2020: 34)

If Lemos and Smilansky are correct, then appeal to concerns about harming the innocent cannot play the role in motivating eliminativism about free will, responsibility, and blame that eliminativists often seem to assume. If Pereboom's quarantine model is representative of eliminativists' best prospects for accommodating a system of criminal

---

[11] For the full development of this argument, see chapter 6 of Lemos (2018).

punishment,[12] then it seems eliminativists themselves are in a particularly difficult position when it comes to explaining how *their own views* are able to sustain a prohibition against intentionally harming the innocent. And so I do not see how this kind of concern could successfully motivate eliminativism. Interestingly, the very same basic moral reason that so powerfully motivates skepticism and the problem of blame in the first place seems to count equally against the prescriptive eliminativist extension of this view.

Pereboom, of course, is aware of these concerns and addresses Smilansky's claim that retributivism and the assumption of basic desert must be retained in order to ensure that only the guilty are punished (Pereboom, 2020: 111). According to Pereboom, Smilansky's proposal that we ought to retain retributivism and the *illusion* of basic desert of blame in order to avoid harming the innocent is actually self-defeating. By appealing to the good of ensuring that the innocent not be targeted by the legal system, Smilansky himself rules out the possibility that such a system preserves genuinely *basic* desert of blame. According to Pereboom, the kind of desert cited as justification for harming "won't be basic if that justification appeals to good beyond such persons receiving what they deserve" (Pereboom, 2020: 111). And so, those who accept Smilansky's own illusionist view cannot retain the kind of basic desert-based prohibition against harming the innocent that he is concerned with either.

However, as Pereboom notes, this response will only be effective specifically against *illusionists* lodging objections about eliminativists' prospects for retaining a prohibition against harming the innocent. But a deeper version of the objection is available to non-skeptics who can consistently invoke basic desert in their argument.[13] In response to this stronger objection, Pereboom argues that in order for commitment to desert-based legal justifications to effectively protect the innocent from punishment, it must also be the case that "someone's *not deserving to be*

---

[12] While Pereboom's quarantine model is one of the most widely discussed, see also Caruso's (2020) public health-quarantine model. Both Pereboom and Caruso emphasize a "principle of least infringement" whereby the least restrictive measures should be taken to protect public health and safety (Caruso, 2020: 61). While this kind of principle may of course *lessen* the harm of punishment to perpetrators who, by Pereboom and Caruso's own lights, are innocent, it will not eliminate it entirely. Nor does appeal to this principle address Lemos' worry that once we are committed to saying that everyone is innocent worries about mere consequentialist rationales for punishment entailing at least some *preventative* harms to those who have not yet even committed any wrongdoing loom large.

[13] Here Pereboom notes David Hodgson's (2012) claim that protection of the innocent from punishment is a benefit of belief in basic desert as an example.

harmed is sufficient reason for the state not to harm that person in the interests of a legitimate state interest" (Pereboom, 2020: 112). But, Pereboom notes, *protection of its citizens* is another prominent state interest that justifies harm, and those who pose a threat may not always be deserving of harm even on the assumption that basic desert *is* sometimes possible. Here Pereboom gives the following examples in support of the claim that protection of citizens is an additional justification for state-sanctioned harm:

> Suppose that an assailant has been given a drug, against his will, that makes him prone to extreme violence for a short time. The only way for the police to stop him from killing someone is to incapacitate him with a painful taser. This is clearly legitimate. Or suppose that the drugged person is about to shoot as many students in school as he can, and the only way the police can stop him is to kill him. This is also legitimate. Or suppose the shooter is mentally ill in such a way that precludes his deserving to be punished. Then we also believe that it's legitimate for the police to kill him. Thus, not being deserving of harm *does not insulate a person* from being justifiably harmed by the state on the basis of legitimate state interests, such as citizen's protections. (Pereboom, 2020: 112)

If Pereboom is right, *any* state sanctioned legal system of criminal punishment will render some degree of harming the innocent tolerable, even those that retain the assumption of basic desert of blame. This is because the prohibition on harming the innocent, while powerful, is not the *only* deontological constraint at issue, and in some cases the prohibition against harming the innocent and other constraints might conflict. This is clear in the examples Pereboom cites earlier.

While I find Pereboom's response to Smilansky here persuasive, it actually makes matters *worse* for the variety of eliminativism I am considering in this chapter, namely those that might hope to motivate elimination over preservation through brute appeal to the unacceptable costs of the dark side of free will and reactive blame. To sum up the dialectic in regard to harming the innocent, I began at the outset by noting that this very concern – which Pereboom himself calls *the basic moral reason* – seems to be one of the central motivating concerns for skepticism and eliminativism. But, as we have now seen, this is deeply puzzling. Skeptical views of free will and blame that attempt to move us all the way to elimination will find themselves stuck with *the very same concern* – once we have abandoned basic desert of blame and any correspondingly deep notion of innocence, there seems no way for eliminativists to sustain any robust, exception-less prohibition against harming the innocent themselves. While Pereboom may be right that such prohibitions always warrant exceptions in the realm of legal punishment given other potentially conflicting obligations of the state anyway, this line of argument fails to save the prospects for appeals to this basic moral reason to motivate eliminativism. What Pereboom's own attempt to rebut this kind of objection shows is that the very same consideration often appealed to in attempting to motivate elimiantivism – that without basic desert of blame, our blaming practices commit us to widespread undeserved harm that *must* be avoided – in fact counts equally against eliminativism itself. At best, therefore, it seems concerns about harming the innocent will leave preservationists and eliminativists with a draw.

7.3 The Dark Side of Eliminativism and an Argument from Empathy

To sum up, I take the previous discussion to largely undermine the prospects for eliminativists to motivate elimination over preservation via some brute pragmatic appeal to the dark side of free will, responsibility, and blame. While it is unavoidably true that there are significant costs to retaining our free will, responsibility, and reactive blaming practices, at present I see no clear way to motivate elimination over preservation via appeal to these costs alone. Here I hope to have acknowledged and addressed head-on what many seem to consider some of the worst features of the dark side. While I acknowledge the force of concerns about both of these costs, I conclude here that in their current form neither adequately motivates a pragmatic argument about gains and losses sufficient to conclude that if we have to make a wager, we ought to wager on eliminativist views that avoid these costs.

For this final section, I would like to shift gears a bit, from the strictly philosophical to a handful of more personal considerations. First, I admit that it has always been puzzling to me that so much discussion of free will, moral responsibility, and blame seems fixed on avoiding appeal to such reflections, especially prior to P. F. Strawson's powerful refocusing of the dialectic in regard to our emotions and relationships. But, even then, there is still a kind of *distance* in the literature. Vignettes and thought experiments are offered, intuitions about blameworthiness are cited, sometimes first personal emotional responses are cited along with them, but there are few examples that make explicit appeal to *the thoughts and emotions of the victim*. Why?

By now, a few noteworthy exceptions will be familiar. Pamela Hieronymi and Christopher Franklin, for example, propose that the *force* of blame has much to do with the *meaning* of wrong actions, namely what they communicate about the way that the wrongdoer views the victim. We need blame, as Angela Smith emphasizes, to *protest* this meaning, and *protect the value of victims*. And, as Margaret Urban Walker notes, failure to do so can sometimes be even worse than the initial harm itself. In failing to blame those who are blameworthy, we *abandon* victims, leaving them (and others!) to wonder if there really is something defective about them. If, after all, they do not merit our defense of them via our blaming practices, then the simplest explanation why is that *they just do not matter enough.*

This picture of the implications of *failures* to blame for victims has always struck me as the weightiest motivating consideration when it comes to our philosophical theorizing about blame. Thus it will come as no great surprise that I have tackled the project of defending the permissibility of blame, and arguing for prescriptive preservationism even if worries about permissibility linger. If Nichols is correct, and my own concern for victims turns out to track our actual weightiest all things considered reasons, then facts about the consideration I take to matter most in this debate render a causal-historical reference-fixing convention operative. And so I have landed on a preservationist account of free will, moral responsibility, and blame that I hope tracks the kind of thing that could get reactive blaming attributions, which *protect and defend victims* of harm off the ground whatever that kind of thing turns out to be. Perhaps, in the end, I have gotten the details wrong, and the violation of non-extraneous expectations turns out not to be the best account of the kind of thing in question. Even so, I take explicitly initiating the project of trying to figure out what *this* kind of thing is to be a valuable one. Perhaps others will be able to offer a better account than I have here. Regardless, I will conclude here with some thoughts about an *actual* victim-based case study in the hopes of motivating why I take such a project to be so important.

This case has much to do with the phenomenon of victim blaming. As Caruso and Waller note, the phenomenon of victim blaming is particularly well-documented in the case of rape victims. I think that if we are to make any claims about the gains and losses of reactive blame based on this phenomenon, we ought not do so without attending closely to *the testimony of actual victims*. Here I will focus on a series of excerpts from the powerful victim impact statement of Emily Doe:

> When I was told to be prepared in case we didn't win, I said, I can't prepare for that. He was guilty the minute I woke up. No one can talk me out of the hurt he caused me. Worst of all, I was warned, because he now knows you

don't remember, he is going to get to write the script. He can say whatever he wants and no one can contest it. I had no power, I had no voice, I was defenseless. My memory loss would be used against me. My testimony was weak, was incomplete, and I was made to believe that perhaps, I am not enough to win this. His attorney constantly reminded the jury, the only one we can believe is Brock, because she doesn't remember. That helplessness was traumatizing . . .

. . . You are guilty. Twelve jurors convicted you guilty of three felony counts beyond reasonable doubt, that's twelve votes per count, thirty-six yeses confirming guilt, that's one hundred percent, unanimous guilt. And I thought finally it is over, finally he will own up to what he did, truly apologize, we will both move on and get better. Then I read your statement.

If you are hoping that one of my organs will implode from anger and I will die, I'm almost there. You are very close. This is not a story of another drunk college hookup with poor decision making. Assault is not an accident. Somehow, you still don't get it. Somehow, you still sound confused . . .

. . . Your life is not over, you have decades of years ahead to rewrite your story. The world is huge, it is so much bigger than Palo Alto and Stanford, and you will make a space for yourself in it where you can be useful and happy. But right now, you do not get to shrug your shoulders and be confused anymore. You do not get to pretend that there were no red flags. You have been convicted of violating me, intentionally, forcibly, sexually, with malicious intent, and all you can admit to is consuming alcohol. Do not talk about the sad way your life was upturned because alcohol made you do bad things. Figure out how to take responsibility for your own conduct . . .

. . . My life has been on hold for over a year, a year of anger, anguish and uncertainty, until a jury of my peers rendered a judgment that validated the injustices I had endured. Had Brock admitted guilt and remorse and offered to settle early on, I would have considered a lighter sentence, respecting his honesty, grateful to be able to move our lives forward. Instead he took the risk of going to trial, added insult to injury and forced me to relive the hurt as details about my personal life and sexual assault were brutally dissected before the public. He pushed me and my family through a year of inexplicable, unnecessary suffering, and should face the consequences of challenging his crime, of putting my pain into question, of making us wait so long for justice.

I told the probation officer I do not want Brock to rot away in prison. I did not say he does not deserve to be behind bars. The probation officer's recommendation of a year or less in county jail is a soft timeout, a mockery of the seriousness of his assaults, an insult to me and all women. It gives the message that a stranger can be inside you without proper consent and he will receive less than what has been defined as the minimum sentence.

Probation should be denied. I also told the probation officer that what I truly wanted was for Brock to get it, to understand and admit to his wrongdoing . . .

. . . The Probation Officer has stated that this case, when compared to other crimes of similar nature, may be considered less serious due to the defendant's level of intoxication. It felt serious. That's all I'm going to say.

What has he done to demonstrate that he deserves a break? He has only apologized for drinking and has yet to define what he did to me as sexual assault, he has revictimized me continually, relentlessly. He has been found guilty of three serious felonies and it is time for him to accept the consequences of his actions. He will not be quietly excused.

He is a lifetime sex registrant. That doesn't expire. Just like what he did to me doesn't expire, doesn't just go away after a set number of years. It stays with me, it's part of my identity, it has forever changed the way I carry myself, the way I live the rest of my life . . .

. . . And finally, to girls everywhere, I am with you. On nights when you feel alone, I am with you. When people doubt you or dismiss you, I am with you. I fought everyday for you. So never stop fighting, I believe you. As the author Anne Lamott once wrote, "Lighthouses don't go running all over an island looking for boats to save; they just stand there shining." Although I can't save every boat, I hope that by speaking today, you absorbed a small amount of light, a small knowing that you can't be silenced, a small satisfaction that justice was served, a small assurance that we are getting somewhere, and big, big knowing that you are important, unquestionably, you are untouchable, you are beautiful, you are to be valued, respected, undeniably, every minute of every day, you are powerful and nobody can take that away from you. To girls everywhere, I am with you. Thank you. (Miller, 2020: 337–361)

The author of this powerful statement, we now know, was Chanel Miller. Chanel was sexually assaulted by Brock Turner behind a dumpster at a party while she was unconscious.[14] Turner was convicted of three felonies, with a recommended sentence of six years, and maximum of fourteen. The judge in the case (since recalled from the bench) sentenced him to a mere three years of probation and six months in county jail. He served only three months before his early release.

Turner's case made national news due in part to the fact that he was an aspiring Olympic swimmer, the fact that his father and friends made shocking public statements about the weight of the negative impact of

---

[14] To try to sum up what happened to Chanel in a single sentence does not – and cannot – capture the full scope of the harm she suffered. Her memoir, *Know My Name*, is a powerful and beautifully written account of that suffering, and an excellent resource for those who truly wish to learn more about the experience of actual victims of sexual assault.

his trial and conviction on *him* (he could no longer enjoy a good steak, for example), and Chanel's powerful public statement as Emily Doe.

Both Turner's conviction and his lenient sentence are a testament to the value of reactive blame and the need for corresponding systems of proportional punishment. Miller's statement conveys this, I think, better than any philosophical arguments possibly could. Here she makes explicit the harm that Turner caused her in terms of both her physical and psychological pain, as well as her struggles with its symbolic meaning in regard to her own intrinsic value as a person. Miller's own words powerfully highlight how the claims made by Hieronymi and Franklin about how wrongdoing creates a standing challenge to the value of the victim operate in practice. Her pleas for Turner to take responsibility for his actions, and for his sentencing to properly reflect the harm that he caused also highlight the *necessity*, from a victim's perspective, of holding wrongdoers responsible in order to combat this claim and protect and defend their value. And finally, her outrage at the probation officer's recommendation of a lenient sentence (which the judge unfortunately endorsed in sentencing) shows just one way in which *failure* to blame can serve to re-traumatize victims, bolster these negative claims about their value, and harm them further.

The approach that I have taken in this book is motivated by the first-person testimony of actual victims like Chanel Miller as the central and *most* morally significant motivating consideration when it comes to theorizing about free will, responsibility, and blame. What can and should eliminativists say to victims like Chanel? While much has been made of the dark side of free will and reactive blame, I think that the answer to this question reveals a dark side for *eliminativism* as well. While skeptics and eliminativists are admirably motivated by a desire to avoid inflicting undeserved harm on the targets of blame, they often seem to overlook the significant costs of doing so for victims.

As Pereboom notes earlier, some degree of undeserved harm might be necessary in order for the state to protect its citizens. Again, I think that Pereboom is right here, but that this analysis stops a step short. *The same is true of our interpersonal relationships more broadly.* Were it possible to protect and defend the value of victims in our interpersonal lives without reactive blame and its corresponding practices of holding responsible, then doing so might be a good thing. But, what adopting a *victim-centered* approach to blame reveals is that this simply is not possible. Given that we find ourselves embedded in a world in which we engage in interpersonal relationships with other morally fallible beings who inevitably harm each other, we must hold those who cause such harm responsible, or risk leaving victims by the wayside. And, as the arguments throughout this book have hopefully shown, reactive blame looks to be our best way to do so.

If in fact, there is some brute pragmatic argument in the offing to adjudicate between eliminativists and preservationists about free will, responsibility, and blame, I think that it is actually a *preservationist* one. Insofar as we care about the value and well-being of victims, we *must* preserve reactive blame and its corresponding practices. To abandon them would require telling victims like Chanel Miller that we ought to let Brock Turner off the hook, at least in the deep sense. He is, after all, largely the product of his genes, environment, and the sexist, classist social structures that he finds himself in. But these, of course, are not *his* fault. He is not the ultimate source of his own character or his actions. Thus if the assessments of his father, friends, the probation officer, and the judge are correct, and a slap on the wrist would be sufficient to teach him the requisite lessons and encourage better future behavior, then so be it. That is all we ought to inflict on him, because there is nothing further that he *deserves* in the basic sense.

This proposed response, to me, boggles the mind. When I put myself in the shoes of victims like Chanel, I cannot even fully imagine the pain and outrage that such a recommendation would cause. But Chanel, herself, goes some way toward eloquently capturing it above. My conclusion, therefore, is that at the end of the day, we ought to place such testimony at the forefront of our philosophical thinking about free will, moral responsibility, and blame. Rather than talk abstractly of gains and losses, costs, and the dark side of free will and blame, we do better to ruminate more carefully on this kind of *argument from empathy*. I think that when we do, preservationist conclusions begin to look like the most empathetic choice. They make the most sense of moral anger, after all.

References

Altemeyer, R. A. (1981). *Right-Wing Authoritarianism*. Manitoba: University of Manitoba Press.

(1996). *The Authoritarian Specter*. Cambridge, MA: Harvard University Press.

Andreasen, R. O. (2000). Race: Biological Reality or Social Construct? *Philosophy of Science*, 67, S653–S666.

Anscombe, E. (1963). *Intention*. Oxford: Blackwell.

Appiah, K. A. (1995). The Uncompleted Argument: Du Bois and the Illusion of Race. In L. A. Bell and D. Blumenfeld, eds., *Overcoming Racism and Sexism*. Lanham, MD: Rowman & Littlefield, pp. 59–78.

Blackburn, S. (1985). Errors and the Phenomenology of Value. In T. Carson and P. Moser, eds., *Morality and the Good Life*. New York: Oxford University Press, pp. 324–337.

Blair, R. (1995). A Cognitive Developmental Approach to Morality: Investigating the Psychopath. *Cognition*, 57(1), 1–29.

Blair, R., Lawrence Jones, Fiona Clark, and Margaret Smith. (1997). The Psychopathic Individual: A Lack of Responsiveness to Distress Cues? *Psychophysiology*, 34(2), 192–198.

Brady, M. (2011). Emotions, Perceptions, and Reasons. In C. Bagnoli, ed., *Morality and the Emotions*. New York: Oxford University Press, pp. 135–149.

Brentano, F. (1969) [1889]. *The Origin of Our Knowledge of Right and Wrong*. O. Kraus and R. Chisholm, eds., R. Chisholm and E. Schneewind, trans. London: Routledge & Kegan Paul.

Brink, D. (1986). Externalist Moral Realism. *Southern Journal of Philosophy*, 24 (S1), 23–41.

Campbell, J. (1957). *Of Selfhood and Godhood*. London: Allen & Unwin.

Caruso, G. (2012). *Free Will and Consciousness: A Determinist Account of the Illusion of Free Will*. Lanham, MD: Lexington Books.

(2015). Free Will Eliminativism: Reference, Error, and Phenomenology. *Philosophical Studies*, 172, 2823–2833.

(2020). Free Will Skepticism and Its Implications: An Argument for Optimism. In E. Shaw, D. Pereboom, and G. Caruso, eds., *Free Will Skepticism in Law and Society: Challenging Retributive Justice*. Cambridge, UK: Cambridge University Press, pp. 43–72.

Churchland, P. M. (1981). Eliminative Materialism and Propositional Attitudes. *Journal of Philosophy*, 78, 67–90.

Churchland, P. S. (1986). *Neurophilosophy: Toward a Unified Science of the Mind/ Brain*. Cambridge, MA: MIT Press.

Ciurria, M. (2019). *An Intersectional Feminist Theory of Moral Responsibility*. New York: Routledge.

Coates, D. J., and Neal Tognazzini. (2013). The Contours of Blame. In D. J. Coates and Neal Tognazzini, eds., *Blame: Its Nature and Norms*. New York: Oxford University Press, pp. 3–26.

Cogley, Z. (2013). Basic Desert of Reactive Emotions. *Philosophical Explorations*, 16(2), 165–177.

D'Arms, J., and Daniel Jacobson. (2000a). The Moralistic Fallacy: On the "Appropriateness" of Emotions. *Philosophy and Phenomenological Research*, 61, 65–90.

(2000b). Sentiment and Value. *Ethics*, 110, 722–748.

(2003). The Significance of Recalcitrant Emotions (or, Anti-quasijudgmentalism). *Royal Institute of Philosophy Supplement*, 52, 127–145.

Daw, R., and Torin Alter. (2001). Free Acts and Robot Cats. *Philosophical Studies*, 102, 345–357.

Deery, O. (2021a). Free Actions as a Natural Kind. *Synthese*, 198(1), 823–843.

(2021b). *Naturally Free Action*. Oxford: Oxford University Press.

Deery, O., Matt Bedke, and Shaun Nichols. (2013). Phenomenal Abilities: Incompatibilism and the Experience of Agency. In D. Shoemaker, ed., *Oxford Studies in Agency and Responsibility*. New York: Oxford University Press, pp. 126–150.

De Sousa, R. (1987). *The Rationality of Emotion*. Cambridge, MA: MIT Press.

Donnellan, K. (1966). Reference and Definite Descriptions. *Philosophical Review*, 75, 281–304.

(1968). Putting Humpty Dumpty Together Again. *Philosophical Review*, 77(2), 203–215.

Döring, S. (2003). Explaining Action by Emotion. *The Philosophical Quarterly*, 53, 214–230.

Elgin, C. (1996). *Considered Judgment*. Princeton, NJ: Princeton University Press.

(2008). Emotion and Understanding. In G. Brun, U. Doguoglu, and D. Kuenzle, eds., *Epistemology and the Emotions*. Farnham: Ashgate Publishing, pp. 33–50.

Feinberg, J. (1970). *Doing and Deserving*. Princeton, NJ: Princeton University Press.

Feltz, A., and Edward Cokely. (2008). The Fragmented Folk: More Evidence of Stable Individual Differences in Moral Judgments and Folk Intuitions. In B. C. Love, K. McRae, and V. M. Sloutskey, eds., *Proceedings of the 30th Annual Conference of the Cognitive Science Society*. Austin, TX: Cognitive Science Society, pp. 1771–1776.

Feyerabend, P. (1962). Explanation, Reduction and Empiricism. In H. Feigel and G. Maxwell, eds., *Scientific Explanation, Space, and Time*, vol. 3 of

Minnesota Studies in the Philosophy of Science. Minneapolis: University of Minnesota Press, pp. 28–97.

Foot, P. (1978). Hume on Moral Judgment. In *Virtues and Vices*. Berkeley: University of California Press, pp. 74–80.

Franklin, C. (2013). Valuing Blame. In D. J. Coates and N. Tognazzini, eds., *Blame: Its Nature and Norms*. New York: Oxford University Press, pp. 207–223.

  (2018). *A Minimal Libertarianism: Free Will and the Promise of Reduction*. New York: Oxford University Press.

Glover, J. (1970). *Responsibility*. London: Routledge & Kegan Paul.

Goodman, N. (1955). *Fact, Fiction, and Forecast*. Cambridge, MA: Harvard University Press.

Greene, J. (2010). The Secret Joke of Kant's Soul. In T. Naddelhoffer, E. Nahmias, and S. Nichols, eds., *Moral Psychology: Historical and Contemporary Readings*. Malden, MA: Wiley-Blackwell, pp. 359–372.

Griffiths, P. (1997). *What Emotions Really Are*. Chicago, IL: University of Chicago Press.

Haas, D. (2013). Merit, Fit, and Basic Desert. *Philosophical Explorations*, 16(2), 226–239.

Haidt, J. (2001). The Emotional Dog and Its Rational Tail: A Social Intuitionist Approach to Moral Judgment. *Psychological Review*, 108(4), 814–834.

Haji, I. (1998). *Moral Appraisability: Puzzles, Proposals, and Perplexities*. New York: Oxford University Press.

  (2016). *Luck's Mischief: Obligations and Blameworthiness on a Thread*. Oxford: Oxford University Press.

Hare, R. (1952). *The Language of Morals*. Oxford: Oxford University Press.

Hart, H. L. A. (1968). *Punishment and Responsibility*. Oxford: Oxford University Press.

Heller, M. (1996). The Mad Scientist Meets the Robot Cats: Compatibilism, Kinds, and Counterexamples. *Philosophy and Phenomenological Research*, 56(2), 333–337.

Hieronymi, P. (2004). The Force and Fairness of Blame. *Philosophical Perspectives*, 18, 115–148.

  (2005). The Wrong Kind of Reason. *The Journal of Philosophy*, 102, 437–457.

  (2020). *Freedom, Resentment, and the Metaphysics of Morals*. Princeton, NJ: Princeton University Press.

Hodgson, D. (2012). *Rationality + Consciousness = Free Will*. New York: Oxford University Press.

Hurley, S. (2000). Is Responsibility Essentially Impossible? *Philosophical Studies*, 99(2), 229–268.

Jackson, F. and Philip Pettit. (1995). Moral Functionalism and Moral Motivation. *Philosophical Quarterly*, 45, 20–40.

Johnson, M. (2001). The Authority of Affect. *Philosophy and Phenomenological Research*, 53, 181–214.

Kane, R. (1985). *Free Will and Values*. Albany: State University of New York Press.

(1996). *The Significance of Free Will*. New York: Oxford University Press.

(2007). Libertarianism. In J. Fischer, R. Kane, D. Pereboom, and M. Vargas, eds., *Four Views on Free Will*. Oxford: Blackwell Publishers, pp. 5–43.

(2011). Rethinking Free Will: New Perspectives on an Ancient Problem. In R. Kane, ed., *The Oxford Handbook of Free Will*, 2nd ed. New York: Oxford University Press, pp. 381–404.

(2017). Free Will Bound and Unbound: Reflections on Shaun Nichols' *Bound*. *Philosophical Studies*, 174(10), 2479–2488.

Knobe, J., and John Doris. (2010). Responsibility. In J. Doris and The Moral Psychology Research Group, eds., *The Moral Psychology Handbook*. Oxford: Oxford University Press, pp. 321–354.

Kohlberg, L. (1969). Stage and Sequence: The Cognitive-Developmental Approach to Socialization. In D. A. Goslin, ed., *Handbook of Socialization Theory and Research*. Chicago, IL: Rand McNally, pp. 347–480.

Kripke, S. (1980). *Naming and Necessity*. Cambridge, MA: Harvard University Press.

Laudan, L. (1984). *Science and Values*. Berkeley: University of California Press.

Lemos, J. (2016). Moral Concerns about Responsibility Denial and the Quarantine of Violent Criminals. *Law and Philosophy*, 35, 461–483.

(2018). *A Pragmatic Approach to Libertarian Free Will*. New York: Routledge.

Lerner, M. J. (1965). Evaluation of Performance as a Function of Performer's Reward and Attractiveness. *Journal of Personality and Social Psychology*, 1, 355–360.

Lerner, M. (1980). *The Belief in a Just World: A Fundamental Delusion*. New York: Plenum Press.

Lerner, M., and Carol Simmons. (1966). Observer's Reaction to the "Innocent Victim": Compassion or Rejection? *Journal of Personality and Social Pyschology*, 4, 203–210.

Levy, N. (2011). *Hard Luck: How Luck Undermines Free Will & Moral Responsibility*. Oxford: Oxford University Press.

Lewis, D. (1973). *Counterfactuals*. Malden, MA: Blackwell.

(1979). Counterfactual Dependence and Time's Arrow. *Noûs*, 13, 455–476.

Lillehammer, H. (2007). *Companions in Guilt: Arguments for Ethical Objectivity*. London: Palgrave Macmillan.

Machery, E. (2009). *Doing without Concepts*. Oxford: Oxford University Press.

Mackie, J. (1977). *Ethics: Inventing Right and Wrong*. New York: Penguin.

Mallon, R. (2006). Race: Normative, Not Metaphysical or Semantic. *Ethics*, 116 (3), 525–551.

McCormick, K. (2013). Anchoring a Revisionist Account of Moral Responsibility. *Journal of Ethics and Social Philosophy*, 7(3), 1–20.

(2014). Holding Responsibility Hostage: Responsibility, Justification, and the Compatibility Question. *Journal of Value Inquiry*, 48(4), 623–641.

(2015). Companions in Innocence: Defending a New Methodological Assumption for Theorizing about Moral Responsibility. *Philosophical Studies*, 172(2), 515–533.

(2017a). Revisionism. In N. Levy, M. Griffith, and K. Timpe, eds., *The Routledge Companion to Free Will*. New York: Routledge, pp. 109–120.

(2017b). Why We Should(n't) Be Discretionists about Free Will. *Philosophical Studies*, 174(10), 2489–2498.

McGeer, V. (2013). Civilizing Blame. In D. J. Coates and N. Tognazzini, eds., *Blame: Its Nature and Norms*. New York: Oxford University Press, pp. 162–188.

(2019). Scaffolding Agency: A Proleptic Account of the Reactive Attitudes. *The European Journal of Philosophy*, 27(2), 301–323.

McKay, T. (1968). Mr. Donnellan and Humpty Dumpty on Referring. *Philosophical Review*, 77(2), 197–202.

McKenna, M. (2009). Compatibilism and Desert: Critical Comments on *Four Views on Free Will*. *Philosophical Studies*, 144, 3–13.

(2012). *Conversation and Responsibility*. New York: Oxford University Press.

Miller, C. (2020). Emily Doe's Victim Impact Statement. In *Know My Name*. New York: Penguin Books, pp. 337–361. [Originally published by Katie J. M. Baker in *Buzzfeed News* on June 3rd (2016), as *Here's the Powerful Letter the Stanford Victim Read to Her Attacker*.]

Moore, G. E. (1903). *Principia Ethica*. Cambridge: Cambridge University Press.

(1962). Proof of the External World. In *Philosophical Papers*. New York: Collier Books, pp. 127–150.

Nadelhoffer, T., Jason Shepard, Eddy Nahmias, Chandra Sripada, and Lisa Thomas Ross. (2014). The Free Will Inventory: Measuring Beliefs about Agency and Responsibility. *Consciousness and Cognition*, 25, 27–41.

Nadelhoffer, T., and Daniela Goya Tocchetta. (2013). The Potential Dark Side of Believing in Free Will (and Related Concepts): Some Preliminary Findings. In G. Caruso, ed., *Exploring the Illusion of Free Will and Moral Responsibility*. Lanham, MD: Lexington Books, pp. 121–140.

Nahmias, E., D. Justin Coates, and Trevor Kvaran. (2007). Free Will, Moral Responsibility, and Mechanism: Experiments on Folk Intuitions. *Midwest Studies in Philosophy*, 31, 214–242.

Nahmias, E., Stephen Morris, Thomas Nadelhoffer, and Jason Turner. (2006). Is Incompatibilism Intuitive? *Philosophy and Phenomenological Research*, 73(1), 28–53.

Nelkin, D. (2013). Desert, Fairness, and Resentment. *Philosophical Explorations*, 16(2), 1–16.

Nichols, S. (2002). How Psychopaths Threaten Moral Rationalism. *Monist*, 85, 285–303.

(2004). *Sentimental Rules: On the Natural Foundations of Moral Judgment*. Oxford: Oxford University Press.

(2013). Free Will and Error. In G. Caruso, ed., *Exploring the Illusion of Free Will and Moral Responsibility*. Lanham, MD: Lexington Books, pp. 203–218.

(2015). *Bound*. Oxford: Oxford University Press.

(2017). Replies to Kane, McCormick, and Vargas. *Philosophical Studies*, 174 (10), 2511–2523.

Nichols, S. and Joshua Knobe. (2007). Moral Responsibility and Determinism: The Cognitive Science of Folk Intuitions. *Noûs*, 41(4), 663–685.

Nichols, S., Ángel Pinillos, and Ron Mallon. (2016). Ambiguous Reference. *Mind*, 125(497), 145–175.

Nolan, D. (1997). Impossible Worlds: A Modest Approach. *Notre Dame Journal of Formal Logic*, 38(4), 535–572.

O'Connor, T. (1995). Agent Causation. In T. O'Connor, ed., *Agents, Causes and Events: Essays on Free Will and Indeterminism*. Oxford: Oxford University Press, pp. 173–200.

Olson, J. (2004). Buck-Passing and the Wrong Kind of Reasons. *The Philosophical Quarterly*, 54, 295–300.

Parfit, D. (2001). Rationality and Reasons. In D. Egonsson, J. Jesefsson, B. Petersson, and T. Rønnow-Rasmussen, eds., *Exploring Practical Philosophy*. Burlington, VT: Ashgate, pp. 17–39.

Paulhus, D. (1991). Measurement and Control of Response Bias. In J. Robinson, P. Shaver, and L. Wrightsman, eds., *Measures of Personality and Social Psychological Attitudes*. San Diego, CA: Academic Press, pp. 17–59.

Paulhus, D. and Jasmine Carey. (2011). The FAD-Plus: Measuring Lay Beliefs Regarding Free Will and Related Constructs. *Journal of Personality Assessment*, 93, 96–104.

Pereboom, D. (1995). Determinism al dente. *Noûs*, 29(1), 21–45.

(2001). *Living without Free Will*. Cambridge, MA: Cambridge University Press.

(2005). Defending Hard Incompatibilism. *Midwest Studies in Philosophy*, 29, 228–247.

(2007a). Hard Incompatibilism. In R. Kane, J. M. Fischer, D. Pereboom, and M. Vargas, eds., *Four Views on Free Will*. Oxford: Blackwell, pp. 85–125.

(2007b). Response to Kane, Fischer, and Vargas. In R. Kane, J. M. Fischer, D. Pereboom, and M. Vargas, eds., *Four Views on Free Will*. Oxford: Blackwell, pp. 191–203.

(2009a). Free Will, Love, and Anger. *Ideas y Valores*, 141, 21–33.

(2009b). Hard Incompatiblism and Its Rivals. *Philosophical Studies*, 144, 21–33.

(2011). Free Will Skepticism and Meaning in Life. In R. Kane, eds., *The Oxford Handbook of Free Will*, 2nd ed. Oxford: Oxford University Press, pp. 407–424.

(2013). Free Will Skepticism, Blame, and Obligation. In J. Coates and N. Tognazzini, eds., *Blame: Its Nature and Norms*. Oxford: Oxford University Press, pp. 198–206.

(2014). *Free Will, Agency, and Meaning in Life*. Oxford: Oxford University Press.

(2020). Free Will Skepticism, General Deterrence, and the "Use" Objection. In E. Shaw, D. Pereboom, and G. D. Carus, eds., *Free Will Skepticism in Law and Society: Challenging Retributive Justice.* Cambridge: Cambridge University Press, pp. 91–115.

Piaget, J. (1965) [1932]. *The Moral Judgment of the Child.* M. Gabain, trans., New York: Free Press.

Prinz, J. (2004). *Gut Feelings.* New York: Oxford University Press.

Putnam, H. (1962). It Ain't Necessarily So. *Journal of Philosophy,* 59, 658–671.

(1975). The Meaning of "Meaning". *Minnesota Studies in Philosophy of Science,* 7, 131–193.

Rabinowicz, W., and Toni Rönnow-Rasmussen. (2004). The Strike of the Demon: On Fitting Pro Attitudes and Value. *Ethics,* 114, 391–423.

(2006). Buck-Passing and the Right Kind of Reasons. *The Philosophical Quarterly,* 56, 114–120.

Rakos, R., Kimberly Laurene, Sarah Skala, and Stephen Slane. (2008). Belief in Free Will: Measurement and Conceptualization Innovations. *Behavior and Social Issues,* 17, 20–39.

Reisner, A. (2009). The Possibility of Pragmatic Reasons for Belief and the Wrong Kind of Reasons Problem. *Philosophical Studies,* 145, 257–272.

Roberts, R. (2003). *Emotions.* Cambridge: Cambridge University Press.

Roskies, A., and Bertram Malle. (2013). A Strawsonian Look at Desert. *Philosophical Explorations,* 16(2), 133–152.

Scanlon, T. M. (1988). The Significance of Choice. *Tanner Lectures on Human Values,* 8, 149–216.

(1998). *What We Owe to Each Other.* Cambridge, MA: Harvard University Press.

(2008). *Moral Dimensions: Permissibility, Meaning, Blame.* Cambridge, MA: Harvard University Press.

Scheid, D. (1997). Constructing a Theory of Punishment, Desert, and Distribution of Punishments. *Canadian Journal of Law and Jurisprudence,* 10, 441–506.

Schlick, M. (1939). *When Is a Man Responsible?* D. Rynin, trans. New York: Prentice-Hall.

Sher, G. (2006). *In Praise of Blame.* Oxford: Oxford University Press.

(2013). Wrongdoing and Relationships: The Problem of the Stranger. In D. J. Coates and N. Tognazzini, eds., *Blame: Its Nature and Norms.* New York: Oxford University Press, pp. 49–65.

Shoemaker, D. (2015). *Responsibility from the Margins.* Oxford: Oxford University Press.

(2017). Response-Dependent Responsibility. *The Philosophical Review,* 126, 481–527.

Smart, J. J. C. (1961). Free-Will, Praise, and Blame. *Mind,* 70, 291–306.

Smetana, J. (1983). Social-cognitive Development: Domain Distinctions and Coordinations. *Developmental Review,* 3, 131–147.

Smilansky, S. (2011). Hard Determinism and Punishment: A Practical Reduction. *Law and Philosophy*, 30, 353–367.

(2016). Parfit on Free Will, Desert, and the Fairness of Punishment. *Journal of Ethics*, 20, 139–148.

(2017). Pereboom on Punishment: Funishment, Innocence, Motivation, and Other Difficulties. *Criminal Law and Philosophy*, 11, 591–603.

(2020). Free Will Denial and Deontological Contraints. In E. Shaw, D. Pereboom, and G. Caruso, *Free Will Skepticism in Law and Society: Challenging Retributive Justice*. Cambridge: Cambridge University Press, pp. 29–42.

Smith, A. (2013). Moral Blame and Moral Protest. In D. J. Coates and N. Tognazzini, eds., *Blame: Its Nature and Norms*. New York: Oxford University Press, pp. 27–48.

Smith, M. (1994). *The Moral Problem*. Oxford: Blackwell.

Stitch, S. (1983). *From Folk Psychology to Cognitive Science*. Cambridge, MA: Cambridge University Press.

Strawson, G. (1993). On Freedom and Resentment. In J. M. Fischer and M. Ravizza, eds., *Perspectives on Moral Responsibility*. Ithaca, NY: Cornell University Press, pp. 67–100.

(1994). The Impossibility of Moral Responsibility. *Philosophical Studies*, 75, 5–24.

(2002). The Bounds of Freedom. In R. Kane, ed., *The Oxford Handbook of Free Will*. New York: Oxford University Press, pp. 441–460.

Strawson, P. F. (1962). Freedom and Resentment. *Proceedings of the British Academy*, 48, 1–25. [All pagination taken from reprint in Hieronymi, P. (2020). *Freedom, Resentment, and the Metaphysics of Morals*. Princeton, NJ: Princeton University Press, pp. 107–133.]

Stroessner, S., and Charles Green. (1990). Effects of Belief in Free Will or Determinism on Attitudes toward Punishment and Locus of Control. *The Journal of Social Psychology*, 130(6), 789–799.

Suikkanen, J. (2004). Reasons and Value – In Defense of the Buck-Passing Account. *Ethical Theory and Moral Practice*, 7, 513–535.

Tappolet, C. (2000). *Emotions et Valuers*. Paris: Presses Universitaires de France.

Taylor, R. (1992). *Metaphysics*, 4th ed. Englewood Cliffs, NJ: Prentice-Hall.

Turiel, E. (1983). *The Development of Social Knowledge: Morality and Convention*. Cambridge, UK: Cambridge University Press.

Turiel, E., Melanie Killen, and Charles C. Helwig. (1987). Morality: Its Structure, Functions, and Vagaries. In J. Kagan and S. Lamb, eds., *The Emergence of Morality in Young Children*. Chicago: University of Chicago Press, pp. 155–245.

Turiel, E., and Judith Smetana. (1984). Social Knowledge and Action: the Coordination of Domains. In W. Kurtines and J. Gewitz, eds., *Morality, Moral Behavior and Moral Development: Basic Issues in Theories and Research*. New York: Wiley.

Unger, P. (1979). There are No Ordinary Things. *Synthese*, 41, 117–154.

Van Inwagen, P. (1990). *Material Beings*. Ithaca, NY: Cornell University Press.

Vargas, M. (2005). The Revisionist's Guide to Responsibility. *Philosophical Studies*, 125, 399–429.

(2009). Revisionism about Free Will: A Statement and Defense. *Philosophical Studies*, 144, 45–62.

(2011). Revisionist Accounts of Free Will: Origins, Varieties, and Challenges. In R. Kane, ed., *The Oxford Handbook of Free Will*, 2nd ed. Oxford: Oxford University Press, pp. 457–474.

(2013). *Building Better Beings: A Theory of Moral Responsibility*. Oxford: Oxford University Press.

(2017). Contested Terms and Philosophical Debates. *Philosophical Studies*, 174 (10), 2499–2510.

Viney, W., Robert McIntyre, and Donald Viney. (1984). Validity of a Scale Designed to Measure Beliefs in Free Will and Determinism. *Psychological Reports*, 54, 867–872.

Walker, M. (2006). *Moral Repair: Reconstructing Moral Relations after Wrongdoing*. Cambridge: Cambridge University Press.

Wallace, R. J. (1994). *Responsibility and the Moral Sentiments*. Cambridge, MA: Harvard University Press.

(2011). Dispassionate Opprobrium: On Blame and the Reactive Sentiments. In R. J. Wallace, R. Kumar, and S. Freeman, eds., *Reasons and Recognition: Essays on the Philosophy of T.M. Scanlon*. New York: Oxford University Press, pp. 348–372.

(2019). *The Moral Nexus*. Princeton, NJ: Princeton University Press.

Waller, B. (1990). *Freedom without Responsibility*. Philadelphia: Temple University Press.

(2011). *Against Moral Responsibility*. Cambridge, MA: MIT Press.

(2013). The Stubborn Illusion of Moral Responsibility. In G. Caruso, ed., *Exploring the Illusion of Free Will and Moral Responsibility*. Lanham, MD: Lexington Books, pp. 65–86.

(2015). *The Stubborn System of Moral Responsibility*. Cambridge, MA: MIT Press.

(2020). Beyond the Retributive System. In E. Shaw, D. Pereboom, and G. Caruso, eds., *Free Will Skepticism in Law and Society: Challenging Retributive Justice*. Cambridge: Cambridge University Press, pp. 73–95.

Warmke, B. (2011). Moral Responsibility and Invariantism. *Philosophia*, 39(1), 179–200.

Watson, G. (2004). *Agency and Answerability*. Oxford: Clarendon Press.

Weigel, C. (2013). Experimental Evidence for Free Will Revisionism. *Philosophical Explorations*, 16, 31–43.

Williams, B. (1981). *Moral Luck*. Cambridge: Cambridge University Press.

Williamson, T. (2007). *The Philosophy of Philosophy*. Oxford: Blackwell.

Wolf, S. (2011). Blame, Italian Style. In R. J. Wallace, R. Kumar, and S. Freeman, eds., *Reasons and Recognition: Essays on the Philosophy of T.M. Scanlon*. New York: Oxford University Press, pp. 332–347.

Yap, A. (2017). Credibility Excess and the Social Imaginary in Cases of Sexual Assault. *Feminist Philosophy Quarterly*, 3(4), 1–24.

Zagzebski, L. (2004). Constraining and Condemning. *Ethics*, 108, 489–501.

Zimmerman, M. J. (1988). *An Essay on Moral Responsibility*. Totowa, NJ: Rowman & Littlefield.

Index

9 781108 827416